The *Art* of the IMPOSSIBLE

The *Art* of the IMPOSSIBLE

DAVE BARRETT and the NDP in Power 1972–1975

Geoff Meggs and Rod Mickleburgh

Harbour Publishing

2 3 4 5 — 16 15 14 13

Harbour Publishing Co. Ltd.
P.O. Box 219, Madeira Park, BC, V0N 2H0
www.harbourpublishing.com

Cover image, detail from I-32413 courtesy of Royal BC Museum, BC Archives
Edited by Silas White
Index by Elaine Park
Cover design by Teresa Karbashewski
Text design by Martin Nichols
Printed and bound in Canada

Canada Council for the Arts   Conseil des Arts du Canada

British Columbia Arts Council
An agency of the Province of British Columbia

Harbour Publishing acknowledges financial support from the Government of Canada through the Canada Book Fund and the Canada Council for the Arts, and from the Province of British Columbia through the BC Arts Council and the Book Publishing Tax Credit.

Library and Archives Canada Cataloguing in Publication
Meggs, Geoff, 1951–
The art of the impossible : Dave Barrett and the NDP in power, 1972-1975 / Geoff Meggs and Rod Mickleburgh.

Includes bibliographical references and index.
ISBN 978-1-55017-579-0

1. Barrett, Dave, 1930-. 2. British Columbia—Politics and government—1972-1975. 3. New Democratic Party of British Columbia. 4. Prime ministers—British Columbia—Biography. I. Mickleburgh, Rod II. Title. III. Title: Dave Barrett and the NDP in power, 1972-1975.

FC3828.2.M45 2012   971.1'04   C2012-904953-0

For Jan and Lucie

"Let us teach ourselves and others that politics can be not only the art of the possible, especially if 'the possible' includes the art of speculation, calculation, intrigue, secret deals and pragmatic manoeuvrings, but that it can also be the art of the impossible, namely, the art of improving ourselves and the world."

–Václav Havel, New Year's Address, 1990

"I found Barrett a most admirable man, a peculiar combination of talent, intuition and good luck, whose government had come to office at the ideal time to make loads and loads of change in BC. It was, and I still think is, a unique situation in North America, and I had to be a great fool not to join it. I thought that the only reason other people didn't see the government this way was because they had been blinded by generations of boring and cynical politics. I knew that Barrett was a raw political force, like the Fraser River … I knew he was cynical about people's motives, but who wasn't? I thought it was a healthy attribute to be this way and still try to work for economic justice. Besides, he was fun to be with."

–Peter McNelly, February 4, 1974

Contents

Preface

In a province that immortalizes the names of former premiers on soaring bridges or massive dams, the only monument to Dave Barrett, BC's first NDP premier, is a simple plaque on the road to the Cypress Mountain park he helped to save from logging. He had told friends he'd most like to be remembered as "the cause of Cypress Bowl," and for ending the practice of jailing children as young as twelve. "It was a tremendous feeling," he said, recalling the day he gave that latter order. "I used the power that was in the office and I ordered it stopped. I hope it never returns." These are strangely simple but powerful memories from a man whose government passed more substantial legislation in its three-year term than any administration before or since. Forty years later, his political legacy remains embedded in BC's political, social and economic life, missing from most histories of the period but all around for those who know where to look.

"Unashamedly I call for love," Barrett told voters on the eve of his 1972 election victory over W.A.C. Bennett, whose Social Credit Party had ruled the province since 1952. "For too long this province has been racked with division—labour against management, teacher against government, doctor against cabinet minister." Voters agreed, handing him an unprecedented NDP majority.

Barrett and his colleagues used their mandate to the limit. The Agricultural Land Reserve dramatically reshaped urban and rural development right across the province. A new environmental and land use secretariat laid the foundation for real protection of BC's wilderness. The welfare system was completely overhauled, human rights were protected and a new labour code came into force. The province undertook major investments in housing, daycare and transit.

Every British Columbian who has ever bought auto insurance, attended community college, ridden in an ambulance, taken the SeaBus, tangled with a boss about wages or benefits, or vacationed in one of scores of wilderness parks has benefited from the Barrett legacy. Barrett's three-year term could be seen as a time of positive change, when a new generation took its turn shaping the province's future, transforming, modernizing and democratizing a government held for nearly twenty years by W.A.C. Bennett's one-man rule.

But that's not how politics works in BC. Barrett wanted love, but he was lucky to get the Cypress Bowl plaque, even at age eighty. His legislative agenda, despite its clear roots in the NDP election platform "A New Deal for People," triggered a firestorm of protest. Hobbled by his own errors, persistent and critical media scrutiny, a party membership that insisted he do even more and an implacably hostile business sector, Barrett found his mandate ebbing away. In 1975, confronting a wave of strikes and a reunited opposition in the legislature, he called a snap election that resulted in the NDP's defeat and another fifteen years in opposition.

Love? There has been no love for Barrett from academics or media commentators, who recall his government as a period of anarchy and darkness, when a colourful but erratic premier "tried to do everything at once," and mistook his victory as a mandate to implement a socialist revolution. Most historians have passed over the NDP's tumultuous time in government in a sentence or a paragraph, dismissing it as an anomaly, "an electoral hiccup," and as a "series of mistakes [that] combined with a growing sense of political crisis in Victoria to create an overwhelming impression of administrative incompetence." Barrett himself has been classed as "a loser" whose "intensely martial personality poisoned politics in the province." The province's corporate leaders were so shaken by Barrett's ascendancy that they launched the Fraser Institute, a neo-conservative think tank that became one of the foremost such organizations in the English-speaking world, to generate the policies and media presence necessary to prevent a recurrence. This book is the story of those unprecedented three years.

In an era when politics—what Bismarck termed the "art of the possible"—has been reduced to a narrow band of budget-balancing and symbolic acts rather than transformative changes, any contrary example is worth considering. Barrett and his colleagues seemed to stand Bismarck's maxim on its head, engaging for three heady years in what Václav Havel would later call the "art of the impossible," boldly walking outside the unstated boundaries of permitted political action to implement their platform. Their work proved remarkably enduring. Despite the silences in the historical record, Barrett's legacy is all around us, not only in the economic and social life of the province, but also in the way politics is practised—or not.

Barrett broke the unstated but fundamental rule of BC politics—indeed, of politics in many jurisdictions—which states that while left-wing, even socialist parties are allowed to run in BC elections, they are not allowed to win. If they do, they are not allowed to implement their program, as the top priority of all right-minded people is to drive them out. When they are driven out, the soil they grew on is to be ploughed with salt, their memory extinguished, and their term in office relegated to the realm of nightmare. There can be no need for radical change, after all, in what until recently was known as the Best Place on Earth.

Too extreme? In 1941, the BC electoral system was reorganized in a wartime coalition of Conservatives and Liberals to thwart an election victory by the surging Co-operative Commonwealth Federation (CCF), the NDP's predecessor. As the coalition crumbled in 1949, its partners implemented a preferential ballot system to achieve the same result, allowing the free enterprise parties to run against each other while keeping the left from power. The governing parties also implemented a system of sprawling two-member constituencies in urban areas that were intended to neutralize a "socialist" member of the legislature with one from the acceptable parties. As the *Vancouver Sun* editorialized prior to these changes, the CCF was poised to at least win a minority government unless the free-enterprise advocates took strong action: "When the minority government is also a socialist one, and the majority of the people would have preferred a non-socialist government, it's a double calamity."

Barrett's election represented just such a disaster to those who considered it their prerogative to run the province. Other parties could rely on the support of each other to govern with only a plurality; social democrats required an absolute majority, and even this hurdle would be raised if they ever seemed close to clearing it. In August 1972, Barrett led his party over that hurdle with a victory that would have given the NDP a clear majority of seats even if all Conservative voters had sided with the Socreds. The reaction was first astonishment, then denial, then anger and, finally, relentless counterattack. Barrett had expected such a reaction, urging his cabinet to govern with the view they were in office for a "good time, not a long time." Inevitably, as he acknowledged later, his own personal shortcomings contributed to his defeat at the hands of a reunited opposition determined to rid the province of "the socialist menace."

Perhaps the most gifted British Columbian politician of his generation, Barrett was a prisoner, as well, of his own apprenticeship in politics. He had studied W.A.C. Bennett's strengths and weaknesses, but had never found the time in opposition to look beyond them. What had become fatal flaws in Bennett's persona—a tendency to do it all himself, an unbounded faith in his own political instincts—proved equally deadly when emulated by Barrett.

Nor did Barrett learn to contend with the emerging electronic media reality of modern politics. The television cameras loved Barrett, the province's first TV-age premier, but he never evolved a strategy to manage his red-hot image. In the post-Watergate era, reporters came to work to bring down governments, not give them the benefit of the doubt. Later generations of politicians, including Bennett's son Bill, who defeated Barrett in 1975, learned the value of message discipline, communications planning and issues management. Barrett did it all on the fly. Like an acrobat performing without a net, he wowed the crowds until the inevitable stumbles contributed to disaster.

An unsurpassed political campaigner, Barrett manoeuvred the NDP to power, then found himself with no long-term strategy. He and his colleagues, so long in opposition, dared not believe in the possibility of their own victory. They took office without a transition plan or any more strategy than their own platform. As Barrett's opposition united, his supporters dropped away. When the momentum of the election ran out, as it inevitably did, his opponents quickly overwhelmed him.

Worse, the man who proudly proclaimed his government to be socialist, and stood accused of seeking what his opponents termed "awesome, sweeping powers" to usher in fundamental social change, was condemned in his own party for his failure to go even further. Once in power, some argued, it was crucial to nationalize telecommunications, to entrench women's equality, to strengthen union picketing rights. These initiatives, too, had roots in the NDP platform, but Barrett refused to implement them, sometimes mocking those in the NDP ranks who proposed them even when the government had valid strategic reasons for inaction. The gap that opened between the party membership and much of the caucus turned into near-civil war until 1974, when Barrett finally put down the rebellion. Thousands of activists who helped win the 1972 mandate refused to volunteer in 1975, unwilling to defend the changes Barrett had brought. Exhausted, demoralized, divided and often feeling deeply betrayed, New Democrats saw their dream extinguished before they could savour its reality, snatched from them, as many saw it, by Barrett's autocratic and destructive megalomania. The result was a continuing tension in the NDP between those who believed Barrett's example was one to be emulated and those whose cautious response was "day one, term two" to any initiatives that seemed likely to rock the party's electoral boat.

These realities, as well, are a vital part of the Barrett legacy. Ironically, voters in 1975 delivered a more balanced assessment of Barrett's government than open-line hosts or party activists. Barrett's share of the 1975 vote was almost identical to his 1972 tally. A consolidated vote for the now-united opposition, led by a reorganized Social Credit, sufficed to end his time in office. In 1979, his third election as leader of the provincial NDP, he actually increased the NDP's share of the popular vote to 46 percent, its highest ever, only to lose to Social Credit for a second time. In the face of a united governing party, the votes that had proved sufficient to win a landslide in 1972 produced a massive defeat in 1975 and would continue to do so for another fifteen years. Barrett's extraordinary party leadership was tacitly acknowledged by absence of challengers. He remained unopposed as leader until his fourth and final unsuccessful contest in 1983, when he resigned.

Why was the electorate kinder than the pundits or even Barrett's supporters? Machiavelli concluded long ago that "one can be hated as much for good deeds as for evil ones," adding that if a leader must choose between being feared and being loved, "it is far better to be feared than loved if you cannot do both ... for love is secured by a bond of gratitude which men, wretched creatures that they are, break when it is to their advantage to do so; but fear is strengthened by a dread of punishment which is always effective." Barrett asked for love, and many voters responded to his unbounded belief in the ability of a democratic society to transform itself for the better. Yet many others feared the consequences of voting for him even more, and with reason. Barrett's opponents left no doubt of their determination to see Barrett defeated, to the extent of liquidating their own BC investments, if that was what it took to avoid a "double calamity."

The pattern set by Barrett's victory, then his defeat, remains the foundation of BC politics. The "free enterprise" and "socialist" labels that had some relevance in the generation after the Second World War are still the basic categories of political combat, despite the long-ago disappearance of the socialist movement that Barrett experienced in his youth. The populist hucksterism of W.A.C. Bennett, the chamber of commerce boosterism that urges voters to "Believe BC" to end the grim prospect of NDP misrule, is as commonplace today as it was in 1952. Barrett and his colleagues laid siege to the political fortresses of their era and, to their astonishment, broke down the gates. For a while, all was new. Aware they confronted an opportunity offered once in a lifetime, they vowed to make the most of it. Despite everything that followed, they all insisted afterward, "it was a good time."

1: The Twenty Years' War

There seemed no reason why the Kelowna hardware merchant, a teetotalling Presbyterian invariably dressed in a dark business suit and black homburg hat, should not rule forever. Certainly that was the near-unanimous view in Vancouver on February 20, 1965, as the leaders of British Columbia's Social Credit Party gathered for a lavish banquet at the Hotel Vancouver to honour Premier W.A.C. Bennett, who had just become the province's longest-serving premier. Preceded by a brass band, the grinning Bennett was carried into the hall atop a model of a BC ferry teetering on the shoulders of young party members. Snaking through the lobby and the banquet hall, they sang choruses of "For He's a Jolly Good Fellow" and "Happy Birthday" before they deposited their hero at the head table, where he joined six of the original Social Credit members of the legislature elected with him thirteen years before.

As the boisterous crowd fell silent, a voice echoed from the speaker system like a message from the Almighty, a recording of Bennett's declaration of faith to the party veterans in 1952, just months before the election that catapulted them to power. It was the famous "hook, line and sinker" speech, calculated to reassure suspicious Social Credit activists that their new recruit, only recently a card-carrying Conservative leadership candidate, was in fact a loyal and committed Socred. "I want you to know we are going to win the next election on June 12," Bennett had intoned. "When I joined, I joined hook, line and sinker."

"Thank God we recorded those words," the master of ceremonies told the now-hushed crowd. Bennett had won that election, and four more after that. Bennett graciously acknowledged the stormy applause of more than eight hundred guests, including hotel shoeshine boy Y.C. Chan, whom Bennett had invited personally. "I know he's a wonderful guy," Chan said. "He makes friends of everybody." His governments had just been lucky, Bennett modestly told his admirers. "We have been able to stand up to criticism. But can we stand up to prosperity? Will it go to the head of this movement?" It's the kind of problem most governments would love to have.

This was an echo of the prophecy he had issued three days before to a non-partisan audience of more than 1,100 gathered in the same hotel. Kicked off with skirling pipers and Mounties in full-dress uniform, Vancouver Mayor Bill Rathie, wearing scarlet robes and his gold chain of office, solemnly gave Bennett the Freedom of the City to celebrate his electoral achievements. The assembled notables, including the province's major industrialists, the leader of every opposition party, religious leaders and even union officials showered Bennett with ovation after ovation. "We are only at the beginning in this province," Bennett told the crowd. "No place in the world has the climate, the people, the natural resources, and yes, the spiritual resources. The foundation only has been laid. Let none of us be satisfied with what we've done, neither the premier, the industrial leader or the labour leader. With God's help and leadership, a tremendous future for BC lies ahead." He sat down to a prolonged standing ovation.

His fifth election as incumbent premier, nearly a year later in 1966, was a cakewalk. In 1969, he scored his highest share of the popular vote ever, shattering his opponents and even knocking the NDP's new leader out of the legislature. It seemed that Bennett's British Columbia operated on distinctive political principles understood only by the premier himself. Canada might have Trudeaumania, Quebec its Quiet Revolution, and the United States could be racked by assassination and the horrors of the war in Vietnam, but in British Columbia there was W.A.C. Bennett and Social Credit, now and forever.

A victor in five general elections since 1952, by 1965 the sixty-five-year-old Bennett dominated the political life of the province. For British Columbians born after the Second World War, Bennett was the only premier they had ever known. He was not only the longest-serving premiers in BC history, he was then one of the longest-serving premiers of any province. For more than a decade, he had presided over an economic boom for forest, mining and oil companies that was without equal in the province's history.

Railroads and highways, the benchmarks of progress in Bennett's world, were the transmission belts carrying the wealth of the province to world markets at rock-bottom prices. Hydroelectric dams, generating vast quantities of cheap energy from flooded valley reservoirs hundreds of miles long, fuelled massive investments in pulp mills, sawmills, smelters and mines. The explosion of private sector investment in the forest sector after the Second World War generated enough revenue to keep taxes low, social spending steady and the budget in relative balance. The Trans-Canada Highway was planned and completed, linking Vancouver and the Interior with Canada by car and truck. The Pacific Great Eastern Railway connected Prince George to the Lower Mainland, and Kitimat and its smelter were cut from the wilderness. For the better part of a decade, BC workers enjoyed virtually full employment and steadily rising incomes, driven in part by a militant, highly unionized workforce that was ready and able to strike for improved contracts. For all this, Bennett humbly accepted credit.

Raised in relative poverty in New Brunswick, Bennett was a

small businessman whose restless drive for self-improvement made him the prosperous owner of a Kelowna hardware business by the end of the Depression. Retail sales and chamber of commerce leadership proved just a stepping stone to politics. By 1951 he had run for office on four occasions, three times winning election to the legislature. He also twice lost bids to lead the provincial Conservatives. Never a charismatic speaker—a slight speech impediment roused sympathy in his listeners rather than passion—he was an outstanding organizer and masterful debater, good-humoured and capable of stinging retorts if challenged or heckled. Bennett's greatest gift was his innate sense of political tactics. He combined a remarkable willingness to take bold risks with a ruthless instinct for the jugular. It was these qualities that brought him first to leadership of the Social Credit Party, a marginal player in BC politics, and then to the premiership of the province three years later.

First elected as a Conservative MLA in 1941, and re-elected in 1945, Bennett had quit to run for federal parliament in 1948, but saw his hopes dashed by Liberal-leaning voters. He returned to the legislature in 1949 just as the province's wartime Coalition, created for the sole purpose of keeping the Co-operative Commonwealth Federation from power, began to collapse. Frightened by a 31 percent vote for the CCF in 1941—only eight hundred votes separated the CCF from a minority mandate—the Liberals and the Conservatives had joined forces, allocating nominations to the Liberal or Conservative candidate most likely to defeat the CCF in a given riding. By 1949, the Coalition partners, no longer able to tolerate each other, created a preferential ballot system to keep the CCF at bay while they went their separate ways. This system assumed that "free enterprise" voters in the Liberal and Conservative camps would assign their second choice to another free enterprise party, not to the CCF. They were proved correct, but not in the way they expected.

Bennett, sensing opportunity and having twice been defeated

in bids to lead the Conservatives, began a quixotic political journey to find a new home, sitting first as an independent and then joining the ragtag rump of Social Credit MLAs who constituted a fourth party in the BC legislature. To reassure his uneasy new colleagues, Bennett did not seek formal endorsement as their leader, but lead them he did into the 1952 election, aiming his main fire at the two old-line coalition parties. He hammered them, in particular, for the imposition of a hated hospital tax to pay for expanded medical care. His campaign demonstrated the combination of populist politics and inspired political calculation that was to mark his career.

Weeks later, when the ballots were counted at last, second-choice preferences had come from CCF, Liberal and Conservative voters alike to vault Social Credit to within a single seat of power. Harold Winch's CCF had 34.8 percent of the vote and was declared elected in eighteen seats. Bennett's Social Credit had only 30.18 percent of the votes, but claimed nineteen seats. The Liberals, despite winning 25.26 percent of the vote, took only six seats. The wild card was Independent Labour candidate Tom Uphill of Fernie, still smarting from Winch's decision to run a CCF candidate against him. Bennett, now confirmed as Socred leader by a vote of caucus, again demonstrated remarkable pragmatism, securing Uphill's support to form a government. After suitable consultations and deliberations, Lieutenant-Governor Clarence Wallace invited Bennett to form a minority government, despite Social Credit's second-place finish in the popular vote.

Within a year, Bennett engineered a confidence vote in the legislature to trigger a new election. The Lieutenant-Governor was again co-operative, rejecting Winch's argument that by precedent, the Opposition should be invited to form government after a minority government is defeated. Winch had even secured Uphill's backing, bringing his support in line with the nineteen seats that had been sufficient to justify Bennett's claim to govern. Given the opportunity by Wallace to go back to the polls, Bennett won a clear majority. The hospital tax was repealed, replaced by cash from general revenue, which the expanding provincial treasury could easily afford. Bennett settled comfortably into power. In three short years, he had gone from rejected Tory leadership candidate to Social Credit premier with an unassailable majority, all the while holding the socialists at bay. The Conservatives and Liberals were relegated to the margins. It was the true dawn of the Wacky Bennett era.

A veteran of the Okanagan's chamber of commerce world of service clubs and church dinners, Bennett looked every inch the small businessman, with dark suit, glossy black shoes and severely parted hair. But his straitlaced demeanour was in stark contrast to his flair for dramatic political gestures that astonished reporters and mesmerized the voters. Determined to accelerate northern development after his 1956 election victory, Bennett personally negotiated an agreement with Axel Wenner-Gren, a Swedish industrialist, to create a monorail to Prince George running at speeds of up to 280 kilometres an hour. This visionary project was to be built on a right-of-way carved from public lands that ranged from 10 to 25 kilometres wide over a distance of 650 kilometres, and included large water concessions on the Peace, Parsnip and Findlay rivers. The scheme foundered when reporters discovered that Wenner-Gren, a friend of Nazi *Reichsmarschall* Hermann Goering, had floated similar schemes in Mexico and Rhodesia with no results.

Nor could anyone forget the scene August 3, 1959, when, from the bow of a boat loaded with dignitaries on Okanagan Lake, Bennett fired a flaming arrow at a raft burdened with sixty-nine boxes of government bonds covered with auto tires, mill shavings and oil. Although the arrow shaft bounced harmlessly off the raft and guttered out in the water, a Mountie hidden out of sight touched off the blaze that signalled the elimination of the province's debt. The stunts were a necessary diversion of attention from a slowdown in the province's economy during the late 1950s that forced spending cuts, the layoff of hundreds of government workers, and reductions in already-minimal welfare payments. Bennett's administration also was dogged by the Robert Sommers affair, a long-running scandal over corruption in the issuance of forest licences that would have brought down many other governments. But time and again, Bennett scattered his enemies and won re-election.

Some of his tactics, to be sure, were unorthodox. Although a devout free enterpriser, he had nonetheless nationalized the Black Ball Ferry Company to create BC Ferries. He did the same to BC Electric in 1961, creating BC Hydro to realize his dreams of massive new dams on the Columbia and the Peace rivers. These socialistic initiatives, which would have triggered a firestorm if attempted by an NDP government, were implemented with only token resistance from business interests.

Bennett's attitude to resource rents, however, more than made up for the odd nationalization. Corporations anxious to exploit natural resources could do so almost for free. Domestic natural gas consumers paid more for BC gas than export customers did in the United States; the "downstream benefits" of the Columbia River dams were postponed for forty years; and a dramatic expansion of copper mining during the 1960s generated negligible royalties. Nor were environmental regulations a hindrance although the province was incubating Greenpeace in the 1960s. Bennett's compliant mines ministry was staffed with industry veterans, and even the province's class-A parks were available for exploitation if profitable deposits were identified. Of seven thousand major polluters in the province, only six hundred to seven hundred held pollution permits.

On fiscal and social policy, Bennett was a model right-winger. Health, education and welfare spending was ruthlessly reined in, although Bennett did fund the creation of Simon Fraser University in the 1960s. The province's budget was always balanced—or at least appeared to balance. Creative use of "sinking funds" and other accounting devices ensured that each year's budget demonstrated the requisite fiscal probity, with liabilities and debts discreetly hidden in the accounts of Crown corporations and other unreported entities. Union rights were sharply restricted, a source of constant friction in a province where more than 40 percent of the private sector workforce was unionized and public sector unions barely existed. The right to strike was accepted in principle, but resisted in practice. The province's union movement confronted court injunctions and imposed agreements at every turn, learning from the earliest days of Bennett's administration that few gains of consequence could be won without militant picketing, hard-fought strikes and even jail time by union leaders. The Vancouver sophisticates who sought to manage the province's affairs from the lounges of the Terminal City Club or the Vancouver Club may have deplored Bennett's populist rhetoric and small-town style, but they much appreciated his open-handed royalty policies and firm anti-labour stance.

In Victoria, government administration remained unchanged from the day Bennett took over in 1952. All significant decisions were made by Bennett alone, in accordance with the Keep It Simple, Stupid (KISS) sign that hung in his office. For most of his career, Bennett was his own finance minister and his cabinet met without officials present. No minutes were kept. Cabinet ministers had no political staff. There were no communications or public relations staffs. It was a one-man government. Travel and even long-distance telephone calls were approved at the top. Politically, Bennett portrayed himself as the ally of the ordinary citizens against the elites. He was the bulwark against victory by the dreaded socialists and "the alternative to socialism." He pioneered what biographer David Mitchell termed the "paranoid style in BC politics: good guys versus bad guys; fear and loathing; class conflict." Once fundraising had been reorganized under Bennett's control, Social Credit became the W.A.C. Bennett party, a political machine organized around a single dominant personality.

Bennett ruled the legislature with an iron hand. Biographer Paddy Sherman, a reporter who rose to become publisher of the *Province*, described him as "a man to whom politics is civil war, a man to whom everything is a potential weapon in his battle for more money to make his province and himself look better ... His unchangeable principles are few. As events change he will freely reverse a stand a year later." Bennett had little patience for grassroots democracy, believing that "if the electors govern, you have anarchy." He had no interest in referendums and consultation, arguing his mandate to govern was virtually absolute. "People in a democratic way select people to do a job," he said, "and they must boldly do that job and they must not ask questions and have royal commissions all the time. They should take responsibility and bold action."

With a few exceptions—Robert Bonner, the gifted but aloof downtown lawyer he recruited to cabinet to link him to Vancouver business interests, and Phil Gaglardi, the Kamloops businessman who had challenged him for leader in 1952—Bennett's caucus was happy to sit back and let him run the show. For the most part they were, in the words of BC political scientist Walter Young, "earnest lower-middle-class men and women who were as much in awe of the trappings of parliament and power as anyone is likely to be ... dependent on the man who was their talisman and the master entrepreneur in a province where politics and exploitation were intertwined."

On the floor of the legislature, Socred members simply did as they were told, waiting for Bennett to resolve any procedural matters that arose. The rules of procedure had remained unchanged since 1920. There was no Question Period. There was no Hansard record of debate. If time ran short at the end of a session, Bennett simply continued debate around the clock until the opposition members sagged with exhaustion. Many members of the press gallery were on the government payroll. This effectively reduced the prospect of negative coverage, particularly in the province's Interior, where daily papers relied on the wire service and the occasional column by low-paid legislature reporters who rounded out their salaries with freelance work extolling the government's achievements. But why staff the legislature with reporters at all, considering how seldom it met?

During the 1950s, Bennett found he needed the legislature in session only about thirty-eight days a year, extending it to nine weeks or about forty-five days during the 1960s, a period in which total government expenditures rose 500 percent. No extra oversight was needed, however. W.A.C. was in control. Only cabinet ministers were full-time. Once the legislature adjourned for the year, both opposition members and government backbenchers were expected to head home to their real jobs. No offices were provided at the legislature, even for the opposition leader, and reporters who covered opposition figures between sessions were upbraided by Bennett for undue partisanship. The Social Credit caucus shared six phones; all the CCF members, later the New Democrats, worked in a single large room with shared desks. "The legislature, in many respects, was not the real world," wrote Walter Young. "It was a yearly venting of steam from an engine that might otherwise become overheated. The real business of government did not concern debate or party politics."

BC sailed through the post-war era in this political time warp. While the United States put a man in space, elected Kennedy, plunged into the Vietnam War, experienced riots, launched a War on Poverty and enacted civil rights, BC's legislature did all the business of Canada's third-largest province in an average forty-five days a year. The Warsaw Pact invaded Czechoslovakia, France was rocked by political upheaval, Canada celebrated Expo 67 and Montreal prepared for the Olympics, but in BC, the man in the homburg simply carried on.

Year after year, in election after election, Bennett outmanoeuvred the hapless socialists, setting up long-suffering CCF/NDP leader Robert Strachan for defeat after defeat. In a world convulsed by change and political upheaval, British Columbia seemed to have perfected a political perpetual motion machine: although the wheels turned, nothing changed. But as the Hotel Vancouver staff cleared away the last of the dirty dishes from the Social Credit banquet in 1965, the people and movements that would end the Bennett era were already gathering strength. In fact, the man who would bring Bennett down had already been twice elected to the legislature, defeating a cabinet minister in his first bid for office.

If the 1965 Hotel Vancouver fete was a tribute to W.A.C. Bennett's successes, it was a reminder to NDP opposition leader Robert Strachan—who gamely attended the non-partisan banquet—of his career's remarkable futility. Strachan had received three electoral drubbings at Bennett's hands by the night of the dinner with another bout scheduled for 1966. Bennett was the longest-serving premier in BC history—and Strachan the longest-serving leader of the opposition.

The upheaval that had catapulted Bennett to power in 1952 had forced the CCF to change leaders three times in as many years. Since 1938, the party had been led by Harold Winch, an electrician and union activist first elected in Vancouver East in 1937. Winch led the CCF to a clear majority of first-choice ballots in 1952, but Bennett's crafty manoeuvring had denied him the premiership not once, but twice. When the Lieutenant-Governor refused his request to form government in 1953, Winch resigned and was replaced by teacher Arnold Webster, who bowed out in 1956 in favour of Strachan. Born in Glasgow, Robert Strachan was a leader of the Nanaimo carpenters' union, a self-educated man of considerable accomplishment and an eloquent speaker with a slight Scottish brogue. He had only to open his mouth to remind voters of the CCF's labour ties, prompting Social Credit

Attorney General Robert Bonner to dismiss him as "the breeze from the Hebrides."

To be fair to Strachan, the CCF, which reorganized as the NDP at a joint convention of the CCF and the Canadian Labour Congress in 1961, had to work hard just to stand still in the face of the lopsided distribution of seats in Social Credit's favour. In 1960, for example, Social Credit needed only 38 percent of the general vote to secure thirty-two seats of the total of fifty-two. A popular vote of 32.7 percent netted Strachan only sixteen seats. This hard reality, combined with the three-way split of the anti-Socred vote among CCF, Conservative and Liberal voters, and his own inability to challenge Bennett's populism, saw Strachan beaten in 1956, 1959 and 1963 by wide margins despite a steady one-third share of the popular vote—a share Strachan proved unable to increase.

Strachan's 1966 campaign, driven by a "People First" program that pledged to apply "democratic socialist principles to government and the administration of public affairs," followed a depressing and familiar pattern. Heavy with proposals for panels of experts on education and federal-provincial relations, the platform was far from radical, but that didn't stop Bennett from demanding a strong mandate to demonstrate stability to foreign investors. Once on the campaign trail, Strachan promised inflation protection through a Prices Review Board, public auto insurance, a new labour code and minimum income for seniors, all of which became planks of the NDP's successful 1972 campaign. But Bennett simply ignored Strachan, declaring "socialism in BC would mean collective farms, state-run stores, control of mines, pulp mills and factories." Editorial writers predicted a Bennett win for the simple reason that voters "will see no real alternative." When the ballots were counted, both Bennett and Strachan remained where they were. Strachan found himself working with a sixteen-person caucus, two more than before the writ dropped but just under half of Bennett's caucus of thirty-three.

With this fourth successive defeat, Strachan's critics in the party began to circle. Then only fifty-two, Strachan had never been challenged for the leadership despite annual reviews under the party's constitution. A *Sun* reporter covering Strachan's election-night party September 12 in Duncan thought the carpenter, "who once flamed with ambition, seemed almost complacent" and relieved at the outcome. At the International Woodworkers of America (IWA) Hall on Vancouver's Commercial Drive, the mood was different. A jubilant Dave Barrett, re-elected to a third term from the newly created Coquitlam riding, noted that opposition candidates from the NDP or the Liberals had won sixteen of twenty-five Lower Mainland seats up for grabs (several were two-member ridings). "This is the beginning of the end for the Socreds," Barrett declared. Others saw it as the end of Strachan. The *Province* reported that labour lawyer Tom Berger, newly elected to the legislature in Vancouver–Burrard, was already "touted in some quarters as a potential NDP leader." The Berger challenge was not long in coming and it would split the party down the middle.

The main challenge to Strachan came from BC's unions, the powerful new partners who had joined with the CCF to form the NDP in 1961. By the late 1960s, the alliance was already bearing fruit outside the traditional CCF stronghold in Saskatchewan, where Tommy Douglas had completed five terms as premier. Manitoba's NDP appeared poised for victory, Ontario's NDP was growing, but BC seemed like the best prospect for a true breakthrough if Strachan's lacklustre leadership could be shaken up. BC's NDP-affiliated unions believed they had found their man in Berger.

The tall son of an RCMP officer and grandson of a Swedish judge, Berger had grown up in Victoria. After graduating from law school, he worked in a small Vancouver firm at every aspect of criminal law, "defending drug addicts, traffickers, thieves, burglars and prostitutes [and] trade unions and their members."

In 1963, he opened his own one-person law practice. Although a Liberal in university, Berger had quickly gravitated to the CCF as the "stoutest defenders of minority rights." A powerful advocate and a very hard worker, Berger joined the party in 1960 at the age of twenty-seven, ran unsuccessfully in the 1960 provincial election and was elected provincial party president in 1961. A year later, Berger was elected to federal parliament in Vancouver–Burrard, but found himself out of office in less than a year, a casualty of the swing that saw the Diefenbaker Conservatives ousted in favour of Lester Pearson. Undaunted, Berger contested a seat in the two-member provincial riding of Vancouver–Burrard in 1963. Again defeated, he returned to law.

Berger's legal career was even more impressive than his political one. By 1966, he had become one of BC's leading labour and criminal lawyers in what was a crowded field, defending striking ironworkers in the dispute that followed the Second Narrows Bridge collapse and successfully suing W.A.C. Bennett for slander in a celebrated 1965 case involving George Jones, the head of the BC Purchasing Commission. ("I am not going to say anything about the Jones boy," Bennett told a large audience in Victoria, despite Jones' acquittal on charges of accepting a benefit. "But I could tell you lots." Berger won Jones a $15,000 cash settlement from the premier.) In 1966, Berger again contested one of the two provincial seats available in Vancouver–Burrard and this time was elected handily. Within the year, he decided to challenge Strachan's leadership. He was thirty-three.

Berger's 1967 drive to unseat Strachan, backed by a number of key NDP labour affiliates as well as a number of party activists, caused an upheaval in the ranks of the BC NDP. The announcement of Berger's candidacy seemed to catch Strachan off-guard, as did his blunt statement that "the social and economic landscape of the province has change immeasurably, but the political landscape has not changed since 1952." Most caucus members immediately declared their loyalty to Strachan, closing ranks against a relative newcomer whose political allegiances seemed uncertain but whose institutional backing by labour made him a serious threat. The confrontation came to a head at the NDP's 1967 convention.

Convention delegates upheld Strachan's leadership by a vote of 278 to 177. "The majority of the delegates had decided that Berger was a young man in too much of a hurry," concluded his biographer, but the struggle to remove Strachan continued, splitting the caucus and the party right down to the riding associations. Berger refused to rule out another challenge. Although party membership was growing, it was a fraction of the level of other strong NDP provinces. Worse, after a generation in the political wilderness, the party was $30,000 in debt and the party office had essentially stopped functioning. Aware that Berger would confront him again, Strachan announced his resignation late in 1968. Not surprisingly, Strachan turned to Barrett—his most vocal supporter in caucus—as he stepped down, privately assuring him he would support a Barrett bid to become the next party leader.

If there was one person the party's old guard believed could replace Strachan, it was Barrett, who had defeated Minister of Labour Lyle Wicks in his first election bid in 1960. From his earliest days in the legislature, he was spotted as a talented up-and-comer. Barrett was different in every way from Strachan, whom he deeply admired. Short, pudgy, with a broad smile, a mischievous sense of humour and a complete inability to seem defensive or calculating, Barrett was the leading edge of a new wave of talented MLAs who joined the caucus during the 1960s. Like Berger, Barrett owed at least some of his notoriety to a clash with W.A.C. Bennett's government, which had fired him from his social work job at the Haney Correctional Institute when he sought the CCF nomination in Dewdney in 1959. He was the son of Sam Barrett, a politically active East Vancouver grocer who supported and revered 1930s CCF leader Ernest Winch, and Rose Barrett, a Communist who participated in many of the Depression-era campaigns against poverty and colonialism. But Dave never took life too seriously. His Britannia school yearbook termed him a "jokester" and he was no stranger to the wilder side of Van East life: "drugs, bootleggers ... We all knew it was going on," he recalled in his autobiography.

During his high school and university years, Barrett worked as a city street worker, a cannery worker and a fruit seller, eventually achieving an undergraduate degree at Jesuit-run Seattle University. In 1953, now unemployed and married to Shirley Hackman, the love of his life, he found a job in Vancouver as a social worker handling a caseload of seventy-eight foster children. He very quickly realized he needed more professional training to advance in the field and won admission to the graduate program in social work at St. Louis University in Missouri.

Despite his childhood immersion in left-wing politics, Barrett later wrote that he approached social justice issues from a religious perspective. He was inspired by Thomas Aquinas, who held "that legitimate power springs not from the divine right of kings but from the commonwealth of people." This conviction, combined with total immersion in the political atmosphere of the southern states at the height of the Red Scare, gave Barrett a distinctive approach to politics that was to shape his time in government. As a social worker, Barrett saw first-hand how quickly the criminal justice system discarded people, whether they were foster children or petty criminals. His decision to enter politics reflected a determination to make the system work better in the interests of liberating the potential of all members of society, as individuals, not to overturn the system to replace the rule of one class with another. But given his upbringing and training, Barrett was able to blend the perspective of social democratic roots of his East Van childhood with his Jesuit training. These formative elements of his philosophy, combined with his exposure to the populist politics of the United States, were expressed with a personal eloquence that made him a powerful and spontaneous speaker.

When an offer came to work at the Haney Correctional Institute near Maple Ridge, Barrett brought his family back from Missouri to British Columbia, where he quickly challenged the operations of BC's antiquated criminal justice system. A natural in political combat, Barrett hungered for a career in politics. Soon after a meeting at Haney with MLA Tony Gargrave, the CCF's justice critic, he buttonholed a local party activist in a parking lot and said, "I want to join the CCF. I want to be an MLA." He quickly got his chance to seek an NDP nomination in his own constituency.

In the 1959 nomination battle in the Dewdney riding that stretched from Mission to Port Moody, Barrett faced off against four other candidates, including high-profile lawyer Stu Leggatt. The contest was far from the headlines in a hot summer dominated by news of a salmon industry strike, a forest strike, contempt of court hearings against workers who had refused to resume construction of the collapsed Second Narrows Bridge, and the Hotel Georgia's decision to put a television in every room.

Barrett's candidacy was ignited by the kind of political lightning strike that can make or break a career when he learned that Attorney General Robert Bonner was about to fire him for criticizing social welfare services on the campaign trail. One of Bennett's most senior cabinet ministers was determined to silence a provincial employee who was not yet even a CCF nominee. Barrett tipped a television reporter, who got confirmation from Bonner on film. Barrett lost his job and won his seat. "Govt. Fires Pro-CCF Jail Worker" blared the *Vancouver Sun*'s front-page headline on July 27, 1959. That and intensive television coverage catapulted Barrett into overnight celebrity. Reading the writing on the wall, Leggatt skipped the nomination meeting and the brash twenty-nine-year-old Barrett waltzed to a first-ballot victory before heading to an upset 1960 election win over Wicks. The campaign not only brought him a seat in the legislature, it cemented a bond with the local leaders of International Woodworkers of America and key figures in the party establishment he would rely on for the rest of his political career.

Barrett quickly became a thorn in the government's side and a star on the opposition benches, forcing government investigations of abuses and exposing the "tragic waste" of institutions like the Willingdon School for Girls, where 30 percent of the young women committed for "incorrigibility" were guilty only of liquor offences. Within months of his election, Barrett was able to question Bonner in the House for twelve hours during estimates, and for the next two terms he was constantly in the news on issues like prison reform, the drug laws and divorce. By 1964, even the *Sun* was applauding him in an editorial headlined "Good for Mr. Barrett ... and his interesting ideas." Barrett became adept at reducing his attacks to a few memorable syllables, suggesting, for example, that a Socred plan to locate four mental institutions in Burnaby would create a "city of madness." On another occasion he warned a meeting of Young New Democrats that criticism levelled by a Socred minister against clerics who opposed government labour policies showed "the raw face of Canadian fascism."

Barrett's most high-profile success in opposition was his campaign to protect Cypress Bowl from logging, a victory he claimed as premier. The $10-million resort development plan, promoted by friends of the government, required the sale of parkland to allow Cypress Mountain to be logged and converted to a ski resort with an artificial lake, high-rise towers and an eight-thousand-car parking lot. Government support included tax-funded hydro lines and road access. When Barrett was able to link the promoters to Meyer Lansky and the mob, he scored a major victory over Social Credit and Vancouver Liberal MLAs Gordon Gibson Sr. and Ray Perrault, both project supporters, to protect an environmental landmark from being scarred by logging that would be seen from most of Vancouver. By 1965, Barrett was a two-term legislature veteran and clearly the most talented frontbencher on the NDP team. The next year, however, Strachan's caucus was joined by Berger, already a veteran of the House of Commons, and urban planner Bob Williams, an East Vancouver activist who had shaken up Vancouver City Council as an alderman. A new generation was taking its place.

The NDP's 1969 leadership contest between Berger and Barrett was a battle between two men who each went on to number among the most important British Columbians of their generation. The stakes could not have been higher. New Democrats were not alone in sensing the end of the Bennett era. "There is no socialist government in North America," wrote *Vancouver Sun* columnist Allan Fotheringham. "The one place it could happen is BC," and Barrett could be the man to do it. Despite his "rumpled, lumpish look," the thirty-nine-year-old Barrett was a hard worker, rushing from an anti-Vietnam war rally to a by-election on the eve of the convention. "If there's one thing I learned from Bennett, it's how to kill," Barrett said. "The time to hit a politician is when he's down."

Like many party veterans, Barrett had "resented it deeply" when he learned of Berger's initial 1966 leadership challenge, believing it reflected untrammelled personal ambition in someone who lacked experience. Berger's ambition and talent clearly rankled his rivals, but more critical for many New Democrats was labour's role in Berger's candidacy. Key labour activists, including BC Federation of Labour staffers like Clive Lytle, the Federation's policy director, were lead organizers for Berger, ensuring that the 180 delegates from affiliated unions—nearly one-quarter of the convention total—were solidly in Berger's corner under the bloc voting practices completely within the rules but deplored by non-labour activists. Barrett later speculated that his vocal opposition to this policy was the main reason organized labour, with some exceptions, never supported his leadership. But Berger also drew support from long-time non-labour activists like Dennis and Yvonne Cocke, the New Westminster operators of the formidable "Cocke machine" that was feared as much as respected in party circles.

Interest in the 1969 contest was so intense that eight hundred delegates registered for the April convention at the Hotel Vancouver, two and a half times the number that had turned out eighteen months earlier to re-elect Strachan and turn back Berger's first assault. News media, sensing that New Democrats could be picking the next premier, provided round-the-clock coverage. Tension ran high at the hotel as the delegates prepared for the historic leadership vote, believing the NDP was finally ready to move, as Fotheringham put it, "from the beer league to the cocktail fringe" of BC politics.

Confident that Strachan's commitment in 1968 would produce an endorsement in 1969, Barrett had thrown himself into the race full of confidence, but the campaign produced one ugly surprise after another. As delegates streamed into Vancouver, Barrett was stunned to learn that Vancouver East MLA Bob Williams had decided to enter the race. Williams now offered himself up as a compromise candidate between Barrett and Berger, though few who knew Williams could imagine him as a conciliator or bridge-builder.

That wasn't Barrett's only problem. Although a majority of caucus members were supporting him, the MLAs had not made a recommendation. Berger's team included newly elected New Westminster MLA Cocke, long-serving Atlin MLA and Nisga'a leader Frank Calder, Surrey MLA Ernie Hall, Berger's Burrard riding mate Ray Parkinson, and at least 75 percent of the union delegates. The night before the vote, another bombshell dropped: Strachan threw his support to Williams. "Bob Williams is the best man," he told a news conference, praising him as smart, unifying and not beholden to "sectional interests," a dig at Berger's union backing. Then the strongest argument of all: "There is no MLA in our party whom the Socreds hate more."

A mob of reporters charged to Barrett's hotel room to get his reaction. "I was churning inside," he wrote later, "but I managed to bore the press into leaving. It was an incredible test, because I was really fuming. Strachan had misled me." (As was often the case when Barrett faced crisis, he had his shoes off when he met reporters.) But Barrett had taken Strachan for granted, apparently making no effort to nail down his support even on the eve of the vote. "I never did find out why Strachan switched," Barrett wrote. "We never discussed it." It was a mistake that may have cost Barrett the leadership, despite a belated endorsement from Williams, who found himself a distant third on the first ballot.

The convention mood was bitter. The Barrett forces not only resented Berger—in their eyes he was a former Liberal, an intellectual without majority caucus support and a product of the labour machine—they felt betrayed by Williams and Strachan, who himself was shaken by the outcome. In the end, Barrett had been able to win support from only half his caucus colleagues, a handful of labour supporters and slightly less than half of the convention delegates after Williams and fourth-place finisher John Conway had dropped out. Berger had won the day and the coming election was his to lose. But Bennett had no intention of giving Berger a moment to prepare. Just four months after the young lawyer took over, Bennett dissolved the legislature and sent the province to the polls.

With its new, bright, forward-looking, thirty-six-year-old leader, the NDP was confident of victory. Party billboards and newspaper ads featured a man in a suit carrying a briefcase, with the headline "Ready to Govern." Berger had told convention delegates, "The time has come to form government," adding that an NDP administration "would implement socialist principles on a non-compromise basis." Nationalization of BC Tel was at the top of the list, along with higher resource royalties. Berger combined the NDP's standard list of platform commitments with bitter personal attacks on Bennett, calling him "a pathetic old man clinging desperately to power." In the days before tracking polls, it was easier to nurse delusions of victory. Barrett told a Mission rally that Berger would take thirty-five seats for the NDP, four more than the Socreds held on dissolution.

The Berger threat was considered real enough in business quarters to require an emergency secret meeting of fifty-six corporate leaders at Hy's Encore on Hornby Street, where Hy Aisenstat himself made the pitch. The group included Jimmy Pattison, the forty-one-year-old self-made millionaire who had got his start as car salesman and was elbowing his way into the province's establishment by purchasing Neon Products, a sign business. Pattison was a Van East outsider at Hy's, which was conveniently located close to Howe Street's Vancouver Stock Exchange, and midway between the Vancouver and Terminal City Clubs on Hastings and the new MacMillan Bloedel and BC Hydro towers on Burrard and Georgia. It was a telling sign of the concentration of power in BC's resource economy that such a gathering of powerful men could meet at short notice to steer provincial politics. The anti-Berger ads that subsequently appeared were linked to a BC Tel ad man.

Berger's presumptuous approach backfired. W.A.C. Bennett stepped up his warnings against "Marxian socialism." At one boisterous rally, he pulled out all the stops to warn that "the barbarians are at the gates," turning the expectation of an NDP breakthrough into his strongest weapon. The wily campaigner also played up Berger's ties to the province's militant labour leaders, almost all of whom had supported Berger in his bitter tussle with Barrett. Bennett's slogan, "Strike pay with Berger or take-home pay with Bennett," struck home.

Berger, the slick city lawyer backed by the labour bosses, proved a perfect foil for Wacky's populist, anti-elite message.

Preoccupied with the inner-party battle, the NDP had been unable to produce campaign signs in some ridings. Not to worry, said long-time Kootenay NDP MLA Leo Nimsick, who held on to his seat by a wafer-thin fifteen-vote margin. "We don't want to peak too soon." When the ballots were counted on August 27, 1969, Bennett had won his greatest victory ever, adding seven seats to take thirty-eight of fifty-five in the legislature. Not only was the NDP reduced to twelve seats, Berger suffered personal defeat in Burrard and the provincial Liberals rebounded to five under new leader Pat McGeer. Berger and the New Democrats were crushed.

By destroying Berger so decisively, Bennett accomplished for Barrett what Barrett had failed to do for himself. The much-reduced NDP caucus quickly united around Barrett as House Leader and the 1970 party convention acclaimed him as party leader. Now all-powerful, Barrett moved against the labour movement, promising to end the system that allowed union locals to "affiliate" to the NDP and wield their membership blocs on the convention floor. The threat brought an immediate counter-threat from BC Federation of Labour secretary treasurer Ray Haynes, but at the subsequent convention, in June 1970, both sides claimed victory: local affiliation was retained but Barrett supporter Paddy Neale beat Haynes for a seat on the party executive.

Barrett, who described himself as a "free-swinging humanist," nonetheless insisted "we are not a labour party. And I think that should be clearly understood. I am not anti-union. I am pro all people of this province, who work for a living ... This is not a labour party. This is a party representing the common interests of the common man." His ambition for the NDP was "to make it human. I want to bring together all of the good ideas that exist in the party and put it in human, understandable terms. I think that more than anything else this party has a great deal to offer the total society in British Columbia. It has a basic concern of man

A gracious Dave Barrett walks across the floor of the legislature to shake hands with his political adversary W.A.C. Bennett, 1972. Photo provided by the *Vancouver Sun*

to man. It has essentially excellent moral values. I want to put all of this into human terms so that every citizen in every walk of life understands that we have good intentions, we have good desires and as Woodsworth says, what we desire for ourselves we wish for all."

"The man Bennett would least like to have seen as BC leader

was Barrett," wrote *Sun* columnist Jack Wasserman. "The reason is simple, Barrett is Bennett with social awareness. Although relatively inexperienced, he has a keen political sense, he has the ability to simplify complex issues and, when necessary, distract the voter with a straight gut issue. He has a thick hide and is completely undisturbed by the fact that he is unloved by the establishment—any establishment. Also, like Bennett, he can laugh at himself in private and become wildly emotional in a debate in the legislature. And whatever the pundits and the establishment may think, the people respond to him, as evidenced by his large vote in a middle-class riding. From the ashes ... who knows?"

Despite the bitter disappointments of 1969, Barrett had reason to be grateful to both Bennett and Berger. It was Berger who had forced the issue of Strachan's leadership, ultimately winning his job. But it was Bennett who laid bare the New Democrats' organizational and political weaknesses in devastating fashion during the election, opening the door for Barrett to take the leadership. It is doubtful that any of Berger's leadership opponents could have won in 1969, given the NDP's lack of preparation, the proximity of the election and the unflinching business support for Bennett. There's no doubt, however, that Barrett's defeat at the 1969 convention made it possible for him to become premier in 1972.

2: Inside the Gates

There was little to suggest the end was nigh for W.A.C. Bennett and his twenty-year domination of British Columbia when the New Year dawned in 1972. The economy continued to tick along, another surplus was recorded in the strange accounting books that passed for Social Credit budgeting, and no one on the opposition benches showed much sign of catching on with the public. Barrett had spent much of the previous year driving the province with his faithful aide Harvey Beech, speaking to tiny meetings of party faithful. The Liberals were in the throes of deposing their leader, UBC neurologist Dr. Pat McGeer, and the provincial Conservatives were test-driving lawyer Derril Warren, a BC native recently returned from Alberta, where Conservative Peter Lougheed had banished the Social Credit regime of Ernest Manning four years earlier. Although Warren had wooed two Social Credit MLAs, Scott Wallace and Donald Marshall, into a new Conservative caucus, no one on the Social Credit benches mourned their departure.

Bennett had begun the year in his usual fashion, with a brief and uneventful session of the legislature. His January 20 Throne Speech was tedious even by Bennett's usual standards. There was a strong focus on the economy, with promises of yet more railways, dams and schools. Bennett vowed to crack down on litter and proclaimed a new hearing aid regulation to be in full force and effect. In his reply, Barrett had flayed the Throne Speech as a hollow document, absent of any mention of the dramatic anti-nuclear voyage of Greenpeace's *Phyllis Cormack* that had stirred "an awareness in all the people of North America" about the threat of pollution and nuclear war. "We have a lazy, tired government," Barrett concluded. "These are modern times, they require a modern government." Bennett was a "man in power who sees himself in an almost divine right position," added Williams, "and he sees not a cabinet around him, but rather a court." The legislature had adjourned only weeks later amid an acrimonious debate about government editing of what passed for the record of proceedings.

Nonetheless, the seventy-one-year-old premier began his annual spring tour of the province in good spirits, leading the way from stop to stop in his large, government-owned black Cadillac. Cabinet ministers followed in their own vehicles. As always, commemorative scrolls, cufflinks and ceremonial teacups were packed up for presentation to appreciative local politicians and their wives. It was a ritual that never failed to work a form of grassroots magic, far from the lights of the big city. This time, however, it was a disaster.

The expedition had barely started before controversial cabinet minister "Flying Phil" Gaglardi was pulled over by the RCMP for driving, in the words of one cop, like "a bloody maniac." At Kamloops, one of the early stops, striking construction unions harnessed their fury at being ordered back to work into a raucous disruption of a ceremony to open a new vocational school. The premier could barely be heard over the crescendo of boos, jeers and angry catcalls that didn't let up throughout his brief speech. As he struggled to make his way out through the packed protestors, surrounded by police, Bennett's renowned, million-watt smile never wavered. Suddenly, a deep, gravelly voice rang out through the din. "Keep smiling, Wacky!" the union man bellowed.

Years later, *Vancouver Sun* reporter Michael Finlay remembered that sarcastic yell as a voice of doom for W.A.C. Bennett, heralding his coming downfall. To Finlay, it was a clear sign the old man was on his way out. There was no more respect, no more reverence. After two decades in power, Bennett had become a figure to taunt, to ridicule to his face. Jeering demonstrators showed up wherever the cabinet cavalcade ventured. And in Lillooet, Ma Murray, the legendary, feisty, eighty-four-year-old publisher of the *Bridge River–Lillooet News*, made her own news that day by pointedly refusing to attend a luncheon for the premier.

The ill-fated tour culminated at the Royal Towers Hotel in New Westminster with one of the most violent protests the province had seen in years. More than five hundred burly building tradesmen, infuriated by a back-to-work order issued by Bennett's Mediation Commission, gathered outside to block the entrance. While Bennett slipped in through a back door, police struggled desperately to force an entry through the surging crowd for beleaguered members of the cabinet. Placards attached to two-by-fours became weapons, raining down on the ministers as they ran a fierce gauntlet into the hotel.

Attorney General Les Peterson was bashed on the head. Minister of Mines Frank Richter was hit on the back. Minister of Highways Wesley Black was punched in the stomach as he stumbled to avoid being struck. Pat Jordan wrenched her shoulder. When he put out his arm to protect cabinet colleague Isabel Dawson from being clubbed by a sign, Minister of Agriculture Cyril Shelford suffered a broken collarbone. The next day, W.A.C. Bennett assured one and all that everything was "Jes' fine," in the words of the little candidate bug in the Pogo comic strip. "A brilliant success," the premier boasted of the cabinet's thirteen-day excursion. Friendly crowds greeted them wherever they went, he told a gathering in Vancouver. Meanwhile, a *Vancouver Sun* reporter with an eye for irony noted that seated in the audience were "cabinet ministers nursing bruises, welts, sore muscles and possibly broken bones."

A month later, the premier upheld another tradition—his annual lawn party on the grounds of his large white Kelowna residence. There were no demonstrators this time. These were the premier's people, ordinary folk in ordinary dress, clutching their invitations, sipping lemonade, munching tiny sandwiches and pastries. As the premier circulated among the four thousand guests, patting children on the head and advising them not to use drugs, it was as if time had stood still.

Outside the premier's safe Okanagan enclave, however, British Columbia, as elsewhere in Canada and the world, was in turmoil. The benign, dope-smoking, free-loving, youth revolution of the 1960s had turned edgy. In Vancouver, there had been the 1971 Gastown Riot and a violent altercation just six weeks earlier between police and hundreds of bottle-throwing fans seeking to crash a Rolling Stones concert at the Pacific Coliseum. Heightening the atmosphere was ongoing conflict between a contemptuous counterculture and Vancouver's hippie-hating Mayor Tom Campbell. Harder drugs were now killing people. Activists plotted about overthrowing the state, rather than calling for peace and love. Greenpeace had been founded by local anti-nuke protesters one year earlier. The environment had emerged as a cause, and feminism was on the march. Revolution was in the air.

While Hollywood revelled in the success of *The Godfather*, Bennett acolyte and Deputy Minister of Tourism Ron "Stagedoor Ronnie" Worley, as he was labelled to devastating effect by columnist Allan Fotheringham, spearheaded production of *Twenty Great Years in British Columbia*, a thirty-minute celluloid paean to Social Credit. When Worley asked for the film to be shown in regular movie theatres, he was turned down flat. Even the narration is appalling, one forthright executive told the *Vancouver Sun*. Beyond BC, there had been the October crisis in Quebec, the Vietnam War continued its deadly path (the famous photo of a naked girl burned from a napalm attack and running down a road, appeared in the *Vancouver Sun* the same day as its coverage of the riotous Royal Towers confrontation), and a two-bit break-in at Democratic Party offices in the Watergate building in Washington was slowly attracting the attention of a couple of reporters named Bob Woodward and Carl Bernstein.

Apparently oblivious to this chaotic atmosphere of change, a man born at the turn of the century sought one last mandate, one final hurrah against the socialist hordes. It had, after all, been three years since his last trip to the polls. It was summer. It was his tradition. An outsider, alien to the strange, polarized politics of British Columbia, would have been stretched to offer a plugged nickel for the premier's chances of an unprecedented seventh term. A week after the election, Bennett would be seventy-two, far older than any premier in the country. Half a dozen incumbent governments had recently been voted out across Canada, including the premier's contemporary, Joey Smallwood, turfed after twenty-three years at the helm of Newfoundland. Nor was Bennett, with his odd, staccato speaking style that regularly jumbled words, a politician for the emerging age of TV.

Worse, he was up against a trio of energetic new leaders, two of whom (David Anderson of the Liberals and Derril Warren of the Conservatives) had been too young to vote in 1952 when W.A.C. Bennett began his two-decade grip on British Columbia. At forty-one, the NDP's Dave Barrett was oldest of the opposition lot, and he was thirty years younger than W.A.C. Bennett. Nonetheless, few if any predicted an end to the Bennett era. There was simply too much political history to look back on. BC after all was land of the "ten-second" Socred. Each election legions of voters—anti-Socred before they voted and anti-Socred after they voted—became party supporters just long enough to mark their ballots to keep out the NDP. This dread of socialists storming through the gates to power, regularly whipped up by

W.A.C. Bennett on the hustings, had never failed to deliver.

But the 1972 campaign turned out to be one too many for the aging premier. Bennett had lost his touch. On the road only three days a week, he bizarrely refused to tell anyone in the media where he was going. He called this peek-a-boo strategy "the new method of campaigning." When he did show up, Bennett appeared wan and tired. In contrast, the roly-poly Barrett smiled and clowned his way around the province, far from the media spotlight of the Lower Mainland, defusing fear wherever he went. He didn't downplay NDP policies, particularly vows to bring in government-owned auto insurance and tax the province's rich resources. But his message was non-threatening: "Enough is enough."

The tone was set on day one. Barrett slammed Social Credit's giveaway of the province's natural resources and its pinched spending on a multitude of social concerns. But at the same time, he insisted the NDP was the underdog. There would be no predictions of victory, no "Ready to Govern" slogans from Dave Barrett. His only goal, he suggested, was a stronger opposition. Then, referring to Bennett's slur that he had something to do with Marx, the NDP leader quipped, "I ask him which one: Groucho, Harpo or Zeppo?"

Soon afterward came Barrett's hilarious dismissal of attempts by Bennett to link him to the Waffle manifesto, a document, signed by Barrett and other prominent NDP MLAs, that called for a greater tilt to the left by the federal party. "When he talks about waffles, I talk about pancakes," Barrett told a TV reporter. "When the premier said I was a waffle, I said he was a pancake. He said I was a double waffle. I said he was a stack of pancakes. Now he says there are waffles in our caucus. I say there are pancakes in his group. It's sheer nonsense. The premier wants to avoid the issues. However, if he keeps this up, knowing how he feels about Quebec, I'm going to call him a crepe Suzette." Not much was heard of the Waffle manifesto after that. More seriously,

Barrett explained that he put his name to it only to stimulate debate within the party.

In the early days of the campaign, Barrett received less media coverage than the new boys, David Anderson and Derril Warren. The thirty-three-year old Warren, especially, attracted a media following, with his youthful sincerity and a belief in some quarters that he was the logical choice to inherit W.A.C. Bennett's legacy as leader of BC's substantial free enterprise forces. That didn't bother Barrett much. It was universal political wisdom that the more the non-NDP vote was split, the better it was for the New Democrats. Barrett concentrated on not being a target. By car and a small rented plane, accompanied only by the tireless Harvey Beech, a railway switcher from Coquitlam who was one of his closest friends, Barrett travelled to the far reaches of the province, lapping up the beautiful summer weather. No group was too small to hear his message.

In the north-central community of Houston, he told a gathering of forty people that it was time for "the little people" to say no to corporate takeovers. "You have a choice," he said. He journeyed even farther north to the mining town of Stewart, where he avoided a speech altogether. Instead, he merely mainstreeted, ate a steak in the community hall and refused a request to be "Hyderized," the well-known ritual just across the border in Hyder, Alaska, involving shots of seventy-five-proof alcohol. "I'm not drinking any snake bite, not in a temperance province like BC," Barrett laughed, and downed a soda pop.

It was up north that he unveiled one of his most effective jokes, an icebreaker that never failed to warm up the crowd. Barrett heard that one of the papers had written about consulting an astrologist to determine various characteristics of the four party leaders. When it came to "sexual proclivities," he told the tittering crowd, the astrologer identified him as a passionate lover. Barrett phoned home that night. Feeling pretty good about himself, he asked his wife, Shirley, if she'd seen anything interesting in the paper that day. "No, Dave," Shirley replied. "Just the same old lies." It was a brilliant joke that showed Barrett as someone unafraid to poke fun at himself, far from the scary figure Bennett was trying to paint of the man aspiring to be premier. The joke also reminded his audience that the media were against the NDP. They were as much a part of the corporate elite as Howe Street; what the press carried should not always be believed. But in mid-August, the headline over a lengthy *Sun* review of the first few weeks of the Barrett campaign read, "Barrett attacks with a smile." He could not have asked for better.

Meanwhile, other major forces were marshalling against Canada's last remaining Social Credit government. For the first time, the independent Teamsters Union and its pro-establishment leader Senator Ed Lawson pledged all-out opposition to Social Credit. Lawson was a bitter foe of the BC Federation of Labour and a regular hobnobber with Vancouver's social elite. But his union had been stung by a ruling of the government's Mediation Commission that denied eight hundred Teamster cement truck drivers $400,000 in retroactive pay. "The time has come for a change," declared Lawson. He directed large sums of union donations to the NDP's twelve incumbents and Liberal Barrie Clark. Classroom teachers also joined the fight. A political action arm of the "non-partisan" BC Teachers' Federation spent hundreds of thousands of dollars on behalf of candidates pledged to improve the province's cash-starved education system. Not a penny went to Social Credit.

Barrett began drawing bigger crowds, though his picture was still a rarity in the *Vancouver Sun*. When he complained, managing editor Bill Galt said the paper had tried to get a newsy picture of Barrett during his swing through the Okanagan "but all we could get was him with a handful of apricots." As election day neared, Social Credit's tried and true scare tactics ramped up one more time. Humorous in their own simplistic way, full-page ads showed a freshly paved highway heading, rightwards, to the horizon. A rutted, dusty road branched off to the left into a dense forest. The ads warned in big, capital letters: "DON'T TURN 'LEFT.'" Bennett lashed out at Barrett as both a "crybaby" and the most dangerous, radical leader the NDP had ever had. He linked him to the Communist Party, and finally, thundered the familiar threat that everyone was waiting for. At a large election rally in North Vancouver, Bennett proclaimed, "The socialist hordes are at the gates in British Columbia." This time, they were.

In the last week, the wheels simply fell off the Social Credit campaign, as it lurched from one public relations fiasco to another. Nothing was more damaging than an inexplicable decision by flamboyant Phil Gaglardi, the veteran Socred cabinet minister and Kamloops evangelist, to spill his political guts to a reporter from, of all papers, the *Toronto Star*. What he told reporter Chris Dennett was astonishing. Bennett was too old for the job. He didn't understand young people. He had stayed on only to thwart Gaglardi's leadership hopes. Bennett would resign after the election and he, Phil Gaglardi, was the only sensible choice to succeed him. Other cabinet ministers were nothing but square pegs trying to fit into round holes. Gaglardi's sensational comments dominated the final days of the campaign. The minister denied making the statements attributed to him. He tried to explain that he was only responding to rumours put to him by the reporter. Bennett was equal parts aghast and furious. He ordered him to sue Chris Dennett. And win. Dennett stuck by his story. Asked why he thought the minister opened up to him, the *Star* man said Gaglardi told him he looked like a sensible fellow who wouldn't print any of it.

Minister of Industrial Development Waldo Skillings, whose temper forever seemed out of place in mild-mannered Victoria, was also making news of the wrong kind. He grabbed a young Liberal volunteer who had taken his picture, shouting at him, according to reports, "You stupid young punk. You're not even dry behind the ears, and you've got all this long hair and beard just like my son. If you don't shut up, I'll throw you out the window." A few days later, Skillings struck fifty-five-year-old Conservative candidate Edith Gunning across the neck during a radio debate. (On election night, after Skillings had been defeated, Liberal leader David Anderson, who had snared one of the two Victoria seats, observed, "Anyone who goes around slugging people is going to lose votes.")

Panic set in. Social Credit organizers began buying up Bennett Burgers in bulk to skew the tally at the Frying Dutchman's annual PNE hamburger poll, which had Barrett Burgers far in the lead. The burger count was always closely watched by pundits as a harbinger of public taste, since, in one of BC's endearing quirks, genuine polling was banned during election campaigns. New Socred ads flooded BC newspapers, including one dealing head-on with the premier's age. "Young is an attitude," the ads trumpeted. There were references to Picasso at ninety, "still dazzling the world with creative genius," and Einstein in his seventies "working on his unified field theory." Alas for Bennett, not even Einstein's unified field theory could save him. For some reason, he held his last big public rally at a high school in the heart of the socialist stronghold of East Vancouver. Several hundred hecklers turned up, chanting "Sieg Heil," and "We Want Phil." A reporter overheard Bennett, struggling to speak over the clamour, instruct constant crony and PR guy Bill Clancey to "turn [the PA] up, man. Turn it up."

By this time, Barrett was basking in adulation. Crowds, large and small, were universally friendly. His low-key campaign, with nary a whisper about forming the next government, had worked to perfection. The fear factor was gone. The *Sun*'s counterculture columnist Bob Hunter, who had sailed with Greenpeace to Amchitka, called the NDP's platform "as radical as aspirin." The party's strategy was confirmed in a late directive to local candidates and organizers from campaign manager Hans Brown. He reminded workers to make no predictions, never introduce

Barrett as the next premier and ignore all smears. He admonished a riding that had produced bumper stickers saying, "Socreds Out!" Brown concluded, "This is bad, bad, bad. Don't do it. The campaign must now be nursed into harbour. We have all stuck to our game plan very well. Please, please. Let's stick with it. Any change now will hurt us all."

On the last Saturday before the vote, Barrett paid a relaxed visit to Nanaimo and danced with Shirley at a social event in Surrey. In a message to voters requested by the *Vancouver Sun*, Barrett expressed a wish for the twentieth century to be known as "a People's Century, rather than a material century ... With your help, the NDP can make the necessary changes to bring about this People's Century." Barrett's last rally was a roaring, foot-stomping meeting in his own Coquitlam riding on the eve of the vote. Before 1,200 enthused supporters, he preached electoral reform, an end to corporate sweetheart deals, and love. "For too long, this province has been racked with division—labour against management, teacher against government, doctor against cabinet minister. Unashamedly, I ask for love."

Yet, even then, almost no one realized that zero hour for W.A.C. Bennett and Social Credit really was at hand. Allan Fotheringham's poll of those in the know—business executives, pundits, academics, reporters—produced not one forecast of an NDP majority. Victoria-based *Province* reporter Peter McNelly easily won his newspaper's in-house election pool. He was the only entrant to pick the NDP to win. Privately, however, Barrett was confident. Shirley Barrett says her husband could feel the mood shifting as he toured the province until, by the last week, he believed the NDP would prevail. "He had a lot of fun during the campaign. He kind of bounced from one thing to another," she recalled. "But finally, towards the end, he really got a feeling from the grassroots that it could happen, that there was a change."

That evening, in their modern-ish suburban home on Western Avenue in Coquitlam, Shirley was on pins and needles, waiting for the returns. She served up hamburgers for dinner to Dave and their three children. "It was all I felt up to." Then, in what seemed mere minutes, the history of the province shifted. The old was out. The new was in. "We've done it. We've done it," Barrett kept exclaiming, as results came pouring in. By 9 p.m., it was a wipeout. Cabinet minister after cabinet minister tumbled to defeat, often to total political neophytes. When Phil Gaglardi's loss to steamfitter Gerry Anderson was confirmed, the roar from exultant, disbelieving NDP supporters was nearly the equal of the eruption to come less than a month later, when Foster Hewitt told the nation, "They score!! Henderson has scored for Canada!" Barrett put on a clean shirt, donned his familiar checked jacket, and the family headed off in their famous green Volvo to the Coquitlam Sports Centre and bedlam. Eighteen-year-old Dan drove. The premier-elect sat in the back.

In Kelowna, shortly after 10 p.m., W.A.C. Bennett climbed onto a box at his sombre campaign headquarters, the scene of so many past triumphant celebrations. With a brave smile, he announced, "I now concede the election to the NDP and Mr. Barrett and I wish him well. I hope he enjoys the position of premier as well as I enjoyed it." For Social Credit, reduced after twenty years in power to a mere ten seats, it was a night beyond all grim imaginings. It was as if they had been transported to an alternate universe. "What kind of a computer is this TV station using?" asked one perplexed supporter. "These results can't be right. They can't be." In Prince Rupert, Speaker William Murray, who lost to cab driver Graham Lea, said simply, "I'm afraid I can't explain the results."

In Vancouver, the Social Credit faithful gathered at the Bayshore Hotel. The same hotel had been abandoned just the day before—perhaps in an early inkling of business concern over imminent NDP rule—by reclusive billionaire Howard Hughes, who had been holed up behind closed curtains in the Bayshore's penthouse suite for months. The appearance of Attorney

General Les Peterson momentarily revived the quiet crowd. A woman rushed up to greet him. "Well, at least you won," she said, shaking his hand. Peering down at her, the tall Peterson replied, "No, I lost. We all lost." Jim Chabot, Frank Richter and minister without portfolio Pat Jordan were the only cabinet members to survive the electoral carnage with their leader Bennett. All of Bennett's heavyweight ministers, men who had presided over the province's affairs for years, went down to defeat: Peterson, Gaglardi, Ray Williston, Dan Campbell, Wesley Black, Ralph Loffmark, Donald Brothers and, of course, the combative Waldo Skillings. In a corner of the room, a woman was overheard telling her husband, "Have a drink. I'm going to get hammered and I hate drinking alone."

For the NDP, it was a night of unsurpassed, unimaginable, delirious joy. Forever in BC's political wilderness, forever doomed to finish second, the sad-sack socialists suddenly, and seemingly miraculously, found themselves elected. Barrett had raised the NDP share of the popular vote to 39.59 percent, enough to take thirty-eight seats. The Liberals, with 16.4 percent of the vote, elected five MLAs. The hapless Conservatives, despite winning 12.67 percent of the vote, elected only two. Derril Warren, their leader, was not among them, running third to Liberal Barrie Clark and victorious New Democrat Colin Gabelmann in North Vancouver–Seymour. The seemingly unbeatable Socreds had been reduced to 31 percent of the vote and only ten seats; even if every Conservative supporter had voted Social Credit, the NDP would have won a clear majority.

As Barrett arrived at the Coquitlam Arena, the overflow crowd spilled into the street, cheering, singing, whooping, hollering themselves hoarse. Many had tears streaming down their faces. The first person to greet the conquering hero was Barrett's mother, Rose, who had wrapped bandages around young Dave's head for a Spanish Civil War float in the 1930s. She gave her son a big hug and began to cry. With mile-wide grins, Dave and

Shirley slowly picked their way through the euphoric crowd to the stage, serenaded by raucous renditions of "For He's a Jolly Good Fellow."

Barrett did not stay long, his brief speech was from the heart. First, he paid tribute to his old adversary, W.A.C. Bennett, evoking laughter from some in the crowd. "No, no," said Barrett. "Any man who gives up the best years of his life to public service deserves recognition, regardless of party." With emotion, he recalled dreaming in his younger days of a CCF government taking over in BC. "I never thought I'd be part of ... " He paused, overcome by the moment, then stated, "I feel a great sense of pride that I'm involved in it now ... I promise you this. I will not let our hopes and aspirations down. We will now move into a People's Century in British Columbia ... We have a lot of hard work ahead of us. The people of British Columbia have the right to expect a great deal from us and we must deliver."

In the crowd, soft-spoken union official Rudy Krickan of the Retail Clerks Union said he'd worked for the CCF/NDP since the 1930s. "This is the greatest night of my life." A younger celebrant, with more than a few beers in him, shouted, "I'm so happy, I've kissed twenty-three women and seventeen men." Up in Lillooet, ageless Ma Murray had threatened to move to "Spain or China or somewhere" if Bennett had been re-elected. Now, she exulted, "God, I'm so glad. I was never so happy in my life."

In Victoria, a group of liquor store employees, scheduled to meet the next morning with management, was staying at the Crest Motel. Knowing the NDP had promised to bring in full collective bargaining for provincial civil servants, they went wild. They got drunk, they got hysterical, they got loud. When guests banged on the walls to protest, celebrants moved to the balcony. "A guy out there started denigrating the socialist victory," recalled their union leader John Fryer. "We held him upside down over the balcony." The next day, somewhat the worse for wear, the workers brought in a few bottles of champagne and cajoled members of the Civil Service Commission to toast Barrett's victory. Then they left, saying they'd be back when they had bargaining rights.

Back in Coquitlam, Barrett left with the party still in full swing. He told reporters he had a bottle of champagne in the fridge back home and wanted to share it with Shirley. ("I don't remember that," says Shirley today. "We never had champagne in the house. It was probably just a bottle of beer.") It was left to columnist Bob Hunter writing in the early-morning afterglow of the NDP's great victory, to pronounce the most colourful message to readers of the *Vancouver Sun,* as they contemplated day one of the socialist hordes inside the gates: "It's 2:30 a.m., August 31, 1972, And The Revolution Is All Over In British Columbia. The People Are In Control. The Czar Has Surrendered. The Next Voice You Hear Will Be That Of The True Voice Of The People. The Capitalist Tyrants Have Been Destroyed ... Welcome To The Glorious People's Republic Of Mainland British Columbia," he wrote in his lavish, psychedelic prose. More calmly, he ended his column with, "Barrett may be just about perfect for the times. And now let's all sing 'The Internationale.' If anybody knows it."

It was that kind of night.

British Columbians awoke the next morning, many nursing hangovers, but still giddy with excitement at what they had done. The news of a socialist government in free enterprise, booming BC made the papers in Europe, through the United States and across Canada, where it jostled with headlines about the coming hockey showdown against the Soviet Union.

Reactions varied. A hastily scrawled sign went up on a crumbling bridge in Barrett's home riding: "We is gona get a new bridge." The open-line shows were humming the morning after the election as Bob Williams roused himself in his East Vancouver home. "Can't they call a meeting at the Vancouver Club and annul the election?" a caller asked radio hotliner Jack Webster. The "oatmeal savage" was not encouraging.

Williams' phone rang. It was Barrett. "Williams, for Christ's sake, we won!" Barrett cried.

"Yes, we did, Dave," Williams replied. "I've been doing some thinking about transition."

"Oh, good," said Barrett, who apparently had not. The two rivals of 1969 had become close friends: Barrett the good cop, the funny guy, and Williams the bad cop, the man the Socreds hated with an incandescent rage. They quickly agreed to meet for lunch at The Only, a hole-in-the-wall chowder and seafood joint at Carrall and Hastings in downtown Vancouver.

It was late morning as Barrett and Williams walked down the street, a stroll they would never forget, as sleepy drunks and down-and-out bums turned to stare, then hail the new premier. "Good for you, Dave!" they shouted. For Williams, it was proof "you were elected by the people." At the tiny restaurant, Williams pulled out a big recycled brown envelope, covered with the "transition plan" on both sides. First, the cabinet: Williams proposed Barrett stick with the "dirty dozen," their term for the thirteen previously-elected MLAs who had fought Bennett in the House during the past three years, each in his or her old critic role. Barrett didn't argue. The fourteenth veteran, Gordon Dowding, considered less than reliable as a partisan, would become speaker.

Then over to the back of the envelope, where Williams had sketched a series of initiatives for both the government and Crown corporations. Williams himself would take over all the functions held by Ray Williston, one of Bennett's most senior and capable ministers, effectively running five ministries responsible for the province's lands, forests and water resources. "I'd made up my mind I wanted to buy up Columbia Cellulose in Prince Rupert and Castlegar," Williams recalled years later, noting these troubled pulp operations employed thousands. "Dave was up for all that." Williams was quickly on the phone, telling Williston to make no decision on the forest company's future before the Barrett government was sworn in.

These decisions remained closely guarded secrets, however, and a province still stunned by the election outcome went into the Labour Day weekend wondering what lay ahead. The *Vancouver Sun*'s main headline the next day did its best to reassure worried British Columbians, after the voter revolution of the night before: "NDP, Barrett slay Socreds; Business takes news calmly." An anonymous banker put it more succinctly: "We're either going to find out if we can live with it or we're going to throw it the hell out."

Bennett did not hurry out of office. Nor did he tell anyone of his departure plans. Not until September 15, more than two weeks after the election, did he convene a final press conference, issue a financial statement and officially leave office without saying a word to his socialist successor. The delay left Barrett mostly twiddling his thumbs at home, with no idea when he would be sworn in as British Columbia's twenty-sixth premier. This did permit time for a decompression trip with Shirley to Seattle, during which Barrett again talked over his cabinet choices. "We had a nice meal one night, and he discussed whom he should put in cabinet," remembered Shirley. "He would write names down on a brown paper bag he had,"—perhaps Williams' brown manila envelope.

When the big day arrived at last, the historic inauguration of the province's first socialist premier had a charming, just-plain-folks quality. Not knowing protocol, Barrett simply waited for Deputy Provincial Secretary Lawrie Wallace to summon him to Victoria. Once the call came from Wallace, on the same morning Bennett announced his departure, Barrett quickly bundled everyone into the family Volvo and they headed over to Victoria on the ferry. The premier-to-be took his place in line with everyone else. When he arrived, Barrett realized he didn't know precisely where the Lieutenant-Governor's residence was. At the Swartz Bay depot, he used his last dime to phone Government House for directions. "I think he got the gardener," says Shirley. They wound up parking in the visitors' lot. Then, the Barretts and their three children walked up the curving driveway to the Lieutenant-Governor's opulent digs, like any other tourists. Barrett wore a light blue suit. Shirley had on a grey knitted dress. Neither of their sons wore a tie. Columnist Allan Fotheringham watched closely and wrote, "The new premier wore a continuing grin of simple pleasure. It was not a smug, greedy look. Just a boyish failure to subdue his true feelings."

The cabinet was sworn in several hours later, this time in the chambers of the legislature. Afterward, the "dirty dozen" ministers adjourned to the oak-panelled cabinet room above the Premier's Office in the West Annex, where a long, oval table, inlaid with green leather, sat ringed with big oak and leather chairs. There was pandemonium as the new gang in town celebrated

After parking in the visitors' parking lot like any other tourists, the Barrett family—Dave, Shirley, and children Dan, Joe and Jane—stroll up the driveway to the Lieutenant-Governor's residence, where Barrett will soon be sworn in as British Columbia's 26th premier and first social democrat to hold the office, 1972. Photo by Brian Kent, provided by the *Vancouver Sun*

their arrival at the seat of power. According to NDP legend, not contradicted by Barrett, the premier suddenly silenced the room by taking off his shoes, taking a running jump to the tabletop and skidding the length of its polished surface. There is no doubt about happened next.

"Are we here for a good time or a long time?" Barrett asked. The answer determined much of what took place during the next three years. "We discussed whether we were going to make fundamental changes in British Columbia," Barrett wrote later, "or whether we would try to hang on for a second term, rationalizing that we'd get the job done next time around. We agreed unanimously to strike while the iron was hot. Our government represented the first real break from the traditional power base in the province. We were free and unfettered to roam in new directions. We were impatient to do something decent and honest and human. It was going to be a good time for the ordinary people of British Columbia."

Barrett quickly laid down some ground rules. Cabinet ministers were to be personally accountable for their decisions: no delegating to bureaucrats. Submissions to cabinet were to be no longer than a single page. Staff would not attend cabinet meetings, and political memos were banned. Barrett gave each minister a single focus, driven "from pent-up policies debated at conventions for forty years." Some cabinet members were to be more equal than others. Contrary to his election promise, Barrett kept finance for himself, as W.A.C. Bennett had done. Thirty-nine-year-old Bob Williams, the youngest and most powerful of the new ministers, stepped into Ray Williston's large shoes in charge of lands, forests and recreation and BC Hydro.

The choice of former leader Bob Strachan for the relatively minor highways portfolio was a surprise, but Strachan was also tasked with delivering one of the NDP's key goals: public auto insurance. Witty Vancouver lawyer and Barrett loyalist Alex Macdonald was not only rewarded with attorney general, where he was expected to overhaul family law, but given trade and commerce as well, making him boss of the province's energy policy. Nanaimo chartered accountant Dave Stupich, who also had an agriculture degree, was tabbed for agriculture and the heavy responsibility of halting the rapid disappearance of valuable farmland. Norm Levi, a tank driver as a young man, recruited by Barrett from the John Howard Society, took over welfare and social services.

Locomotive engineer Bill King got the labour ministry, a massive undertaking in an NDP administration committed to major reforms. Veteran Kootenay MLA Leo Nimsick, a retired Cominco storekeeper, took mining, while Burnaby MLA and schoolteacher Eileen Dailly assumed education. She was also named deputy premier, the first woman to hold that position in Canada. The sharp but cautious Dennis Cocke from New Westminster went to health, and Manchester-born Ernie Hall was put in charge of the civil service as provincial secretary, with added responsibility for tourism.

Other ministers received lighter portfolios. Bill Hartley, a flighty MLA from Yale–Lillooet, was given public works. Burnaby lawyer and ex-alderman Jim Lorimer, who had a tendency to doze off in the House, received municipal affairs. The province's first aboriginal MLA, Nisga'a leader Frank Calder, also entered the cabinet as a minister without portfolio. Gordon Dowding proved an effective, if occasionally pompous, speaker. Of Dowding, Barrett once said, "He wears that tri-cornered hat to fit his tri-cornered head."

The new government was far from Howe Street. Diversity presided. The province now had its first Jewish premier, its first aboriginal cabinet minister, and its first two black MLAs: ex-BC Lion and Grey Cup champion Emery Barnes and Rosemary Brown, the brainy, articulate feminist and human rights campaigner from Vancouver–Burrard. Brown was the first black woman elected to a legislature in all of Canada. When Socred

Rosemary Brown raises her fist in triumph on election night, 1972, as she becomes the first black woman in Canada to be elected to a provincial legislature. The *Vancouver Sun* described Brown's gesture as a "black power salute." Photo by Bob Dibble, provided by the *Vancouver Sun*

MLA Pat Jordan referred to August 30 as a black day for British Columbia, Ms. Brown, describing herself "as a person who feels very strongly that black is beautiful," endorsed the remark. "August 30 was indeed one of the blackest and most beautiful days for the people of this province." The government backbench also included a Dairy Queen operator, a fisherman, two railway workers, a former airline stewardess, a United Church minister, a hunting guide, several plant workers, an insurance salesman, farmers and housewives.

Change arrived on a charger with Barrett's first major press conference. An "emergency" fall session would be held, the premier announced, to bring in the NDP's long-promised guaranteed annual income for seniors, an increase in the minimum wage, and a series of other measures including of all things a return of liquor and cigarette advertising. There would be a real Question Period, a full Hansard of all House proceedings, research staff for the Opposition, and a boost in the paltry pay of MLAs. Barrett warned corporations to be ready for tax increases. He also made public the whirlwind of assignments he was giving his new cabinet. Williams would create an environment ministry, Strachan was to start work on auto insurance, public servants would get the right to bargain and the right to strike, Calder was asked to produce a report "on all aspects of Indian life in the province," and King would begin drawing up a new labour code. Those interested in preserving farmland were told to direct their questions to Bob Williams, not Stupich. Barrett predicted some "surprising moves."

Bill Hartley began work to upgrade the imposing, but crumbling, turn-of-the-century legislature building, where pails and special drains had become commonplace to handle rainy-day leaks. A few days after the premier's flurry of news, Dennis Cocke announced a complete review of health care services would be conducted by Dr. Richard Foulkes, and King confirmed that charges against eleven unions for violating the *Mediation*

Commission Act were dropped. Offstage, meanwhile, "Stagedoor Ronnie" Worley, the deputy minister of tourism and fawning author of *The Wonderful World of W.A.C. Bennett,* was shown the exit. News of his firing was read out on the CBC by broadcaster George McLean, the same fellow Worley had hired to narrate *Twenty Great Years.*

Jim Lorimer quashed long-standing plans for a costly third crossing of Burrard Inlet through a tunnel, pledging to launch the SeaBus program instead. The project had been strongly endorsed by local federal Liberal MPs and then Vancouver Mayor "Tom Terrific" Campell, who derided opponents of the proposed crossing as "Maoists, Communists, pinkos, left-wingers and hamburgers." Harnessing his inner hamburger, Lorimer said it was time to choose between the automobile and public transit. He promised ninety-nine new express buses. At the same time, Norm Levi delightedly discovered the difference between opposition and government. A week into his new job, he learned a woman on welfare had her power cut off because she couldn't pay the bill. Now, Levi could do something. He ordered her power restored. When BC Hydro hesitated, Levi informed the publicly owned utility, "I don't want to know why it can't be done. I want her service connected. You can send the bill to my department. We'll settle up later."

During a combative give-and-take session with reporters, Barrett proceeded to scare the pants off the province's powerful, corporate establishment. Although there was no timetable, the NDP's long-standing policy to nationalize BC Tel was still in play, he affirmed. Inland Natural Gas could also be a takeover target, and Westcoast Transmission, the large pipeline firm, might face similar action, the premier continued. BC investors should expect partnerships with government, not "corporate welfare." If companies didn't want to play ball, the province could create its own industrial development corporation, he warned. Resource industries that spurned secondary processing in BC would be penalized. If they refused to pay, the resources could stay in the ground. "Why, it's a love feast," the premier concluded. "All we are saying is 'no welfare.' We want to be partners ... The day of the rip-off is over."

Calculators were soon working overtime in the business pages. Since the NDP victory and Barrett's musings, share values in prime BC companies had dropped more than $300-million, readers learned. *Sun* business writer Bill Fletcher told them that their social worker premier, unschooled in the ways of business, was creating a wave of terror—unintentionally, of course. Later, in the legislature, under attack for causing stock losses, Barrett fired back. "You believe in the trickle-down theory, you so-called free enterprise capitalists," he said, gesturing towards the Social Credit benches. "[You] are living in an era that is long gone—and thank goodness the people of British Columbia said on August 30, good riddance. Good riddance!"

A new party was in power. The flavour of government rhetoric had undergone a seismic shift. "We don't believe in jungle capitalism to create jobs," said Barrett. "We believe in sharing the wealth of this great province in a prudent and responsible manner, and that's why we are going to bring in, and have brought in, legislation." Attorney General Alex Macdonald chipped in, too, ridiculing concerns over Barrett's reiteration of the NDP goal to nationalize BC Tel. "The Liberal leader says he was shocked to find the only BC news in the *Wall Street Journal* was that we planned to own our own telephone system," gibed Macdonald. "How they must have felt on Wall Street. The peasants were getting restless again. First, it was the Dominican Republic, now it was British Columbia."

The historic first Throne Speech by the province's first socialist government, however, was an odd duck. As short on occasion as on length, the address was the skimpiest on record, a mere four hundred words. It did nothing more than enumerate thirteen bills the government planned to pass and pay a brief tribute to "the first guaranteed minimum income of $200 per month for senior citizens anywhere in North America." The pioneer "Mincome" program would cost a substantial amount of money, the speech acknowledged. "But this wealthy province has the funds available, and it is a matter of some urgency that these funds be put into the hands of our senior citizens as quickly as possible. Without their energy, dedication and commitment to the province in its early days, none of us would be in a position to enjoy our great province as much as we do today." The next day, Norm Levi called Mincome "the unfinished work of the socialist movement in its concern for people of all ages." The government's first order of business, Mincome proved to be the most popular of all the moves made by the NDP over the next three years. By the fall of 1975, nearly 130,000 residents were receiving some form of Mincome assistance, by then raised to a maximum of $250 a month.

Over the session's ten days, the government also passed an amendment to the quaintly titled *Male Minimum Wage Act*, raising the minimum wage from $1.50 to $2 an hour, and to $2.50 by 1974. The chauvinist name of the act was changed, and the same rate extended to women workers, as well. The *Public School Act* was amended to give teachers collective bargaining rights, minus the right to strike. Impasses would still be settled by binding arbitration. Bennett's wage and budget restrictions were wiped out, and school boards were allowed to determine their own spending without interference.

And a wide-ranging committee was struck to introduce democratic reforms to legislative procedures that had operated in a backwater unique in Canada under W.A.C. Bennett. Under Bennett, government could not be sued. The chair of the Public Accounts Committee, against parliamentary tradition, was a member of government rather than the opposition. Revenue locked away in Crown corporations such as BC Hydro and BC Railway could not be scrutinized, nor was there much chance for opposition members to properly investigate the regular public accounts. With no formal question period, opposition members were reduced to submitting written queries, leaving cabinet ministers plenty of time to consider how to reply, if they answered at all. Hansard coverage was severely limited, making BC, in the delightful phrase of Liberal Garde Gardom, "the land of the legislative hush-hush." Now all that would change. As non-Socred MLAs swapped yarns of past legislative horrors, Gardom, who was to run for Social Credit himself in 1975, congratulated the NDP for their A-1 start on reform. "The former administration seemed to take unto itself the philosophy of the divine right of kings," he reminded the House.

But it was not a captivating session. The disintegration of Social Credit, BC's once-immortal free enterprise party, continued. Bennett, who had left the province for a cruise, announced by news release September 25 that he would not attend the fall session, would soon resign his seat, and would step down from the Social Credit leadership by May 1973. But former Attorney General Les Peterson, nominated by Bennett to replace him, point-blank refused. Bennett quietly put his plans on hold and was back in the capital, when Dowding called the legislature to order for Barrett's first Throne Speech. Bennett, perhaps lost in memories of his twenty years at the top, barely said a word, asking only a few minor questions. There was one brief but vintage moment, however, for the seventy-two-year-old warhorse. Outraged by a ruling from Speaker Gordon Dowding, the anti-socialist synapses fired up for one of the last times. "The heavy hand of state socialism is on this province today. We see it clearly," Bennett burst out, before lapsing into silence for the remainder of the day.

A rain of announcements continued outside the legislature. Private hospitals were told their funding would be brought under public control. "It is not this government's policy to favour profit-making in the health field. Let's have that clear," said Barrett. "We do not believe in hospitals operating on a profit." Municipalities learned the province would increase its share of college operating costs and take on construction costs, easing a major burden on property taxes. After twenty years of Bennett's dead hand, Barrett's energy, openness and engagement were stunning to the press gallery. Hallway encounters could quickly turn into freewheeling impromptu news conferences. Barrett was everywhere, plunging in to solve problems and get things moving.

The "socialist hordes" are officially inside the gates, and members of the first NDP cabinet in BC history display fitting grins, moments after their swearing-in at the legislature. From left to right: Dave Stupich, Norm Levi, Jim Lorimer, Bill King, Dennis Cocke, Dave Barrett, Lieutenant-Governor John Nicholson, Bob Strachan, Eileen Dailly, Bill Hartley, Alex Macdonald, Ernie Hall, Frank Calder, Bob Williams and Leo Nimsick. Photo provided by the University of British Columbia Library, Rare Books & Special Collections, copyright *Vancouver Sun*

President of Canadian Pacific, Ian Sinclair, then one of Canada's highest-paid executives, arrived in Victoria to complain about the minimum wage increase, which he warned would slash profits at the Canadian Pacific Railway's luxurious Empress Hotel across the street. He demanded the minimum wage remain frozen. Alex Macdonald, who had joined the meeting, watched Sinclair's expression darken as Barrett "went into orbit," ripping CPR for its disgraceful, predatory practices and challenging Sinclair to go on television to declare CPR couldn't afford to pay chambermaids $2.50. Failing that, Barrett threatened to "take back all the acres the CPR had got for nothing." In the silence that followed, Macdonald, acting as interpreter and twiddling a soggy cigar, turned to Sinclair and said, "What the premier means, Mr. Sinclair, is that the minimum wage is going to $2.50."

The NDP's first few months in power exhilarated the party's base. One reporter calculated that Barrett committed his government to forty-two new policies during its first fifty-five days. In November, Barrett's speech to the BC Federation of Labour, despite his past rocky relationship with Fed leaders, produced round after round of applause and a standing ovation for his clarion call for a new era of co-operation and sharing among all British Columbians. A few weeks later, Bob Williams brought NDP convention delegates to their feet with a promise to add as many as two million acres to the province's parks, a one-third increase. As one of the most tumultuous years in BC's ever evolving political history neared an end, Barrett and his government were riding high. But only days before Christmas, with a freeze on the sale of all farm land in the province, the anti-socialist forces would find themselves a target that revealed, they charged, the true, dictatorial face of the Barrett socialists.

3: Awesome, Sweeping Powers

Tanned, relaxed and rested after a two-week Mexican vacation, Dave Barrett stopped briefly outside the legislature on a cold day in January 1973 to chuck snowballs at reporters as he walked to a meeting. In stark contrast to W.A.C. Bennett—always appearing formal in a suit, drinking tea from a china cup, riding in a chauffeur-driven limousine—Barrett was often wearing shirt sleeves, personally driving his kids to school. Many mornings he could be found drinking coffee in the cafeteria with the regular staff. He was well on his way, a *Victoria Daily Colonist* story indicated, to becoming "the people's premier." A regular day at the office began soon after he dropped off his kids at school, and although he had slept only four hours a night for his first few weeks in power, he now felt relaxed enough to get a good night's sleep. He was skipping breakfast in a desperate and losing effort to keep his weight down, but his hair remained jet black. He tried to keep weekends free for the family, but still had not had time to ride the new five-speed bike his son Joe had set up for him weeks before.

Just ten days ahead of his first full legislative session as premier, Barrett saw nothing but sunny skies in all directions. Despite a growing uproar over Stupich's land freeze, which cabinet was about to extend but reduce in scope, the opposition remained deeply divided. Appeals by defeated Conservative leader Derril

Warren for a merger of the Conservatives and Social Credit had been shot down by W.A.C Bennett, who saw the NDP victory as an anomaly to be rectified by a Socred return to power. Warren compounded his problems by telling the *Toronto Star* that he was advising businesses to pull out of BC, an action both Barrett and Liberal leader David Anderson deplored as shameful for someone who sought to lead the province.

Barrett, meanwhile, was undertaking a charm offensive with the business community, telling *Province* publisher Paddy Sherman that his upcoming budget would prove New Democrats were "not here to kill the goose that laid the golden egg." In fact, Barrett claimed, "there are many people in the business community that are socialist voters," who identified with his new brand of "pragmatic democratic socialism that has at its base a philosophy [of] providing a framework of society that allows people to reach their maximum potential with a minimum of influence from government." Sherman cautiously concluded, "Mr. Barrett is learning fast that policies should conform as much to circumstances as to ideology."

The New Democrats' first year in office was unfolding against the backdrop of dramatic changes in national and international politics. The 1972 federal election had ended in a dead heat between Pierre Trudeau's Liberals and Robert Stanfield's Conservatives, with federal NDP leader David Lewis holding the balance of power. Lewis' strident campaign against the tax breaks, subsidies and concessions available to "corporate welfare bums" had struck a chord with voters, whose record level of support suggested the NDP tide was still rising. There were contrary signs south of the border, however, where Republican President Richard Nixon had won a second term with an unprecedented 62 percent of the popular vote, a victory built in part by splitting labour votes away from the Democrats. Nixon's tactics, both legal and illegal, had destroyed the ragtag coalition built around Democratic Party candidate George McGovern, who had seen his candidacy resisted at every turn by union powerbrokers determined to maintain their control of the party against insurgent feminists, black activists and anti-war campaigners.

In British Columbia, the economic boom of the Bennett years continued. By year's end, the economy would deliver record job growth, with the provincial gross domestic product increasing 16 percent, the largest gain in ten years. Canada's economic growth was the best in twenty years and unemployment was sliding to the lowest level since 1966. Few premiers had enjoyed so much provincial good news as they fashioned a government agenda. Yet the NDP's Throne Speech January 25 was a cryptic sixteen-paragraph "working document" that promised a renewed BC bill of rights, changes to the ambulance service, one thousand more civil servants, action on public auto insurance and little else. "The administrative and legislative programs will be carefully designed and will be based on the clear necessity to plan our future," the speech said, "so that we may live in harmony with our special environment and at peace with our fellow men, and to depart from the acquisitive North American values that have seen profligacy and waste on all sides. To implement these programs, our Government will bolster services to our country, our people, industry, and labour, to catch up with modern society's demands for quality services provided by skilled people." The government's legislative agenda would stretch to more than eighty bills, reporters learned later, but details would not be forthcoming until the February 9 budget speech. Cabinet ministers, however, were quick to fill in the gaps during the Throne Speech debate.

Minister of Municipal Affairs Jim Lorimer advised the House that the government had realized "that there had to be a decision made as to whether or not we were going to go down the road with the automobile or whether we were going to move into the field of transit. The decision was reached that we would move to the transit solution." Ninety-nine new buses had already been ordered for April delivery to transit operations in Victoria and the Lower Mainland. What's more, Lorimer had ordered amalgamation of the scattered municipalities in Kamloops and Kelowna, secured federal funding for housing investment, and begun acquisition of land for home construction.

Robert Strachan announced that he had ordered all the "BC No. 1" signs on the Trans-Canada Highway, installed by W.A.C. Bennett to spite Ottawa, to be replaced with the same signs found in every other province—a demonstration "to the people of this province and to the people of Canada that BC [is] a part of Canada and intended to remain a part of Canada." Minister of Health Dennis Cocke, not to be outdone, reported that he had secured funding for collective agreements negotiated by health unions, was taking steps to move mental health treatment into the community, was considering licensing of acupuncturists, and was preparing for a comprehensive review of health care services. Minister of Labour Bill King was next, reviewing his improvements to employment standards and announcing comprehensive reviews of workers' compensation and labour law. Then it was Minister of Lands, Forests and Water Resources Bob Williams' turn, pledging five new parks—a massive 1.5-million-acre expansion—combined with a ban on mining in parks, effectively wiping out the claims of companies then operating in Strathcona Park, Wells Gray, Kokanee Glacier and others.

Within a week it was clear to reporters there was a new reality emerging in the legislature, as stark a contrast in political culture as Barrett's shirt sleeves were to Bennett's dark suits. The long-slumbering capital came alive. An awakened and engaged press gallery, inspired by the truth-seeking, crusading investigative journalists circling around Nixon, found Barrett's hallway musings more newsworthy than his legislature orations. Where Bennett' s backbenchers had sat in mute silence, Barrett's team members slammed the omission of a Ministry of Women's Equality from the Throne Speech or smiled ruefully in the background as he was handed a "Male Chauvinist Pig Award" by the BC Committee on the Status of Women. Where Bennett's opposition had struggled to find gaps in his legislative juggernaut, knowing their efforts would ultimately be ended by all-night sessions, Barrett's opponents were reaping the benefits of Question Period, expanded committee mandates and Hansard "blues," the first drafts of each day's proceedings. Barrett and the New Democrats were delivering on their promise to open up the legislature, handing their opponents the democratic tool kit Bennett had always denied them. The opposition parties were quick to seize the opportunities, and there were many.

Barrett's February 9 budget speech, some of it clearly improvised on the floor of the House, marked the real beginning of the New Democrats' mandate, what the premier termed "a new era for the people of our province, an era where the rights of the individual are supreme ... a just and open era.

"I have said before that the economy should serve the people, not people the economy," he continued. "This approach calls for a new perspective, both in government and in private sectors. We do not desire more growth for growth's sake, but rather growth on terms suitable to this province." Resource revenues would rise, polluters would pay and the government would seek to reopen the Columbia River Treaty to recover growing downstream benefits. The record $1.7-billion budget, balanced by raising the corporation tax and petroleum royalties, assumed revenue growth of 11 percent, well below the 13.5 percent Barrett argued would be reasonable. "This expenditure budget, in an effort to catch up on some of the shortfalls of the past, will be by far the largest budget in the province's history," Barrett said, "with the largest single-year increase of any previous administration." Barrett's "people-orientated policies" saw expenditure increases showered across ministries that had struggled for years under Bennett's heel: more funds for education, cash for seniors' Mincome benefits, gas tax breaks for farmers and fishermen, increases for highways, hospital beds, buses, parks and homeowners' grants. For the first time, the budget presentation included details of BC Hydro and BC Rail operations.

Barrett closed with a tribute to his caucus, starting with the cabinet. "I have been rather harsh and cruel at times with the cabinet," he said. "I have given them agendas, projects and goals that would tax any person. Not once has any single cabinet minister come to me complaining that his workload is too heavy." Perhaps, but behind the double doors of the West Annex cabinet room, Barrett's team had become deeply split over what would later be considered one of its greatest achievements, the protection of BC farmland. Legislation that was not yet before the House had triggered a wave of fear and opposition across the province, in part because of Minister of Agriculture Dave Stupich's unilateral attempts to force the Barrett government to pay massive compensation to affected farmers. Barrett's "advance on all fronts" philosophy, with each cabinet minister solely responsible for major initiatives, was about to trigger his first serious crisis.

Stupich's task seemed simple at first glance: to implement legislation, as promised by the New Democrats for nearly a decade, to stop the loss of the province's precious farmland to subdivisions and commercial development. The need for urgent action had been a matter of political consensus for at least a decade. With only 5 percent of the province suitable for farming, the accelerating loss of the best valley bottomland was obvious to anyone who left Vancouver city limits. By 1973, 20 percent of the total was already under subdivisions, flooded for hydroelectric power, held by speculators, or lost to hobby farms, and more was disappearing at the rate of four thousand to six thousand hectares a year. An attempt to protect Fraser Valley farmland through regional planning during the 1960s had foundered when the province took four thousand acres out of production to build the Roberts Bank super-port.

By the 1970s, local municipalities and the BC Federation of Agriculture were all clamouring for action. From the Fraser Valley to the orchards of the Okanagan and the wheat fields of the Peace River district, agricultural land was threatened by development. Increasingly unable to earn a decent living, farmers often had no alternative but to sell or rezone. Sigurd Peterson, a policy analyst in the provincial agriculture department, had drafted up a new plan in response. Peterson's scheme would use federal land inventory data to impose a freeze on agricultural land. Although he had no idea what it would cost, Peterson proposed that the government assess the "development value" of the land and compensate owners for that cost. Bennett, wary of the financial risks, rejected Peterson's plan in favour of a $25-million greenbelt fund that satisfied no one. Loss of farmland continued.

Public opinion was so united on the need for action that all three opposition parties had promised some solution in the 1972 campaign, the NDP proposing to create a "land zoning program to set areas aside for agricultural production." The New Democrats also recommended a land bank to acquire farmland for lease to producers, but made no mention of compensation. At an end-of-campaign rally in Richmond in support of local farmland campaigner and environmentalist Harold Steves, who had helped put the issue front and centre in the NDP's platform, Barrett brought the crowd to its feet with a pledge to end the loss of agricultural land. Steves was representative of a new generation of New Democrats whose politics were rooted in the emerging environmental movement. The son of the farming family that had given Steveston its name, he had been alerted to the threat to agricultural land when Richmond denied his father a permit to build a barn. Their land had been rezoned quietly for housing. Steves became a key organizer of campaigns to stop the dumping of raw sewage in the Fraser, oppose oil tanker shipments to Cherry Point and protect farmland. Yet Steves, despite his expertise, had no idea how Stupich would implement the campaign commitment.

Stupich seemed like the ideal man to lead the change. An accountant with a degree in agriculture, the Nanaimo MLA was a Barrett loyalist, a veteran of the legislature and a former agriculture critic with a wealth of contacts around the province. Articulate, businesslike and down-to-earth, Stupich looked poised to lead the government to its first legislative victory when he told reporters in September 1972 that legislation would be ready for a fall session, then just a few weeks away. Peterson, now Stupich's deputy minister, was hard at work behind the scenes, turning his rejected 1971 proposal into draft legislation, including a commitment to compensation.

Stupich not only failed to seek a cost analysis of the compensation pledge—an astonishing oversight for an accountant—but began to execute a deliberate strategy of public statements designed to lock Barrett and the cabinet into the compensation plan before either had a chance to review the bill. Stupich later said he had no regrets over the rush to launch the *Land Commission Act* because "the odds are we wouldn't have done it otherwise." Why Stupich doubted Barrett's commitment has never been clear. Stupich had quietly circulated a copy of Peterson's 1971 report to Barrett and Williams that autumn, suggesting it provided the basis for legislative action. The memo attracted little notice; his cover letter gave no hint of any urgency. Taking silence as consent, Stupich chose the most high-profile way possible to close the door on his cabinet colleagues.

No one could fail to notice the extraordinary keynote address Stupich made to the BC Federation of Agriculture in New Westminster November 29. "My advice to developers right now is not to gamble by investing their money in farmland," Stupich told the farmers, who were stunned to learn that a freeze on rezoning agricultural land had been in place since September. A secret freeze? How could this be? As Minister of Municipal Affairs Jim Lorimer quickly ascertained—his ministry would have implemented such an initiative—Stupich's statement was false.

Stupich, undeterred by the headlines he generated, went even further in a scrum with reporters the next day: the government would buy farmland and the development rights that would be lost by a freeze, he vowed, in legislation due after Christmas. In the meantime, the government would step in to stop the speculative sale of land, if necessary, before the law came into effect. Stupich's remarks triggered a predictable province-wide rush to apply for rezonings and subdivisions. By December 21, with Barrett out of town, Stupich convinced an angry cabinet to make good on his threat, freezing the sale of all agricultural land in the province until further notice by order-in-council. Stupich claimed, according to one account, that Barrett had approved the freeze. He had not.

The bombshell announcement landed on the front pages just as the Christmas holiday effectively shut down the legislature. With the new session just a month away, Barrett had not yet seen Stupich's legislation nor approved the freeze, but his options were limited. He could either repudiate Stupich's comments and force him out of cabinet or find some way to deliver legislation. He chose the latter. Stupich's coup had partially succeeded. There would be a bill in the House, although that had never been in doubt. All that was left was to approve its provisions.

Barrett's four-month-old cabinet was plunged into crisis, what Williams later described as a "tough, bitter battle" to rein Stupich in. Despite his friendship with Williams, Barrett was also close to Stupich, having roomed with him for six years during legislative sessions before the 1972 victory. Barrett struck a cabinet committee of Stupich, Hall, Strachan and Williams to resolve the split. At the heart of the debate was the issue of compensation. As a planner who had clashed with the Delta council over the question of agricultural land, Williams was opposed to compensation in principle and fearful of the total cost in practice. He believed the province had the right to zone land and owed nothing to owners if it denied them the opportunity to upzone or subdivide. The wealth generated by public land use policies was a public benefit, Williams believed, not private property held by the landowner. Although neither Barrett nor Williams have ever confirmed it, it appears likely, based on Barrett's early-autumn reference to Williams as a leader on the farmland file, that Barrett had assigned his Van East ally to monitor Stupich from the earliest days of the administration. In the wake of Stupich's BCFA fiasco, the Minister of Lands, Forests and Water Resources unofficially added agriculture to his already massive responsibilities.

Williams dispatched Norman Pearson, his deputy, to investigate Stupich's work. The reports were disturbing. Not only did Stupich confirm to reporters December 27 that the entire province would bear the compensation cost of the land reform, he went further in a private January meeting with the BCFA to urge demonstrations on the legislature steps to strengthen his hand in debates with his colleagues. But Pearson, himself a former planner, had done calculations on the cost of compensation that dealt Williams a trump card: Stupich's approach could cost as much as $1 billion, equivalent to 60 percent of the province's annual budget. With that number in his hand, Williams was able to stop Stupich and force a showdown.

Stupich's comments and the freeze had triggered a firestorm of controversy in rural areas of the province. In the absence of legislation, opponents were free to characterize the NDP initiative as they saw fit. Far from worrying about the cost of compensation, farmers feared it would be insufficient. Driven by farmers anxious to cash out and fuelled by real estate developers desperate to protect speculative profits, the opposition to Stupich was the most intense political observers could remember in the modern era. An attempt to dilute the order-in-council in mid-January by narrowing the definition of farm land and allowing subdivision of parcels under two acres was seen as "an extension of the freeze."

The land freeze handed the Social Credit opposition a political gift. It was an apparently arbitrary and unanticipated action that appeared to strike at the heart of property rights. Critics denounced the "awesome, sweeping powers" sought by the New Democrats to interfere with property rights without compensation. South Peace Social Credit MLA Don Phillips was tireless in his attacks. "Let me warn the people of British Columbia today that this order-in-council gives opportunity to a radical, wild, socialist government to put their grasping claws of power on each and every home in this province," he bellowed February 2. "Who is safe, Mr. Speaker?" If Barrett's opponents were looking for an action that would contradict his soothing words to business, they could hardly have improved on Stupich's destructive comments.

Brushing aside the Throne Speech, the Social Credit MLAs launched a series of non-confidence motions based on the order-in-council that put the normally combative Barrett on the defensive. The use of orders-in-council rather than publicly debated legislation was "not a healthy pattern," he conceded, that could "damage the whole legislative process." He made it clear that the strategy was Stupich's, one the cabinet had supported. Faced with the rush to subdivide and eliminate farmland, his government had "agonized" and then acted, knowing it would be judged at the polls for what he believed was a major step forward, "unique [in] North America, to save farmland and the family farm." After a marathon debate that ended at 10 p.m. on a Friday night, the New Democrats defeated the non-confidence motions. Barrett now had to end the split in cabinet.

Behind the scenes, he finally sided with Williams against Stupich on the compensation issue, placating the agriculture minister with a pledge to implement a range of support programs to help farmers stay on the land. The way was finally clear to draft acceptable legislation that created an Agricultural Land Commission to classify and protect BC's farm land—a total of 4.7-million hectares. Experts in Alex Macdonald's ministry literally spread drafts of the new law across the floor of the Attorney General's office, inserting boilerplate appeal provisions and administrative refinements, working around the clock to get the bill ready for first reading.

Barrett had barely restored order on the farmland front when he was blindsided by the reaction to Minister of Education Eileen Dailly's sudden announcement of a ban on corporal punishment in BC schools. The abolition of the strap was a matter of principle for Dailly. As a teacher in a one-room schoolhouse, she had tried the strap and seen the futility of it. In one case, she later told the legislature, she had gone to see the parents of a particularly disruptive student, only to have the father take his own strap down from the wall and proceed to beat his son. A review of school records disclosed that some schools did not use the strap at all; others reported strappings more than two hundred times in a three-month period.

Dailly had made a personal vow not to serve as minister as long as corporal punishment was permitted, but unlike Stupich, she took the precaution of meeting with Barrett before announcing her new policy, making him confirm three times in a private meeting that he supported the change. "Up until that time I had considered myself to be a pretty perceptive politician," he wrote later, "but in no way did I understand the political significance of this seemingly trivial exchange." When Dailly, a former teacher, rose in the House February 14 to defend the NDP budget she set out her educational philosophy and key priorities in a speech that unveiled at least six major initiatives. The pledge to abolish the strap would have sparked an uproar on its own, but it was accompanied by the promise of special commissions on both primary and post-secondary education, the implementation of province-wide kindergarten, expansion of French-language education, and a province-wide family life and sex education curriculum.

"I cannot as Minister of Education in all consciousness, preside over a school system which condones and permits the use of corporal punishment on the children in the schools of British

Columbia," Dailly said. "Surely, Mr. Speaker, if we want to reduce acts of violence in our community and in the world, we must eliminate acts of violence in our schools. If we want to develop future generations into more humane people, we must practice more humanity ourselves."

Thousands of BC parents believed otherwise. Unlike agricultural policy, an offbeat topic to the majority of voters, everyone could understand the strap. Dailly's policy shifts, most of which were never reversed, seemed at the time like a can of gas poured on a blazing political fire. "Talk-show hosts launched into an absolutely maniacal attack," Barrett recalled later, suggesting that normally placid children were turning into wild animals in the classroom "who needed the strap to keep them in line." Confronted by intense criticism in public meetings, Barrett gave as good as he got, demanding in one Williams Lake showdown to know "why the hell we should use taxpayers' money to beat your child? If you want your child beaten, do it on your time and at your expense. We will not be like free enterprise governments. We will not usurp parents' responsibilities. As socialists, we don't believe the state has that right. But watch out. If you do beat your kid, you could get charged with abuse." If any British Columbians doubted the New Democrats were intent on making change, those doubts were banished by the strap debate.

While the cabinet struggled over the agricultural land freeze and open-line hosts fulminated over corporal punishment, Barrett had been conducting a national and international campaign to transform the province's energy policy. BC drivers had recently been stung by a round of gasoline price increases, sparking demands for action to rein in the oil companies. US plans to bring Alaskan oil to southern markets by tankers sailing the length of BC's coast had united the province in opposition, both to integration of Canada's energy system with that of the United States and to the environmental threat to BC's coast. Nor had Barrett forgotten his election promise to wring a decent return to taxpayers from BC's growing natural gas exports. For reasons he had never been able to explain, W.A.C. Bennett had tolerated a price structure that saw British Columbians pay one-third more to burn BC natural gas than American consumers paid for the same product.

The energy file offered Barrett a potent combination of issues with a direct impact on taxpayers' pocketbooks, the provincial budget and federal–provincial relations—not to mention BC's coastline, now threatened by oil tankers. Barrett could stand up to Ottawa and Washington, fight the oil multinationals and defend the environment, all at the same time. Unlike Bennett, who had championed maximum rates of resource extraction at minimum royalty rates, Barrett believed in planned development, secondary processing and what later would be called "sustainable development." Barrett's clear support of the "limits to growth" theories emerging from the nascent environmental movement had inspired Greenpeace founder and *Sun* columnist Bob Hunter to declare the premier "the most forward-thinking politician in the country."

Barrett had two of his most able and loyal cabinet ministers helping him. Alex Macdonald was assigned the task of developing the NDP's long-promised energy commission, a new public entity to regulate oil and gas production and sales. Williams, responsible for other natural resources, had already undertaken a shake-up of BC Hydro, ordering the corporation to submit its dam projects to environmental review, replacing the board and appointing a new chair with experience as the head of Manitoba and Saskatchewan's power corporations. While Williams warned Washington State that the province would take a harder line against flooding of the Skagit River, Barrett complained that "the Americans are skinning us" on downstream benefits from the Columbia River Treaty and demanded improvements.

The long-standing provincial debates over hydroelectric development were being overshadowed by the widening controversy over oil tanker shipments down the BC coast. American markets hungry for newly discovered oil on Alaska's Prudhoe Bay were driving US authorities to consider the Trans-Alaska Pipeline System to carry crude oil from the Beaufort Sea across hundreds of kilometres of Arctic wilderness to a proposed new oil terminal in Prince William Sound. From there, tankers would head south to terminals in the Juan de Fuca Strait due south of Victoria. Canadian public opinion was overwhelmingly opposed to the idea. Just eight months earlier, federal parliament unanimously endorsed a May 15 motion from NDP MP Frank Howard opposing the project and the House of Commons plunged into a two-day emergency debate June 8, 1972, after a small oil spill at Cherry Point terminal in Washington. Among those in the thick of the controversy was former Victoria Liberal MP David Anderson, who had led the fight against tankers in Parliament.

Barrett plunged into the energy battles with gusto, triggering enough headlines in any given week to keep reporters distracted from the trench warfare unfolding in the legislature over auto insurance and agricultural land. He had conducted a visit to Alaska in mid-November to seek agreement on pollution controls and signal his opposition to the tanker project. Barrett then called oil and gas executives on the carpet to press for the price rollbacks and higher royalties he had promised on the campaign trail. When the oilmen unsurprisingly refused to roll back prices or support higher government royalties, he warned reporters he would soon set up his energy commission with unprecedented scope to manage energy prices: "I'm talking about electricity, I'm talking about natural gas, I'm talking about gasoline and oil products—all things that are essential commodities." Within days, Barrett was warning producers that "dramatic increases" in the wellhead price of natural gas would produce windfall revenues for taxpayers. "No gas company is going to skin the people of BC." Barrett's budget, which increased oil royalties, produced a non-confidence vote from the Social Credit members that Barrett was happy to debate.

As President Richard Nixon's commitment to the Trans-Alaska project firmed, Barrett told the legislature he was planning a sudden trip to Washington, DC, to fight the project in face-to-face meetings with top US officials. A series of small but troublesome oil spills in Alert Bay, Cherry Point and Cold Bay, Alaska, had kept the serious pollution risk in the news for more than six months. Always the dramatist, Barrett released the full text of his February 15 emergency telegram to Prime Minister Pierre Trudeau to the legislature, including details of his personal calls to senior American officials. Anderson could only complain of "political gamesmanship at its worst." If so, it was effective. As the legislature remained mired in budget estimates and debate on agricultural land, the premier flew to Washington to meet directly with the Americans, leaving Ottawa's foreign affairs experts fuming on the sidelines. Wondering "why there has been no positive leadership from the federal government," he proposed a $4-billion alternative pipeline and rail route down the Mackenzie Valley. Exasperated federal officials asked for a copy of his submission.

Barrett's Washington foray infuriated federal Minister of Energy, Mines and Resources Donald Macdonald, who had been assuring Canadians in January that Ottawa had no intention of integrating Canada into the US market. Canada, he said, would maintain enough oil and gas reserves to meet present and future domestic needs and only sell the surplus. But as Barrett fired off his telegram, the National Energy Board began to limit rising exports to the United States. Price controls followed in September 1973 to protect Canadians from sharp rises in the price of oil driven by the Yom Kippur War between Israel and its Arab neighbours. The reality was that Canada lacked a national energy strategy and Ottawa was improvising.

BC had never been a major oil producer and energy had

not been a significant issue in the 1972 campaign, apart from consumer anger at the export price for natural gas. Nearly three-quarters of the province's expanding gas production was exported. Thanks to Bennett's policies, British Columbians paid one-third more to buy BC natural gas than American customers in the Pacific Northwest. Westcoast Transmission purchased all gas produced by the province's sixty-five producers, but was partly owned by Pacific Petroleum, which alone accounted for half of BC's gas production. Another 19 percent of Westcoast was owned by El Paso Natural Gas, one of Westcoast's largest American customers. To complete the circle, Phillips Petroleum exercised effective control of both Westcoast and Pacific Petroleum.

Due to these comfortable arrangements and long-term contracts, El Paso was able to buy BC gas for only thirty-one to thirty-two cents per thousand cubic feet at a time when the market price was closer to fifty-eight cents. BC Hydro was paying much more than El Paso to buy gas for its BC customers. The Canadian Petroleum Association estimated gas prices needed to rise 70 percent to match the energy value of alternative fuels, but Ottawa was not interested and BC lacked the regulatory powers to make the necessary changes. Energy pricing, like farmland protection and auto insurance, were areas British Columbians had long widely agreed needed action, even if they were unsure what a real solution looked like. Barrett was quite prepared to make up for Bennett's negligence.

Barrett was not impressed by corporate arguments that oil and gas exploration was risky and costly work, often warning that BC would create its own oil company if the existing ones did not perform. "God did not place the resources there for Imperial Oil, Standard Oil, Come-by-Chance, Fly-By-Night, Running Shoes or any other outfit," he told the legislature on March 11, 1974. "Those resources ... can be found by technologists and geologists in the employ of the government as well as private companies. If the private companies can't use their divining rods with their mysterious monopoly and multinational corporation approach, we'll find oil." Attorney General Alex Macdonald was equally emphatic, warning on February 27, 1975, that "we in this province ... are not going to be drilled and bored and punished and blown and flared and capped by the international oil companies."

Macdonald's *Energy Act,* introduced March 22, not only proposed to regulate gasoline prices, but created a BC Energy Commission to regulate wellhead prices for oil and gas. Refusing opposition requests to send the bill off for detailed committee review—"we have lost twenty years in protecting the vital energy needs of the province ... and this government is not prepared to lose another six months"—Macdonald forced it through the House to final reading April 17 with all opposition parties opposed. It was during this debate that Macdonald took the true measure of Socred MLA Don Phillips, "who can tell you everything he knows in ten minutes [but] spoke for four hours ... We clocked him at 105 words per minute with gusts up to 165."

The first Energy Commission chair, former NDP MLA Jim Rhodes, was a businessman who surprised many with his administrative competence and went on to head both BC Petroleum Corporation and BC Hydro. Macdonald's first assignment to Rhodes, however, was a complete review of natural gas pricing, a project that would lead to the creation just a few months later of "thirty-second socialism," one of the Barrett government's most lucrative innovations.

The delay of Stupich's legislation, which had not even been mentioned in the Throne Speech, had opened the door on February 16 to Strachan to introduce two bills necessary to establish public auto insurance. For Strachan, whose career had been studded by bitter disappointments, the introduction of Bills 34 and 35, the *Insurance Corporation of BC Act* and the *Automobile Insurance Act,* must have been deeply satisfying. Unlike the agricultural land freeze, which had never been tried anywhere, public auto insurance was already functioning with great success in Saskatchewan and Manitoba, thanks to NDP administrations in those provinces. The commitment to create a similar program in BC had been a staple of the NDP platform for a decade and options for its implementation had been considered by a Social Credit royal commission and outlined in a private member's bill in the previous session. But Strachan's legislation and the launch of the Insurance Corporation of BC triggered a political debate that would dominate the next three years, gravely damaging the government and ending Strachan's political career.

The auto insurance bills set off a period of what the press gallery dubbed "legislation by thunderbolt," the ceaseless introduction of major initiatives that overwhelmed reporters and the opposition. Just days after Strachan's bill—itself hard on the heels of the strap uproar, the energy crisis and the record budget—Norm Levi tabled legislation to amend the *Social Assistance Act*, raising rates and easing eligibility. The next day, it was five more bills from three ministers, including two agricultural bills and Stupich's long-awaited *Land Commission Act*. Twenty bills received first reading in the first two weeks of March, but when second reading debate began March 5 on Strachan's bills, auto insurance quickly joined the agricultural land freeze as the opposition's key battleground against the NDP. Despite Strachan's excellent preparation, his battle would ultimately prove the most difficult. While tens of thousands of British Columbians were involved in agriculture, relatively few actually owned or speculated in farmland. Virtually everyone over sixteen, however, drove a car and most made the costly annual pilgrimage to an insurance agent.

The Social Credit government had been plagued by the auto insurance issue, struggling for years to find a solution to BC's soaring premiums that would help drivers without offending the insurance industry. W.A.C. Bennett, who had been unflinching when he nationalized BC Electric and Black Ball Ferry Company, seemed to quail when confronted by insurers and their massed battalions of small-town agents. It was no accident that Barrett had focused in opposition on the plight of a twenty-three-year-old widow—denied insurance payments despite the death of her husband in a crash—to highlight the callous indifference of Bennett's Attorney General, Les Peterson, to the insurance industry's penny-pinching. Barrett's tactic of appealing to Peterson sixty-seven times to intervene had resulted in Barrett's ejection from the legislature to the front pages of the daily papers.

The crisis over auto insurance had been building for the better part of a decade. BC's rates were the highest in Canada and rising. The public believed the industry operated as a cartel, effectively conspiring to set rates and payments. Fees were high, but claims were handled slowly, with lawyers taking a big chunk of the payouts resulting from litigation. In a classic delaying manoeuvre, Bennett had appointed a royal commission in 1966 to investigate the "losses and expense" resulting from car accidents. Headed by Supreme Court Judge R.A. Wooten, who had two able deputies, the commission took more than two years to report, but recommended far-reaching changes, including no-fault insurance. Wooten opened the door to government operation of car insurance. Socred Attorney General Les Peterson hailed the findings as "an imaginative and revolutionary approach to the problems."

Peterson spoke too soon. The province's trial lawyers were shocked by Wooten's betrayal in proposing a no-fault system that eliminated the costly civil suits used to assess blame. This tort-based system provided a rich source of income for trial lawyers. (Workers' compensation, by contrast, is a no-fault system. An injured worker is guaranteed coverage but is prohibited from suing an employer. Employers face penalties, however, for violations of safety codes.) Despite his legal background, the judge had concluded that the existing system "has failed to provide British

Columbia with optimal protection per dollar of premiums paid." Worse, the commission laid the blame at the door of the "tort reparation system" that allowed insurers and drivers to sue and countersue in costly civic actions to allocate the blame in accidents. With more and more accidents resulting from driver error rather than true negligence, the litigation was extremely wasteful and poor at generating real compensation in serious cases. Victims of uninsured drivers faced even greater obstacles recovering funds from an industry-run indemnity fund. As for competition, Wooten found that the Insurance Bureau of Canada, the industry's national organization, "effectively eliminated price competition over a larger segment of the industry than was the case with any other price-fixing arrangement of the past decade," a line that found its way into many NDP speeches.

Wooten proposed a BC Automobile Insurance Board (BCAIB) to regulate private insurers in a no-fault system providing basic insurance for as little as $16.75 a year, a fraction of what many drivers faced in the existing system. Crucially, however, Wooten did not propose public ownership of the auto insurance industry. The outcry from the trial lawyers—who saw the report as a "step toward anarchy"—as well as the insurance industry, which insisted that "the negligent and careless driver should be held accountable," inspired Bennett to seek even more delay by referring the matter to a committee of the legislature, which quickly split along party lines. Bennett introduced a range of reforms in time for the 1969 election that maintained the tort system, created the BCAIB as a regulator, improved some benefits, regulated some premiums and opened the door to more government intervention.

Within a year, however, the changes were deemed inadequate. Even the Social Credit convention considered government takeover, only backing off after direct appeals from Peterson. When the BCAIB called for a rollback of basic no-fault premiums in December 1971 to $14 from $21, the industry refused, despite the board's determination that only 41 percent of the premium revenue was being returned in settlements. When the board ordered a rollback the following month, Barrett calculated that $14-million in premiums had been improperly collected from BC drivers.

There was no doubt Barrett had a mandate for public auto insurance: it had been recommended, in part, by a royal commission; Bennett's stopgap measures had been proven inadequate; the New Democrats had proposed legislation for public auto insurance in 1972 as a private member's bill; and the promise had been front and centre in the NDP's election platform. Every British Columbian with a driver's licence knew exactly how bad the system was and how resistant insurers and trial lawyers were to change.

Even better, there was strong evidence of success elsewhere. Autopac, Manitoba's program, then heading into its third year, was running a surplus, had not increased premiums significantly since it was created and had won the confidence of agents, who now were fewer in number but doing better than ever. Strachan quickly enlisted Norman Bortnick, the head of Saskatchewan's public auto insurance company, to manage the launch of ICBC. But the bills Strachan ultimately put before cabinet went further than any province had before.

Although the legislation did not abolish the tort system, Strachan built on the Wooten report to require every driver in the province to have insurance effective March 1, 1974. Every existing agent would be authorized to sell the insurance on behalf of ICBC, but private carriers were prohibited from doing so, which was not the case in the two prairie provinces with public insurance. What's more, the legislation authorized ICBC to sell other types of insurance and required the province's schools to use the corporation as their insurer. The legislation was accompanied by a booklet of explanatory notes, leaving the press gallery and the opposition little room to complain about "thunderbolts," but the expanded scope of the BC legislation was enough to send the entire insurance industry, along with trial lawyers, to battle stations.

As Strachan rose in the House to lead off debate at second reading, the veteran MLA was at ease and well prepared. He reminded the Socreds of the two occasions on which their own party had passed motions seeking a government-operated insurance program and recalled the 1971 disclosure by Socred MLA Alex Fraser that the Bennett government was not only committed to a takeover but had been on the verge of executing one that spring. Strachan marched through the bill, promising that the new ICBC plan would be non-profit, dedicate all revenues to benefit motorists, invest in highway safety and be "self-sustaining." Where private carriers returned sixty-three cents of every dollar to drivers in payments, public plans could achieve eighty-five cents, Strachan declared. Since 1967, Saskatchewan drivers had seen their premiums rise 6 percent, while BC drivers saw their average premiums rise 27 percent.

Opposition MLAs focused their attacks on the impact on insurance agents, arguing their businesses would be "terminated" in favour of a new, bloated bureaucracy in Victoria, but Barrett, fully on the offensive, mocked the Socreds. "The bill is here because the people of BC want it," he cried. "One reason you lost the last election, remnants of the Social Credit hordes, is that you didn't serve the little people anymore."

The opposition attack had little success against Strachan's well-developed plan. As second reading debate closed March 8, Strachan pulled out postcards from all over the province, printed by the industry for angry voters to mail to their MLAs. Strachan's examples had pro-ICBC messages written on them, including one from a West Vancouver voter who scribbled "I am in complete favour of the government takeover." Strachan triumphantly concluded with a challenge to the opposition "to stand up and be counted, for or against the people of British Columbia and government auto insurance." Second reading was approved, as was third reading on April 18, and ICBC was born.

Strachan looked like a statesman in contrast to the beleaguered Stupich, whose disastrous strategy stretched out the agricultural land debate for five months. In reality, however, Strachan had completed only the first, most straightforward stretch of a political battle that ultimately destroyed him. Stupich was simply passing a law to stop certain transactions. Strachan was seeking to create something new in the face of attacks from powerful stakeholders who would fight him every step of the way.

It was not until February 22, nearly three months after Stupich had ignited the agricultural land debate with his remarks to the BC Federation of Agriculture, that Bill 42, the *Land Commission Act* produced by Williams' legislative pressure cooker, was finally tabled in the House. Immediately recognized as surpassing "any legislation now in force in Canada for the control and preservation of both agricultural and other open space land," the bill created a five-person commission to supervise the identification and protection of agricultural land across the province, as well as a $42.5-million fund to acquire land for a provincial agricultural land bank. The new clarity did nothing to quell the opposition. The new commission had what the opposition quickly dubbed "awesome, sweeping powers" over land use across the province and compensation was explicitly prohibited for land included in the Agricultural Land Reserve.

Frustrated backbenchers like Steves, who first saw Bill 42 just hours before it was tabled in the House, believed the government had conceded too much during the drafting stages, particularly on environmental protection. But critics in the BCFA were demanding even more and won a commitment from Barrett March 8 to consider further amendments. Even Stupich was on the defensive, admitting that the bill had "been widely misunderstood and the fact that it is misunderstood might mean that we have misjudged the situation."

Farmers descended on Victoria March 15 to march around the legislature and lobby the MLAs. Sharp-eyed Steves, despite his disappointment in aspects of the bill, was one of its most eloquent defenders, noting that every one of a tidal wave of protest postcards arriving in MLAs' mailboxes had passed through the same developer's postage meter in Richmond. Angry farmers again besieged the legislature, forcing Barrett to make a province-wide radio address promising to refer many outstanding issues to the legislature's agriculture committee. "Farmland is fast disappearing and we've had the guts to face it. We'll stand or fall on this in the next election," Barrett declared. "But I want to predict that when the election comes three years from now there won't be a single opposition leader who will stand on a platform and say, 'Elect me and I will rescind this legislation.' If I have any regret in connection with this bill it is that we have done a very, very poor job of public relations in preparing ourselves and the community on this bill," he concluded, adding that despite the outcry, "farmers and landowners will be treated fairer than ever before."

The controversy had energized the opposition. They made the most of Question Period and Barrett's commitment to avoid "legislation by exhaustion," filibustering the *Land Commission Act* for weeks. Social Credit MLAs launched their careers in the hectic new atmosphere of confrontation and media scrutiny, the long shadow of W.A.C. Bennett finally banished. The leader had disappeared from the scene for weeks, reportedly calling in suggestions from a stopover in Buenos Aires on a South American cruise. "He has been driven out of the House by his own party's filibuster," laughed Barrett. Bennett had been telling rallies they must "not allow the socialist menace to destroy freedom," Barrett said, "but he has completely missed the debate in the House." When Bennett did return March 5, to pose the first question in the new Question Period format, the result was a fiasco. Declaring that three of Barrett's bills—for auto insurance, agricultural land

and the BC Development Corporation—would cause "hardship across the province," Bennett asked demurely, "Would the Premier agree to withdraw all these bills?" Barrett never said a word as Dowding ruled Bennett out of order for violating the basic rule of procedure that no questions may anticipate legislation currently before the House. He then rejected Bennett's request for a supplementary question because he hadn't asked a proper main question. Bennett exploded: "I want the people of this province to know that we have closure! We have a dictatorship! Those are sick things!"

Amid the detractors, there were supporters. The tide seemed finally to be turning in the NDP's favour as fruit growers announced their support for the *Land Commission Act*. Yet the Social Credit filibuster went on late into the night, day after day. Phillips, who delivered a six-and-a-half-hour oration denouncing "this disastrous bill, this dictatorial bill, this vicious bill," declared Barrett had made "monkeyshines in these chambers" and predicted "the people will never trust you again."

It was not until March 28, when Barrett forced the House to sit from 10 a.m. to 11 p.m. daily, that the bill finally passed. The filibuster had recharged the reservoirs of partisanship and bitterness emptied by the election. Normally mild-mannered Liberal MLA Allan Williams (West Vancouver) pounded his fist on the desk as he denounced the bill for "no natural justice." NDP backbencher Graham Lea, referring to one anti-Bill 42 rally, was able to draw a line from the opposition benches to the Ku Klux Klan: "the only thing missing was the burning crosses outside and the bedsheets." Not to be outdone, W.A.C. Bennett shouted that the New Democrats were no more than "communist dictators." Stupich ended the debate by accusing the opposition of heaping confusion upon confusion, a charge better levelled at him. But the impact of the bill was clear, and Stupich underlined it: "There will be no further alienation of agricultural lands in this province except in cases where it is judged to be in the public interest."

When the budget was moving through the House, the *Land Commission Act* and the ICBC legislation heading for second reading and a score of other bills swamping the opposition, Barrett and Williams had opened up yet another front. Barrett announced March 16 that the province had purchased the isolated central coast town of Ocean Falls and its faltering pulp mill from Crown Zellerbach just weeks before the town was scheduled to close for good. Despite claims that the New Democrats had purchased the mill without legislative approval through a Crown corporation that didn't exist, the $1-million takeover by the newly created Ocean Falls Corporation split the opposition. No one wanted to take the blame for killing a town.

"We wanted to protect jobs in a region that had been left listless and on the vine by the previous administration," Williams told the House. Years later he would recall how he had been moved to make the purchase by watching a television documentary on the plight of the families stranded in the remote company town by the threatened closure of the mill. "I thought, damn it, we can't let them down." After a flurry of calls to Crown Zellerbach and the Canadian Imperial Bank of Commerce, the province's banker, Williams was able to acquire the entire community and the massive mill in a cash sale. He was not flying blind. Quick research had disclosed that newsprint prices were on the upswing, suggesting that if the firm halted operation of two kraft and specialty lines and reactivated both newsprint production lines, it could break even. He then drove CZ's asking price down to $1-million from $10-million and extracted timber supply guarantees through to 1975.

Rumours of the purchase had begun circulating a few days before Barrett's stunning announcement, but the late Friday news release caught the opposition off guard. When the storm burst at Monday's session, Barrett immediately put Williams' estimates on the agenda to allow a full debate. One of his proudest moments as premier, he said, was executing a purchase that proved "we consider jobs and the resources of this province to be paramount, and we would not let that town die as Social Credit had allowed it to." Bennett, who had demanded an emergency debate on the purchase, slipped out of the House rather than face Barrett and Williams, who were keen to review the terms of the Wenner-Gren concessions. The New Democrats reminded the opposition that 140 jobs remained at Ocean Falls, 400 homes, a power plant, a hotel, townhouses, apartments, shopping facilities and scrap metal that was probably worth $1-million on its own.

The crisis facing northern communities would have to be confronted, Williams warned, making it clear he was not finished intervening: "The future of those mills and those towns is dependent upon major change and major action." On April 2 he delivered, announcing that the government had acquired all the assets of Columbia Cellulose (Colcel) from the Celanese Corporation, including two pulp mills, two sawmills, a mixed lumber operation, nine-million acres of timber and a paper mill in Belgium. This time Williams had acquired the Colcel operations, supporting three thousand jobs in several communities, through the newly created BC Cellulose, which took over Colcel without any direct cash payment by assuming the firm's $73-million debt.

Once again, Williams had shown he was a tough negotiator. Celanese, fed up with years of losses, had been seeking to unload its Colcel interests for some time. Williams' post-election call to Williston had thwarted a Celanese plan to sell off the profitable Castlegar operations to Weyerhaeuser, opening the door to possible closure of the Prince Rupert operations. When Williams, now the minister, refused the transfer of critical timber rights, the Weyerhaeuser deal collapsed and Celanese came to Victoria to explore a sale. Given Colcel's long record of losses—more than $95-million since 1966—the opposition parties vied with each other to disparage the deal. The purchase was "like buying the Brooklyn Bridge," said Bennett, while Anderson feared

Williams was "buying a share in the *Titanic* after it hit the iceberg." The forest sector purchases, combined with legislation to create a BC Development Corporation to invest in BC firms to create jobs and support business, were met with cries of "communism" and "dictatorship" from the Social Credit benches. It had all been in the platform, but few had expected it to become reality.

When the legislature finally prorogued on April 18, it had been the most productive session on record: sixty-one sitting days, ninety-six pieces of legislation adopted and four new Crown corporations created. Between the agricultural land legislation, the BC Development Corporation, pulp mill purchases and public auto insurance, the New Democrats had also found time to mandate province-wide kindergarten, provide new rent protection to tenants, raise welfare rates and much more.

A land freeze, energy price controls, ICBC—they may have all been in the NDP election program, but outside observers could see where this was heading and many didn't like it. The New Democrats could rule forever in backwater prairie provinces without causing much concern; the NDP in power in Canada's third-largest province was another matter. "For whatever a New Democrat may be in Manitoba and Saskatchewan, in [BC] he is unquestionably a socialist of strong left-wing philosophy," wrote one national columnist. "It is dramatically clear that Premier Dave Barrett is taking BC on a swift march to the left and the question now is just how far left he will move and how long he can survive politically by doing this." *Province* publisher Paddy Sherman was also revising his early sympathy for Barrett, now finding him "incredibly unaware as a politician. His government is turning out to be naive, arrogant, inept, prone to gallop headlong into danger ... creating the widespread impression of arrogant and impatient amateurism." A *Vancouver Sun* editorial writer saw the New Democrats as "the most radically socialist government in Canada's history."

One Toronto journalist read the tea leaves differently. Barrett's popularity was soaring, he believed, producing "a personal popularity even greater than that with which he led the NDP to power eight months ago, and quite possibly unsurpassed by that of any Canadian politician, at any level, since the Trudeaumania of 1968." The *Sun*'s Allan Fotheringham agreed. "The boys down at the Tycoon and Typhoon Club," he said, "where Barrett is known as the Red Baron," would be discombobulated by the sustained applause that had greeted the premier as he came out from behind the curtain as mystery guest on the CBC's *Front Page Challenge*. "The boy's got it."

As Barrett prepared to head out of Victoria for a post-session provincial tour, he received another unexpected and unequivocal grassroots endorsement. On March 16, when the battle in the legislature had been at its most intense, Barrett had gone on Jack Webster's CKNW open-line show head-to-head against celebrity prostitute Xaviera Hollander, the Happy Hooker, who was taking calls over at Judy LaMarsh's show on CKWX. According to the Bureau of Broadcast Measurement, Barrett's ratings crushed the Hooker's.

4: Little Chief, MiniWAC and the Northern Kingfish

Three weeks after the spring session adjourned, Barrett was again on the road in his old Volvo, driving with Harvey Beech from one end of the province to the other to spread the good news about his eight months in office. They staged town hall meetings that drew massive crowds—one thousand in Prince George, six hundred in Kamloops—including both supporters and opponents. When Barrett began to recognize a few individuals who turned up in every town, heckling and stamping their feet to disrupt his speeches, he adopted the tactic of introducing them to his audience and inviting them to speak. Along with the disruptions came RCMP warnings of death threats; Barrett declined a police escort. For the most part, the mood and the coverage were good. His visit to the Williams Lake Stampede produced pictures in the *Sun* of Barrett swilling beer, pitching a ball and holding a prize, but readers were most impressed by the premier's prowess in the "barnyard Frisbee contest," which required entrants to hurl dried cow dung as far as possible. Despite a throw that travelled an astounding 132 feet, 4 inches, Barrett was apologetic: "In Victoria, we do most of our bull-throwing indoors, so this is my first outdoor event."

Before departing the capital on May 15, Barrett had expanded

Premier Dave Barrett taking part in the annual "bull throwing" competition for politicians only at the Williams Lake Stampede in 1973. Barrett beat out the previous winner, local Mayor Jim Fraser, by tossing his piece of dung more than 132 feet. Photo by Deni Eagland, provided by the *Vancouver Sun*

his cabinet beyond the bare-bones list scratched out on the envelope at The Only. Gary Lauk, a sharp-tongued lawyer from Vancouver Centre, picked up part of Williams' industry and trade work; Prince Rupert MLA Graham Lea took Strachan's highways duties; Jack Radford of Vancouver South took on the recreation duties in Williams' care; Levi's ministry was renamed "Human Resources" from "Rehabilitation and Social

Improvement"; and BC Federation of Labour researcher and Status of Women activist Phyllis Young, from Vancouver–Little Mountain, took on consumer affairs. More notable than the appointments were those passed over. Rosemary Brown, believed by many to be the perfect choice for a minister of women's equality, was not appointed to the post, nor was anyone else. This decision by Barrett would raise a simmering feud with the women's movement in his party to a full boil. Some reporters thought Strachan had been slighted by the loss of highways, but he retained control of the crucial ICBC file. No one believed, by contrast, that Williams had suffered a setback through the allocation of two of his responsibilities to others. It was clear Williams remained first among equals in Barrett's cabinet.

Even more reassuring for Barrett as he headed up the Fraser Canyon was the steady flow of new talent to Victoria to staff cabinet ministers' offices and the bureaucracy. Each minister acquired a ministerial assistant, some two, Bob Williams three—a stark contrast to Bennett's practice of leaving his ministers without staff support of any description. Barrett had been careful not to do anything like a purge of the civil service. Some deputy ministers were demoted to associate deputy, but were mollified when advised they would not lose pay. In their stead came some of the most talented new administrators in the province and Canada: Burnaby Mayor Bob Prittie resigned to become deputy of municipal affairs; Williams' mentor Alistair Crerar moved into the lead at the Environmental and Land Use Secretariat; lawyer David Vickers became Alex Macdonald's deputy attorney general; labour law specialist Paul Weiler joined Bill King's team, as did employer-side labour lawyer Jim Matkin. This new horsepower on the policy front meant the New Democrats would be well armed for a fall session, but Barrett had still not built the coordination and planning capacity that was already routine in almost every other province's cabinet.

After the BC road trip, Barrett had flown to New York and then

Europe, assuring BC's Wall Street bondholders the province remained open for business. Comforted by the government's decision to retire $30-million of $250-million in outstanding parity bonds, the rating agencies sent him on his way with BC's credit rating intact. From New York it was off to Paris, Vienna, Munich and Bonn, where Barrett's group was feted by Chancellor Willy Brandt. A buoyant Barrett conducted a wide-ranging scrum at the airport on his return, regaling reporters with promises of British investment in a new steel mill and a pledge to overhaul BC liquor laws to give them a more European flavour. Although he had always resisted the expansion of taverns and wine gardens, he found that "in Paris, the sidewalk cafes are just fantastic, just fantastic ... I think there is room for it in BC now, I really do."

Yet it was alcohol, its over-consumption, and a demand for complete honesty in cabinet dealings that cast a pall over Barrett's summer just as he prepared to head out for an August family vacation. According to press secretary John Twigg, who hurried to brief the premier in the dying days of July, rumours were circulating that Frank Calder, MLA for Atlin and cabinet minister without portfolio, had been detained by Victoria police in connection with a drinking and driving offence. According to police records released later, the incident occurred around 5 a.m. on April 27, when police approached a car stopped in an intersection a stone's throw from the legislature to find Calder and a female companion in the front seat, both drunk.

Although little known outside his small Atlin riding, Calder was a fisherman, logger, theological school graduate and hereditary chief of the Nisga'a First Nation. He had not only won eight elections for the CCF and then the NDP, he was the first aboriginal cabinet minister in Canadian history and lead plaintiff in the historic Nisga'a case that had just been adjudicated in January by the Supreme Court of Canada. After coming to know Tom Berger when he served as NDP leader, in 1969 Calder and the other Nisga'a chiefs retained Berger to sue the province for a declaration that the aboriginal title of the Nisga'a people had never been extinguished.

The historic split decision in that case, handed down January 31, 1973, transformed the legal status of aboriginal rights and title for all of Canada's aboriginal people. The case had Calder's name on it for good reason: the "Little Chief," as he liked to be called, was one of the most senior and prestigious leaders of the Nisga'a council. The Nisga'a had pursued the case over the objections of many other First Nations, who feared a defeat would spell the end of the battle for aboriginal rights. BC had fought the Calder case every step of the way, even after the New Democrats were elected and Calder himself became a minister without portfolio. The Supreme Court verdict forced Prime Minister Pierre Trudeau to concede in a meeting with Calder and his fellow chiefs that "perhaps" they had more rights than he thought. In the three years since the Trudeau government had urged the "termination" of aboriginal rights in a white paper, aboriginal people had mobilized across Canada in opposition. BC was no exception, with roadblocks and demonstrations a regular occurrence. Calder's appointment as a minister without portfolio to "investigate" the circumstances of aboriginal people had been attacked by groups like the Union of BC Indian Chiefs as an attempt to co-opt the aboriginal rights struggle. For all these reasons, Calder's encounter with the police needed to be considered as much more than a simple misdemeanour. Calder was not only one of the NDP's longest-serving MLAs, he was the leader of an aboriginal First Nation that had just led a court case rewriting the rights of Canada's aboriginal people. What, if anything, had he done wrong?

The night of the incident, both Calder and his companion were taken to the station, where they were held and released in the morning, Calder without charges and the woman after paying a fine. There the matter stood until news of the incident finally reached Barrett's ears. Barrett recounts in his memoirs how he quickly asked Alex Macdonald to join him in his office, phoned Calder, who had been tracked down in his riding at Cassiar, and asked him point-blank, "Frank, were you arrested in a car with a woman in the middle of an intersection and were both of you inebriated?"

"No," replied Calder, "that did not happen." That was enough for Macdonald, but Barrett decided to check Calder's statement with Victoria's chief of police. Indeed, the chief said, Calder had been brought to the station. The moment Calder returned to Victoria, Barrett summoned him to his office and fired him from cabinet—not for the incident itself but for lying about it. Barrett told reporters of Calder's dismissal in an emotional news conference July 31, refusing to say what had triggered the decision, but that "I've lost confidence in him as a cabinet minister." The decision had been his, but had been endorsed by cabinet. That wasn't good enough for the opposition, who demanded that Barrett either explain the dismissal or hold an inquiry.

Not necessary, said Calder, now quite prepared to tell his side of the story. "This is not Watergate," he said, his voice choked with emotion. Calder denied the incident was serious enough to warrant dismissal. "This is not a criminal act," he told reporters. "It didn't involve public funds. As a matter of fact, I paid for my girlfriend's fine, so what the hell are they worrying about?" The police report confirmed Calder's statements; he had not been at the wheel. He had not been candid with Barrett because he had taken the call in the presence of a number of people, he said. Nor did he wish to name his companion, a "close friend."

"I have to respect her and her family." There was also the matter of explaining the entire affair to his own family. The Little Chief tearfully told reporters he was selling his home in Victoria and returning to the Nass, but he bitterly warned Barrett that "if he keeps blowing it up, I'll fight him." Calder was as good as his word. When Barrett later appointed veteran MP Frank Howard as a special consultant on aboriginal issues, Calder, still in the

NDP caucus, denounced Howard as nothing more than a "glorified Indian agent," adding "I'm rather disgusted with Barrett." Calder would have ample opportunity to avenge his humiliation.

Although his actions were supported by cabinet, caucus, the party president and the BC Association of Non-Status Indians, Barrett soon found himself fending off accusations that he'd been especially hard on Calder because his landmark court case had targeted BC as well as Ottawa. The dismissal seemed drastic, given Calder had not been charged, nor was at the wheel. Calder's dissembling was unacceptable, most agreed, but a firing offence? Critics noted how reluctant Barrett was to move out other cabinet ministers whose poor performance qualified them as deadwood.

Nor was Calder's close relationship with Berger lost on party insiders. Not only had Calder supported Berger for the leadership, he had worked side by side with him in a court case that had taken many years to come to fruition. During that period, Calder's political message had remained closely aligned with official party policy that considered aboriginal rights a federal issue. The problems facing aboriginal people were posed as questions of discrimination, not violations of fundamental rights. Barrett, Williams and Macdonald had all made it clear the NDP administration would tackle the problems of aboriginal groups—few thought of them as First Nations—with affirmative action and economic development, not comprehensive treaties. Calder did little to contradict this perspective as a sitting MLA, but as a hereditary chief of the Nisga'a he was advancing a different view altogether.

Was Barrett's much-vaunted loyalty a one-way street, there for some but not others? If Stupich or Strachan had behaved in like fashion, would they have been dumped from cabinet? Some noted, as well, how long it took for news of the incident to reach Barrett. There were many on both sides of the House—and in the press gallery—who would be wary about finger-pointing for drinking and driving, perhaps especially with someone who was not your wife.

When the legislature resumed in September, opposition members were quick to express sympathy for Calder, who now sat fuming on the NDP backbenches. Barrett had been adamant, as the controversy lingered over the August long weekend, that the issue was lying, not drinking. "I have no intention of being responsible for any individual who does not come to me and honestly tell me exactly about any incident or occurrence that may hamper his work as a cabinet minister," Barrett said. The episode said much about Barrett's leadership style. From the moment Twigg passed him the rumour, Barrett handled the matter himself, right down to phoning the police chief. While some commentators hailed his toughness, others wondered if the penalty really fit the crime. Perhaps most critical of all, Barrett had put an absolute premium on complete truthfulness. It was this standard his opponents would hold him to in the months to come.

The relaxed good humour of Barrett's spring tour was in stark contrast to the confusion and disarray gripping his opponents. As the New Democrats hit their stride and the tempo of legislation increased, panic began to spread through the ranks of the business community. Despite the exertions of remaining frontbenchers like Don Phillips and Pat Jordan, the Social Credit caucus had demonstrated a near-complete inability to land more than a glancing blow during Barrett's "legislation by thunderbolt." Social Credit House Leader Frank Richter was virtually silent, unable to muster a convincing attack on the wave of "socialist" legislation. W.A.C. Bennett, who had spent much of the fall at home in the Okanagan or travelling in Europe, had lapsed into semi-retirement after Peterson had declined the offer of party leadership. The Social Credit Party, which had seen its membership decline to a few thousand, was moribund. None of this seemed to matter to Bennett, who returned from Europe and then left the country again, this time on a round-the-world cruise. The opposition had neither leader nor a coherent plan to get one.

Conservative leader Derril Warren, without a seat in the House, was casting about for a new strategy. It had been a miserable few months since the election for the tall, spindly Warren, a lawyer who had been defeated in North Vancouver–Seymour by upstart New Democrat Colin Gabelmann, the former political action director of the BC Federation of Labour. Although a BC native with roots in the Okanagan, Warren was a veteran of Peter Lougheed's Alberta Conservative machine, which had demolished Premier Ernest Manning's thirty-five-year Social Credit bastion in 1971. Warren was finding BC a very different proposition.

His initial efforts had shown promise. In 1971, Warren had lured Social Credit MLAs Scott Wallace, a Victoria physician, and Donald Marshall of South Peace River, to his party to form the nucleus of a Conservative caucus. Marshall, however, had been narrowly defeated by Social Credit's Don Phillips, leaving Wallace and Saanich MLA Hugh Curtis as the only two Conservative victors from the forty-nine candidates Warren had been able to field. Not only had Warren failed to increase his caucus or get elected himself, he was widely blamed for Social Credit's defeat. Early in 1973, the chastened Conservative made a pilgrimage to Kelowna to meet directly with Bennett. Sitting in Bennett's living room, as W.A.C.'s son Bill looked on, Warren urged Bennett to combine the two parties and to endorse the election of a new leader at a wide-open convention. His only condition: the new party could not be called Social Credit. To Warren's shock, the elder Bennett pointed to his son, who had never stood for elected office, and declared, "There's the new leader of the party." Bennett declared, "You have only one choice, and that is to join the Social Credit Party."

Unbeknownst to Warren, W.A.C. had cut short his eleven-week world cruise at the request of his son Bill, who had cabled his father, then off the coast off South Africa, with this dramatic message: "If you're going to save the party, you must come home." The telegram had re-energized the defeated and humiliated Socred leader, who found himself revitalized by the prospect of sweet revenge, the re-election of Social Credit with his own son at the helm. For the next year, he would sacrifice himself to that cause. W.A.C. and his wife, May, immediately disembarked at Durban and undertook the thirty-six-hour flight to Vancouver, where W.A.C. arrived shaking a clenched fist, announcing "I am back, now, to spearhead the attack against socialism for all the people of BC. Labour will lose from this socialism just as bad as the farmer. Merchants will lose. Housewives will lose." After demanding an immediate election, he pledged a province-wide tour to rally the voters against the NDP.

The younger Bennett's telegram had been triggered by his secret decision to seek the leadership of the Social Credit Party. Ambitious and successful in business, Bill Bennett had lived his life in his father's shadow. A solid family man, W.R. "Bill" Bennett had none of his father's spontaneous flair for the dramatic gesture, nor his instinct for populist politics. In their place, he had qualities that would prove more valuable: a relentless work ethic, a strong intellect and a tendency to be underestimated. Where Bennett—and Barrett—saw politics as theatre and the legislature as the stage, the younger Bennett saw it as a business problem to be solved by forceful execution of a careful strategy that used every possible modern resource. The relationship between W.A.C. and his son, who would soon be dubbed MiniWac, had been strained and would remain so, but the younger Bennett was prepared to reach out to his father where politics was involved. Like many others, he had expected W.A.C. to retire after the 1966 election and then the 1969 election. Barrett's 1972 victory had finally opened the door to new leadership on the right, but there were many contenders trying to walk through it. Most were uninterested in Social Credit.

About the same time Bennett was rushing back from Africa, a group determined to bring down the New Democrats was meeting in the Kamloops home of self-made millionaire Jarl Whist, a sometime Liberal who proposed to unite all the anti-NDP forces under the banner of SOS, the "Stamp out Socialism" movement. With the assistance of Burnaby lawyer Arnold Hean and activists like Kamloops lawyer Rafe Mair, Whist quickly turned SOS into the Grassroots Movement and then, for real clarity, the Majority Movement, which had the goal of restoring free enterprise by "unifying the three free enterprise parties or, failing that, the free enterprise vote." Like Bennett and Barrett, Hean undertook his own barnstorming tour of the province, selling memberships and speaking to any audience he could find. The widespread opposition to the land freeze and ICBC gave him plenty to work with. Without quick action, Social Credit would find itself outflanked on the right.

For the next six months, W.A.C. Bennett conducted a secret campaign to install his own son as the leader of Social Credit and the next premier. Soon after his ignominious humiliation in Question Period, the elder Bennett gave a stormy address to seven hundred Socreds gathered in Vancouver to plan for a leadership convention, the first in the party's history. It was Warren, not Barrett, who bore the butt of Bennett's wrath for "putting the socialists in" with his vote-splitting on the right. It was time for a new, young leader, Bennett cried, someone who could take the battle straight to Barrett. He persuaded the delegates to schedule a leadership convention for November and went back on the road. Every move W.A.C. made was designed to secure his son the Social Credit leadership. By the time W.A.C. formally resigned his seat on June 5, Bill Bennett had recruited veteran organizer Hugh Harris to manage the Kelowna by-election triggered by his father's resignation. A week after his father's announcement, Bill declared his decision to contest the seat in a by-election that Barrett soon called for September 7.

The timing of W.A.C.'s resignation had the effect of barring anyone other than his son from contesting the leadership, unless he or she was already a caucus member. Only Bill Bennett would have a seat in the legislature when it reconvened that fall, a clear advantage over pretenders like Phil Gaglardi and Herb Capozzi, one of the elder Bennett's old business partners. Even more significant was the likelihood that Bennett could defeat Derril Warren in the local contest, effectively extinguishing the Conservative threat on the right. Warren quickly took the challenge laid down by W.A.C. in March, declaring he, too, would contest the Kelowna seat. It was not as crazy as it seemed; Warren had his own family ties to Kelowna, but nothing compared to Bill Bennett's.

When the ballots were counted, Bill Bennett had won his father's former seat and Warren trailed the New Democrats. The Liberals ran a dismal fourth. It was a double, decisive victory for Bill Bennett, who won a seat and eliminated the Conservatives in a single night. W.A.C., declaring "a victory for free enterprise," was quick to appeal to the Conservatives and the Liberals to "unite behind Social Credit." The *Vancouver Sun* reviewed the results and agreed. "It seems to leave Social Credit as the possible alternative to the NDP at the next general election." On November 24, Bennett closed the deal, sweeping to an overwhelming victory against leadership hopeful MLA Bob McLelland in the largest political convention the province had ever seen. Grace McCarthy, one of his father's most loyal lieutenants, became party president.

Although Barrett could not have known it at the time, his decision to call a quick by-election in Kelowna played into W.A.C. Bennett's hands, not only putting his son on track to win the leadership but effectively eliminating the Conservatives as a source of vote-splitting in the next election. Warren resigned the Conservative leadership and Scott Wallace grudgingly agreed to assume the leadership on the condition he not be responsible for debts. With the Conservatives effectively destroyed as a political force, only the Liberals remained as an alternative to Social Credit on the right, but as Barrett was to learn soon enough, they were vulnerable to splits of their own

As summer turned to fall, the mood in North America darkened. The Watergate crisis, the American withdrawal from war in Vietnam, and the success of Woodward and Bernstein's book *All the President's Men* all combined to produce an increasing sense of dislocation and breakdown that proved fertile ground for fantasy, conspiracy theories and cults. By year's end *The Exorcist*, a tale of demonic possession, would be packing theatres. "Deprogrammers," people who snatched young members from secret cults and sects for return to frantic parents, generated headlines across the continent. By late August, mainstream media were reporting a wave of UFO sightings, flying saucers and other unknown objects that darted across the sky but never showed up on NORAD's radar screens. On September 11, Chile's military unleashed a bloody coup to bring down the elected government of Salvador Allende, rounding up thousands to be tortured and killed in Santiago's soccer stadium. Three days later, the BC legislature convened for its fall session and MiniWAC took his father's seat as the Kelowna MLA.

The NDP's reforms to BC's energy sector during the spring session had been hotly opposed by the oil companies and the opposition. But as summer began to turn to fall, the global economy was seized by its first systemic energy crisis, unleashed by the Yom Kippur war that began with the invasion of Israel by Egypt and Syria on October 6. OPEC, the cartel of Middle East oil producers that dominated world markets, sharply reduced supplies and increased prices. The actions taken by Barrett's government that spring to ensure appropriate returns from BC natural gas production produced a gusher of cash as crucial to the government's fortunes as the collapse of Social Credit had been a year before. The provincial treasury, already benefiting from a strong economy, filled with an unprecedented rush of resource royalties that W.A.C. Bennett had steadfastly refused to collect. The new revenues not only funded Barrett's dramatic expansion of government programs; they ensured he maintained a balanced budget.

As soon as the BC Energy Commission legislation had passed, Jim Rhodes and resource lawyer Martin Taylor plunged into a round of hearings to determine how badly BC taxpayers were faring under the old regime. Their report, released September 14, concluded the province's losses exceeded $100-million a year as BC gas was sold to US customers at 40 to 50 percent less than the sale price of alternate fuels. At the root of the problem were long-term contracts negotiated in the 1960s to spur the development of the northeast gas fields. Westcoast Transmission purchased the gas and moved it to US markets where distributors, including two firms that held significant ownership stakes in Westcoast, reaped massive profits by reselling at significant markups. American consumers had enjoyed a decade of bargain energy prices thanks to W.A.C. Bennett's mismanagement of the resource.

As if the pricing problems weren't complex enough, Westcoast announced September 18 that Amoco, a major American-owned producer, was unable to meet its production commitments because of water flooding the gas formations at its Beaver River field, a consequence of excessive rates of production. Barrett called on Ottawa to release Westcoast from its export obligations to protect thousands of jobs at industrial gas consumers in Trail, Prince Rupert and Kitimat. But Ottawa's Liberal government, which was struggling to develop a coherent energy policy in the midst of a global crisis, refused. Determined to protect BC consumers, Barrett and Macdonald prepared emergency powers legislation to allow them to override the Westcoast contracts, only to shelve the bill without introducing it when Westcoast found new suppliers in Alberta.

Rhodes and Taylor made wide-ranging recommendations to overhaul royalties and pricing. By November, Barrett and Macdonald had created the BC Petroleum Corporation to purchase and resell the province's oil and gas, acquiring 120 contracts with eighty producers who had been dealing with Westcoast. The pipeline firm became a simple utility firm, moving fuel to market with a guaranteed return on investment. BCPC became the price-setter, collecting tens of millions of dollars in what Macdonald dubbed "thirty-second socialism." BC Hydro's new chair, NDP appointee David Cass-Beggs, quickly raised the price to domestic consumers, triggering a further increase for American buyers. When American regulators later ordered El Paso Natural Gas, a Westcoast shareholder, to sell its 13.5 percent interest, Barrett arranged for the government to purchase the shares, giving the province a window on both the production and transmission of natural gas. By the end of the decade, this investment produced $700-million for taxpayers.

But the immediate financial impact was just as dramatic. The new policy allowed the government "to garner the huge profits that had been going to American producers and put them in the hands of BC taxpayers and producers," Barrett wrote later. In just over four months, BCPC alone recorded a profit of $19-million, three times what Social Credit royalties had generated in a year. Within a few months, BC had introduced a two-price system similar to Alberta's. Henceforth about half of BC consumers would receive gas at subsidized prices while export customers paid full fare, but everyone paid more than they had under Bennett. The Amoco crisis had highlighted another Social Credit failure. Unlike Alberta, whose Energy Resources Conservation Board regulated the industry, monitored reserves and ensured domestic demand was satisfied, BC had no solid information on long-term supply or conservation needs. "Too long have the profits of the natural resource of the province ... been siphoned off to multinational corporations," Macdonald cried. "Too long have the levers of economic power over the resources of British Columbia been handled outside of this province."

Barrett's strategy made for great politics and even better revenue increases; on the downside it infuriated enormously powerful forces from the United States government to the Trudeau cabinet and Alberta's oil multinationals. For Barrett, the provincial interest was important, the national interest even more critical, the public interest paramount. "If we are to keep Confederation alive," he told the legislature, "we have reached the point ... where the basis of a national energy policy should be the complete public ownership nationally of all gas and oil resources in this country." In the following months, Barrett would offer BC assistance to Alberta to develop the oil sands, then seen as a solution to Arab blackmail, provided the resources remained publicly owned. Despite the rhetoric, however, BC's intervention was minimal. Apart from the open-market purchase of Westcoast shares, the New Democrats did not interfere with producers or the transmission sector except to raise their prices and reduce their risks while improving the public return. Rhodes moved to head up BCPC and left the Energy Commission, where he was replaced by economist Andrew Thompson. As British Columbians began to purchase their Christmas trees, OPEC announced it would double oil prices effective January 1, 1974. This decision by a distant Middle Eastern cartel triggered another revenue increase for BC's taxpayers, finally reaping the benefits of one of their most valuable resources.

But Barrett, unlike his peers, could foresee the day when those resources were exhausted. In a remarkable comment on March 8, 1974, he foreshadowed the debates of a generation to come and the fate of politicians who engaged in them without careful preparation. "In quieter moments of my life, I asked myself the question as to where are we going in North America?" Barrett said in a legislature exchange with Liberal Allan Williams. "I admit that I don't have the answers, but the question frightens me.

You asked today, what do we do when we reach the point when it's the last quart of oil, or the last gallon of gas? I'll tell you, we don't have any answers. We have absolutely no planning in any jurisdiction in North America for that cataclysmic end that will be here unless we have energy alternatives.

"It is my opinion that the only way we can coordinate energy alternatives is again through government action—grants to private research, grants to private foundations, stimulation of university experiments—not the continuation of the standard things, but new exciting programs. That's a hope.

"But even if you double or triple the time frame to extend the existing resources through prudence, through control, and through conservation, there's still that inevitable end. When you think of the billions of years it's taken to create all those energy reserves, and how rapidly we're finishing them now, man has to be considered to be living in the golden age, because it simply can't last another 100 or 150 years at the rate we're going now ... Can we ration gasoline? Can we force people to share cars instead of one per car driving across the Lions Gate Bridge and politicians having to respond to that problem by saying, 'Build another bridge?' Can we ask people, 'For goodness' sake, travel in car pools'? ... Can you tell people to park and ride? Can you ask somebody who spent $20,000 for a Mercedes-Benz and lives in West Vancouver, to keep it parked there all week and come into town on the bus? How about those of us who own Volvos?

"The point is, I don't think you can legislate people's behaviour. If you tried it, you'd be thrown out of office. Yet you know and I know that it makes sense that there should be four and five people in that car going into Vancouver and coming back every day. But it makes sense for whom? It makes sense for my neighbour; it doesn't make sense for me. When a decision comes down to us, we can't give up those creature comforts we've been really spoiled to accept." Sage words, but just a few months later the New Democrats would attempt to change when all British

Columbians got up in the morning and when they went to bed.

It seemed like a good idea at the time, a pre-Christmas heads-up to British Columbians that the entire province, just like many American states, would move to Daylight Savings Time several months earlier than planned on January 6, 1974. Barrett hoped the surprising move would reap significant energy savings in the face of skyrocketing oil prices, and fully expected the rest of Canada to follow suit. The OPEC oil embargo had already triggered shortages, massive lineups at the pump, and a conservation-driven, US-wide reduction in the speed limit to fifty-five miles an hour by presidential decree. But when Provincial Secretary Ernie Hall announced BC's Daylight Savings Time decision December 20, just as the province headed into the holiday season, he triggered a wave of anxiety. This edict, even more sweeping than Stupich's dramatic pre-Christmas land freeze a year earlier, touched everyone, from parents worried about sending their children to school in the dark, to airline executives whose schedules had been locked in for months. As BC emerged from New Year's Day festivities, the Barrett government found itself facing scathing criticism.

Under Barrett's plan, the sun would not rise in Vancouver until 9:08 a.m. on January 6, reporters laughed. The premier was unmoved. Forest firms and financial institutions would be better off aligned with American practice, he argued. Yet not a single Canadian province followed his lead. On January 4, panicking business leaders, forest industry executives prominent among them, made a last-minute appeal, warning of hazardous working conditions, lost wages and higher energy costs. The growing outcry finally forced a course correction, the first of Barrett's mandate. With just twenty-four hours to go, Barrett relented and postponed the shift to February 3. On January 29, after a month of ridicule, caucus revolt and scathing editorial cartoons—one showed him as a chicken hatching a Daylight Savings Time egg—Barrett conceded the initiative was dead.

It was the overture to a terrible year. As Minister of Education Eileen Dailly reflected ruefully, "They were trying to create an image out there that we were a government that was bumbling, incompetent and couldn't make decisions, didn't know what the hell we were doing. And the daylight savings [proposal] focused on that." No plan, arbitrary, dictatorial, out of touch—the Daylight Savings Time fiasco did much to raise doubts about the New Democrats in the minds of hundreds of thousands of voters who otherwise had no interest in agricultural land, no problem with rational natural gas prices and were happy at the prospect of cheaper auto insurance.

Within days of the first climb-down on Daylight Savings Time, Barrett found himself in another whirlwind of controversy when he effectively fired a senior official live on television. John Bremer, Dailly's one-man commission of inquiry on education reform, had been a "bit of a flop," Barrett told host Jack Wasserman on CBC-TV's *Hourglass*. Barrett had spent the afternoon at a Coquitlam high school assembly where teachers had given him an earful on the opinionated commissioner. Did that mean Bremer, already on the job for nine months, was being terminated? "You can interpret it any way you want," Barrett replied. Dailly, returning from a trip to Ontario, told reporters she knew only what she read in the papers. Bremer's termination, confirmed the next day, thoroughly undermined Dailly and effectively spelled the end of the Barrett government's planned reforms of the education system.

To the Daylight Savings affair and the Bremer firing, the open-line shows added municipal tax assessments, which had changed dramatically as the result of long-overdue reforms introduced by Barrett the previous year. Angry mail was pouring into the Premier's Office from confused ratepayers. Peter McNelly, the former *Province* columnist Barrett had recruited to be his senior aide in the finance ministry, quickly realized the government had a problem. "People were angry," he wrote in his journal, "and the people who were complaining were not the ones the bill was designed to hit." Worst of all, "people were making fun of the government and this was something new."

McNelly represented one of Barrett's early moves to stabilize his faltering government. Barely twenty-nine when Barrett recruited him in February 1974, the lean young journalist with a well-trimmed moustache was an American expatriate counting the days to his Canadian citizenship. McNelly had enjoyed a meteoric rise from city hall reporter in a Victoria newsroom to become the *Province*'s top political writer and legislative reporter. The only person in the press gallery to forecast an NDP win in 1972, McNelly had been one of the Barrett government's most astute, and balanced media critics. Convincing McNelly to move to a political post in the finance ministry gave Barrett eyes and ears both in his key portfolio and the press gallery. With a desk in Barrett's West Annex office, he sat close to the centre of power and could compensate, in part, for Barrett's tendency to rely on gut instinct in handling reporters. Despite his weakness for sharp suits that made him look more like a mafia enforcer than a senior finance official, McNelly became a trusted adviser of Barrett, just outside the inner circle of lifelong confidants like Beech and Williams. He turned his attention to helping Barrett, who was convinced a particularly rainy winter was contributing to the general gloom he was feeling, to regain his momentum.

The Throne Speech was once again a scattershot affair, bouncing from pledges to recreate a BC Police Commission to changes in the *Landlord and Tenant Act* and hints of what became the Gulf Islands Trust. The real news, Barrett told reporters, was still to come, a "Robin Hood" budget that would boost the fortunes of working families. In the House, Social Credit was watching newly elected leader Bill Bennett begin his painful initiation in Question Period. What was covered in an order-in-council approving $86,000 for "furnishings, etc.?" Bennett wondered. What did the "etc." include? Was it "paper clips, paper dollars, dancing girls?" Barrett ran circles around Bennett, then exploded in glee when Liberal leader David Anderson bungled a procedural matter, allowing the New Democrats to end debate on the Throne Speech days ahead of schedule. "The opposition ran out of criticism for the first time in history," Barrett crowed. Things were looking up.

Barrett began to roll out what he called the "most spectacular and progressive budget" in BC history, in which mining royalties would fund reductions in school taxes and resource revenues would support a larger share of provincial expenditures. Behind the scenes, McNelly had been polishing the unwieldy speech drafted by Barrett's finance bureaucrats. The $2-billion blockbuster budget released February 11, again the largest budget in provincial history, was riding a rising tide of income that boosted provincial revenue 25.6 percent in the first three months of the 1973–1974 fiscal year. Not only could Barrett make record expenditures across the board, raising spending by a staggering $453.8-million, he could do so without raising taxes, borrowing or drawing on the accumulated cash surplus. These "resource dividends," a term coined by McNelly and Barrett as they fine-tuned the speech in the early days of February, helped reduce school taxes, increase farm assistance, provide free drugs for the elderly and funnel thirty dollars a year in direct aid to tenants—eighty dollars if they were elderly.

Most of this revenue came from economic growth, not tax or royalty increases, Barrett boasted, and "not a single firm has been nationalized." The government was committed to a mixed economy, but "we have made clear to industry that super profits, special tax concessions granted by former administrations, or blatant exploitation of natural resources will no longer be tolerated. Business also must demonstrate more responsiveness to changing social and environmental values."

The budget was populist, McNelly noted, not socialist. It extended Mincome coverage for seniors, restated the commitment to keep the minimum wage the highest in Canada and pledged to bring in extensive reforms to protect consumers. Barrett's budget speech included good news for tenants, with pledges to "consolidate, rationalize and accelerate housing programs ... because adequate housing is a basic human right." Awash in cash, Barrett was able to live a premier's dream by allocating $140-million in surplus revenue to build ferries, provide mortgage assistance to homebuyers, build community recreational facilities, purchase the BC Medical Centre complex around Vancouver's Shaughnessy Hospital, and add $5-million each to the BC Cultural Fund and the Physical Fitness and Amateur Sports Fund. Additional cash flowed to municipalities, which were relieved of the cost of justice administration and guaranteed much larger per capita grants. School boards were promised support to reduce class sizes and universities were offered additional funding for "bold, imaginative and thoughtful programs." The parks and recreation budget almost doubled to $25.6-million and Barrett promised to hire seventy-seven more conservation officers and fourteen more biologists. The budget speech lasted well over an hour.

"Mr. Speaker, it's a great budget," Barrett concluded. "But I'm not so proud of it for myself as an individual; I'm proud of it because it embodies, in terms of the many people who work with our party—and many people outside of our party, and the ordinary people of this province—a step toward the dream of really being masters in our own house and sharing far more equally in the beautiful revenues and the resources and the lifestyle of this wonderful province."

Business commentators could find little to criticize. The budget was Robin Hood with a difference, Barrett explained: it took nothing from the rich. "The people in Shaughnessy and British Properties can sleep well tonight." He forecasted continued growth at 10 to 12 percent, including inflation, but warned that energy prices could drive that number down. Forest and mining royalties worried business columnists, but the revenue expectations from those sources seemed modest. All in all, wrote one, "it looks like more of the same type of conservative budgeting practised [by Social Credit] for twenty years prior to the NDP sweep."

In fact, Barrett's 1974 budget contained enough good news to last most administrations an entire term. "Barrett really likes the idea of giving money to people," McNelly noted. "He once said that the basic problem facing the poor is that they didn't have enough money." With increases budgeted for health, education, welfare, housing and more, there was plenty for the poor. McNelly believed the New Democrats could get re-elected on the resource dividend concept alone, driving home the message that fair returns on natural resources were being invested directly in public benefits like schools and homes. Homeowners benefited from the budget in many ways: the $30-a-year renters' grant, mortgage relief, property tax relief, new housing investments and school tax reductions. A newly created housing ministry had a budget of $75-million, with $50-million directed to "housing and development" and $10-million for grants to non-profits building seniors' housing. When someone suggested the renters' grant was too small, Barrett scoffed. It could rise in time for the next election and, in the meantime, the family "could go out and buy themselves a dinner on the NDP."

During the late-night budget planning sessions and long plane flights home from First Ministers' conferences, McNelly was learning more about his boss. Barrett was "totally political," he wrote, drawing inspiration from the star-crossed career of Depression-era Louisiana governor Huey Long, the fabled "Kingfish," who had been immortalized in Robert Penn Warren's Pulitzer-winning *All the King's Men* and Randy Newman's song "Kingfish" (1974):

> Who built the highway to Baton Rouge?
> Who put up the hospital and built your schools?
> Who looks after shit-kickers like you? The Kingfish do …

> Who took on the Standard Oil men and whipped their ass
> Just like he promised he'd do?
> Ain't no Standard Oil men gonna run this state
> Gonna be run by little folks like me and you
> It's the Kingfish, Kingfish, friend of the working man
> Kingfish, Kingfish, the Kingfish gonna save this land

Long, who died at the hands of an assassin, was a prototypical populist, maintaining grassroots support by paving roads to backwoods towns and issuing free school textbooks while lashing the "Standard Oil men" who sucked untold riches from the state's oil fields. The state's vested interests responded to Long's ascendancy with undisguised hatred and used every tool at their disposal to bring him down. "Barrett has studied Huey Long's political career in some depth," McNelly learned, "and likes to imagine sometimes what 'Old Huey' would say if he were alive in BC today."

If Barrett was comparing his own career to Long's, there were striking parallels in the turbulent days after the 1974 budget, as well as dramatic differences. Barrett, like Long, had enjoyed a successful first year in office and believed it was time to take additional steps to rein in the province's vested interests. Riding high on a wave of popular support, Long had plunged into 1929, the second year of his mandate, with a determination to bring Standard Oil to heel by imposing a manufacturing tax, much like Barrett's new oil and mineral royalties. Here the Kingfish's career held a bleak warning for Barrett if he chose to hear it. Long had underestimated the strength of Standard Oil's hold on legislators and, in the face of direct intimidation and bribery, lost control of Louisiana's House of Representatives. His opponents in the state's ruling circles seized the initiative and impeached the Kingfish for a number of alleged crimes and misdemeanours, turning the battle into a trial of Long's character rather than a debate about oil royalties. The months-long impeachment struggle paralyzed state politics until Long was able to mount a counterattack that included mass rallies and state-wide distribution of his own "circulars," political flyers that his poll captains could put on every door in Louisiana. Ultimately the Kingfish defeated the impeachment drive, but his victory came at a heavy price. He used every weapon at his disposal, discarding even the minimal rules of political warfare then in force in Louisiana. When it was over, Long's friends saw a changed man, a reformer who had concluded that the ends justified the means, a populist and pragmatist who had been hardened to believe it was better to give no quarter in politics than to risk all that he had won.

If Barrett knew he was heading into such a battle, he gave no sign of it. The weapons Long wielded so effectively—access to political funding, a loyal organization, a grassroots base ready to march in his support—were not available to Barrett. In retrospect, it is clear that the days leading up to Barrett's 1974 budget were a pivotal moment in the NDP administration. Control of the legislative agenda—and the political direction of the province—was hanging in the balance. Within days, the debate would no longer be about "resource dividends" and the right of British Columbians to a fair share of their province's wealth. The debate would turn to Barrett himself: his personal character, his ability to lead, even his emotional stability. It would be an impeachment hearing, without the specific charges. Barrett's response would say as much about his personal values as Long's did about his, and Barrett's political strategy—or lack of it—would prove just as central to the outcome.

5: The Chicken and Egg War

By 1974, sixteen months after the NDP's decisive electoral triumph, what honeymoon existed between the Barrett government and the media was long gone. Government missteps spurred concerted attacks from the editorial and business pages of the province's major newspapers. Hostility from media owners, editorial writers and the business press was to be expected, but that enmity often spilled onto news pages, as well. While many journalists liked Barrett, who was genuinely funny and a hoot to be around, this was the era of Watergate and the dawn of investigative reporting. Government announcements were no longer routinely regurgitated by the media. Reporters dug for better stories; if they were critical of the government, so much the better. Such was the case in the soon-to-come, so-called "Chicken and Egg War," which lasted through February and much of March and which took a big chunk out of Barrett's personal reputation.

This was a new experience for the NDP. During their long years in opposition, they rarely faced media scrutiny. But in a government without media handlers, the premier and cabinet ministers were perpetually one inadvertent comment away from the front page. Bob Strachan never lived down his early, rash complaint that ferry workers held "a gun to the head" of the government during their strike for hefty wage increases. Thin skins rather than toughened hides prevailed, and those gored, particularly Barrett, lashed out repeatedly against what they perceived—often correctly—as unfair coverage. The result was a tempestuous relationship between the NDP and the media that worsened the longer they were in government. As disparagement mounted in the media, the government began to develop a siege mentality, regularly railing away at the unfairness of it all. Controversy was always the media's fault, since the government's heart was pure, and the media was frequently cited by Barrett and the party as a major factor in their devastating defeat in 1975.

Of course, the new media, with its new attitude, would have been a big shock to anyone accustomed to the drowsy bunch that covered W.A.C. Bennett. When Barbara McLintock walked into the legislative press gallery on her first shift for the *Victoria Daily Colonist* on a wintry January morning in 1971, she found a world lost in time, little altered from the 1940s. Going through the gallery's imposing door just off the Speaker's Corridor was like entering a set from *The Front Page*. Its modest two rooms housed a dozen old wooden desks, decrepit chairs, battered filing cabinets, stacks of unread reports and black rotary-dial telephones. Aging typewriters sat on large green blotters to avoid further damaging the well-scarred desktops. A large, ungainly Telex machine sat in one corner. There was a beer cooler, a big, broken-down reclining chair, a small TV set attached high above one of the desks, and a few, rickety wooden phone booths that offered some privacy, unless one had a booming voice like veteran radio and television reporter Andy Stephen.

But Stephen's lack of concern about competition was commonplace. When stories broke, reporters often checked with each other before filing, to ensure they were on the same page. There was little duelling for scoops, since so few were to be had. With no regular Hansard, no Question Period, no regular access to ministers or the premier, no TV cameras and only one relatively short session a year, the legislature under the one-man show known as W.A.C. Bennett was a news backwater. As a wide-eyed twenty-one-year-old, McLintock was the first female to cover a full session of the legislature. Until then, the cozy coterie of gallery reporters was a bastion of hard-drinking men. Bottles of Scotch stowed away in bottom desk drawers were *de rigueur*.

Worse, lines between the Social Credit government and the media were seriously blurred. Reporters often earned extra money by writing speeches for cabinet ministers or helping with press releases. Others wrote the weekly reports Socred MLAs sent back to their local paper. McLintock remembers MLAs trooping into the gallery every Friday, each dropping off $20 to their media ghostwriter. "Everyone worked on the side," she said. "It was incredible how corrupt the press gallery was." The second woman to invade the men's world at the gallery was *Vancouver Sun* reporter and columnist Marjorie Nichols, who showed up in early 1972. She, too, was taken aback by what she found. "Wacky had everyone in his pocket, including the press gallery," she recounts in her autobiography, *Mark My Words*. "It was a very grim experience taking over a bureau and discovering that Wacky had these little side deals going with reporters. A lot of people were on the take." Disgusted by this and the lack of physical privacy, Nichols soon moved the *Sun*'s operation to the ivy-covered Empress Hotel across the street.

The election of Barrett and the NDP blew the cobwebs off. Not only was the downfall after two decades of the province's domineering, one-of-a-kind premier a huge story in itself, but the NDP victory also represented the first time an affluent province—its economy charged by Wild West capitalism—had elected a socialist government. For the next thirty-nine months, BC politics would be one gigantic fishbowl for a fascinated outside world to peer in at. Suddenly the sleepy press gallery in equally sleepy Victoria—home of "the newly wed and nearly dead"—was swamped with people. Both the *Sun* and *Province* quickly posted two permanent reporters to the press gallery. Other media outlets beefed up their coverage, too. Many assigned a full-time correspondent to the gallery's ramshackle facilities for the first time. During sessions of the legislature, the *Sun* would send in a phalanx of reporters from across the pond in Vancouver. They worked in shifts to ensure not a single moment of House proceedings was missed. Some legislation was printed verbatim. Barbara McLintock became a legendary figure, sitting for long hours up in the legislative gallery, knitting. "I did it to stay awake," she explained.

After two decades of W.A.C. Bennett, who would be as likely to smoke a joint as let out a scrap of information he didn't want to let out, Barrett was a reporter's dream. It was hard for him not to make news. He loved headlines. He loved shocking the status quo. He was funny. He was passionate. He could be vitriolic, often outrageous. No one gave speeches like Dave Barrett, his colourful, overblown rhetoric and voice rising and falling for effect like a Mozart sonata or a cantankerous chainsaw, depending on one's point of view. Rare was the week when Barrett wasn't on the front page or leading a newscast at least a couple of times. You never knew what he was going to say or do next. Quips, quotes and denunciations were often blurted out with nary a sober second thought. Barrett did not want to be a controlled, cautious premier. With an excessive belief in his own infallibility and gut instincts, he preferred to freewheel it. That could mean hitching a ride with a reporter, spontaneously going for Chinese food after bumping into a reporter on the street, or just yakking it up in the press gallery. For those in on the coverage, it was manna from heaven.

Barrett's wide-open style, however, created problems for the government. Although he loved attention, he did not really understand how the news business worked. He thought he could charm everyone and be treated positively, because, after all, he was on the right side. He would wander into the gallery, toss off a bunch of zingers and expect reporters to love him. But it didn't work that way anymore. Barrett rode the newspaper winds like a sailboat: favourable coverage could buoy him for days, while excessive criticism darkened his mood. He paid too much attention to the headlines and not enough to devising ways to counteract inevitable government–media tension that was exacerbated by the NDP's socialist agenda.

Media antagonism should not have been a shock. Owners and editors of newspapers do not, as a rule, support a party that campaigns for more public involvement in the economy and higher corporate taxes. Despite their unhappiness with W.A.C. Bennett, not one major media outlet during the 1972 election endorsed the NDP. In the bitter 1975 election, there was one: the *Victoria Times*. Seven months after the NDP's win, *Vancouver Sun* editorial writers were already calling Barrett's crew the most radical government in Canadian history. Business reporter Mike Grenby helpfully chipped in with a list of dozens of government measures that had harmed business. In a 1980 interview with media researcher Carol Gamey, *Victoria Times* editor George Oake explained, "The editorialists in this province, the ones who controlled the newspapers, were against Barrett from day one. They would praise individual things he did, but they were against the general philosophy."

Elements of a double standard crept into the media. While all governments make mistakes, NDP mistakes were often blown out of proportion. There were those who felt the NDP had some sort of hidden agenda, that they must be up to something because they were socialists. As a result, a relatively benign matter could suddenly seem sinister, if looked at it through anti-socialist spectacles. Marjorie Nichols was the most prominent of those who seemed to have it in for the government. As formidable, bright and hard-working a journalist as the province ever had, Nichols believed it was a reporter's duty to keep governments honest, hold them to account and find out what they were up to. But there was an anti-socialist fervour to Nichols' reporting during the Barrett years that often appeared to leave objectivity behind. A volunteer for Republican presidential candidate Barry Goldwater during her college days in the United States, Nichols didn't like unions—vowing to quit if she were forced to join the Newspaper Guild—and she didn't like NDP governments.

"Trust me, there is such a thing as an NDP government ... Higher pay for medical workers, better pay for teachers, legislation to make unionization easier, legislation to outlaw scabs. It's like they get it out of a little dictionary of dogma ... What these first NDP governments were doing was implementing every little resolution that had been passed by every socialist convention since the Winnipeg General Strike," she observed in *Mark My Words* with a touch of the snideness that often surfaced in her coverage of the Barrett years. Her criticisms stung, too, since the *Vancouver Sun* was far and away the paramount media voice in the province, and in those days one of the most influential papers in Canada. When the government announced the purchase of Plateau Mills on June 27, 1973, Nichols collaborated on a story that produced an inflammatory headline across the front page of the final edition of the *Vancouver Sun*: "'Terror tactics' in mill purchase."

The headline was based on a single quote from a disgruntled prospective buyer who claimed Plateau shareholders were warned by the government of repercussions if they did not agree to sell to the province. "You better believe there were some terror tactics going on," said Vancouver financial consultant David R. Beach. The story ran without comment from mill owners or the government. They were given no opportunity to defend themselves against Beach's outlandish charge, because, according to the article, they could not be reached before the paper's deadline. The next day, after Barrett, Bob Williams, and Plateau president William Martens categorically rejected the accusation as "absolute nonsense," the *Sun*'s banner headline read, "'Terror tactics' in Plateau deal denied." Sometimes, it was tough to win.

Nichols' anti-socialist ardour hit its peak shortly before she left Victoria for Ottawa in June, 1975, when Provincial Secretary Ernie Hall brought in his *Emergency Programme Act*. The bill was a replacement for the long-standing *Civil Defence Act*, which provided the government with emergency powers in case of natural disasters, such as a flood or earthquake. Although Hall's bill failed to define "emergency" and gave a few added powers to the government, including the right to expropriate property, the benign intent of the legislation was clear—but not to Marjorie Nichols. Alone among gallery reporters, in a classic "Reds under the bed" reaction, Nichols saw the dreaded spectre of arbitrary government. The next day, the *Vancouver Sun* splashed her story all over the front page under the banner headline, "All-powerful 'emergency bill' raises storm." The sub-head read, "BC move called worse than *War Measures Act*."

The only storm raised by the bill, however, was whipped up by Nichols herself, who asked opposition members to comment on the dangers she saw in the bill. They were horrified, right on cue. After her news story, which included Ernie Hall's pledge to withdraw or amend any flaws in the bill, Nichols donned her columnist's hat and ripped into "this odious legislation ... this little disgrace." It was, she said, "the most terrifying bill ever churned out of the NDP mill." The proposed measures far outdistanced other "sloppy, scary bills that epitomized the first few sessions of socialist rule" and yes, it was worse than the *War Measures Act*. Her column concluded, "Every citizen of this province must be gravely concerned about this NDP government that would award itself total powers on the grounds that they might come in handy sometime. That is not democracy."

The ranks of "gravely concerned," however, did not include other members of the media. The *Province* carried nothing about the *Emergency Programme Act*. Other publications ran only a few straightforward paragraphs. The day after Nichols' alarmist story and column appeared in the *Sun*, a *Province* editorial, rarely restrained in anti-government criticism, downplayed the alleged furor. "Mr. Hall can be believed when he says his government wrote the bill with genuine natural disasters in mind. He can prove it to everybody's satisfaction ... by introducing some simple changes," the paper mildly advised. In his journal, Peter McNelly pointed out that the bill had been written by civil servants and was barely discussed, if at all, in cabinet—hardly evidence of a government with a calculated, Machiavellian plan to seize arbitrary powers in the event of an emergency. Increasingly perturbed, however, by media attacks on the government, McNelly yielded to despair: "Are we really that frightening a group of people? I mean, what about the free ambulance service? Human rights act, Pharmacare program, etc. Is this all to be swept away in a battle of engineered rhetoric? What a sickness."

Eventually, the emergency powers bill died on the order paper. The *Sun* buried the news in a six-paragraph story tucked away in its back pages. Noting that the original *Civil Defence Act* may have actually provided more powers in total, Barrett ridiculed the opposition's "silly and hysterical" criticism. "If we brought in the Ten Commandments, they'd probably vote against it." Discussing the controversy several years later, the normally mild-mannered Hall called Nichols' attack on the bill "a single-handed piece of venomous rubbish ... I couldn't understand why she did it."

Nichols did not work alone. She formed close relations with dominant radio hotliner Jack Webster, fondly known as "the oatmeal savage," and the *Vancouver Sun*'s brilliant columnist Allan Fotheringham, who never seemed able to get a handle on Dave Barrett. A superb wordsmith, Fotheringham's bread and butter was skewering the pompous, the inane and the incompetent. But the NDP premier fit none of those categories. Fotheringham could write movingly about the experience of attending a Barrett public meeting, then turn on him with surprising harshness. After Barrett's early election call in 1975, the columnist derided "the idealist socialist worker [for doing] what any Tammany ward heeler did: call an election when he best thought he could win … What he has just done is as cynical as could be imagined. He has demonstrated that what he likes above all is power, and that he will go to any lengths to retain it." It was a strange analysis of someone who had done more to bring social justice to British Columbia—regardless of how skilfully—than any premier before or since. Webster and Fotheringham had both been strong critics of Social Credit. They welcomed the election of Dave Barrett and the NDP. As time went by, however, they became increasingly critical.

They began hanging out with Marjorie Nichols. The three shared gossip, news, views and booze, rarely to the benefit of the NDP. One reporter labelled them "a daisy chain" of information. Peter McNelly records an occasion when Barrett, scheduled to appear on Webster's hotline show, showed up a bit early: there was Marjorie Nichols feeding Webster tough questions to rattle the premier. Individually, each was a media powerhouse. Together, the threesome had inordinate capacity to damage the Barrett government in the eyes of the public. "When all three of them would be in agreement on a story, you had a triple whammy with a devastating impact," observed long-time Victoria journalist and columnist Jim Hume. "The whole world believed it had to be true." In a 1980 interview, Webster acknowledged the trio's influence and, as he saw it, duty. "You must be querulous, critical, cynical and 'agin the government,' because there are enough people licking their boots without individual reporters with clout doing the same thing," he said. "I'm talking particularly about the Nichols, the Websters, the Fotheringhams. You've got to be 'agin the government.' Otherwise, you get brainwashed, and swamped in no time." In his autobiography, Webster said he was so vitriolic in his hammering of the government that, near the end, he received "a neatly-typed death threat.' The note warned Webster that if the NDP lost the election, he would die. He began carrying a gun.

Yet not all was unrelenting attack. The sixties were in full flower, and that was reflected in the ranks of the media, as well. In contrast to veterans from the Wacky Bennett era, many reporters were young, loved to party at the pub and/or smoke dope. To a degree, they were sympathetic to the professed goals of the Barrett government—righting wrongs and making the province a more just and equitable place. The divide extended to where one drank. The old guard, and many opposition politicians, quaffed wine and hard liquor at the quiet Bengal Room inside the Empress Hotel, with its curry and tiger skin on the wall. Younger reporters chose The Beaver, a rowdy, rambunctious pub with its entrance outside the Empress. Stops at The Beaver were rarely brief.

Reflecting back in 1980, George Oake said there was a clear division in the gallery between those who might be considered somewhat pro-Barrett, or at least neutral, and those who were con. "People like Andy Stephen, Jim Hume (of the Victoria *Daily Colonist*) and Marjorie Nichols were very critical of him all the way through," he said. Stephen was a legendary gallery figure. He pioneered TV coverage of the legislature for local station CHEK and later for BCTV. With his distinctive foghorn voice and large frame, at a time when television was beginning to challenge newspapers as a source for news, he was as recognizable to the public as the politicians he covered. Incorrigibly cheerful, a hearty backslapper and helpful to other reporters when the news was unfolding as it should, his ten-decibel laugh, in the words of one gallery wag, could be heard all the way up Douglas Street. Stephen hosted a weekly TV show from the gallery called *Capital Comment*, which paid $45 a gig to grateful reporters for appearing on a panel. Given the often bleary state of hungover reporter/panellists at its early Friday-morning tapings, the show also became known as "Capital Coma." Like his contemporaries, Stephen had ties to the Social Credit government under W.A.C. Bennett, getting paid for helping with publicly funded sports festivals and the like. Although a fount of political lore, Stephen didn't like change. He had trouble relating to the NDP government and the younger reporters crowding into the gallery.

Reporters would also come from elsewhere in Canada and the United States to witness the remarkable socialist government presiding over British Columbia. Their stories, especially those by Canadian correspondents, were often favourable. They saw Barrett's politics and the government's achievements in a broader context, and few leaders could be as personable and fill up a reporter's notebooks with as many good quotes as Dave Barrett. The tone was different from some reporters south of the border, where government intervention in the economy and any hint of socialism, no matter how soft, were considered akin to Communism. There were more than a few examples of apocalyptic prose full of howlers. On the first anniversary of Barrett's election, *Newsweek* magazine labelled him "Norman Thomas, North," a reference to the pacifist who ran six times for president as a candidate for the Socialist Party of America. The article referred to Barrett's press secretary, John Twigg, as a twenty-four-year-old "former anarchist." It went on to describe the premier's recent, "see-what-it's-like" day on a fishboat as "the first of a number of quasi-Maoist forays that Barrett has planned."

The prominent US financial weekly, *Barron's*, took it even further. The ultra-conservative publication weighed in with a full-page editorial that ran under the headline, "Chile of the North? That may be the fate of British Columbia under the Socialists." According to *Barron's*, Barrett and the NDP were moving ahead "with a Socialist program rivalling that of the Allende government in Chile." The anonymous writer scorned efforts by Barrett to downplay concerns on Wall Street. "The fact is that he has teeth like Mack the Knife. Investors should mentally hang a sign on British Columbia that says: 'Cave Canem' (Beware of the Dog)." The piece ended cheerfully with a quote from a disgruntled Abbotsford farmer, said to have come to Canada after being

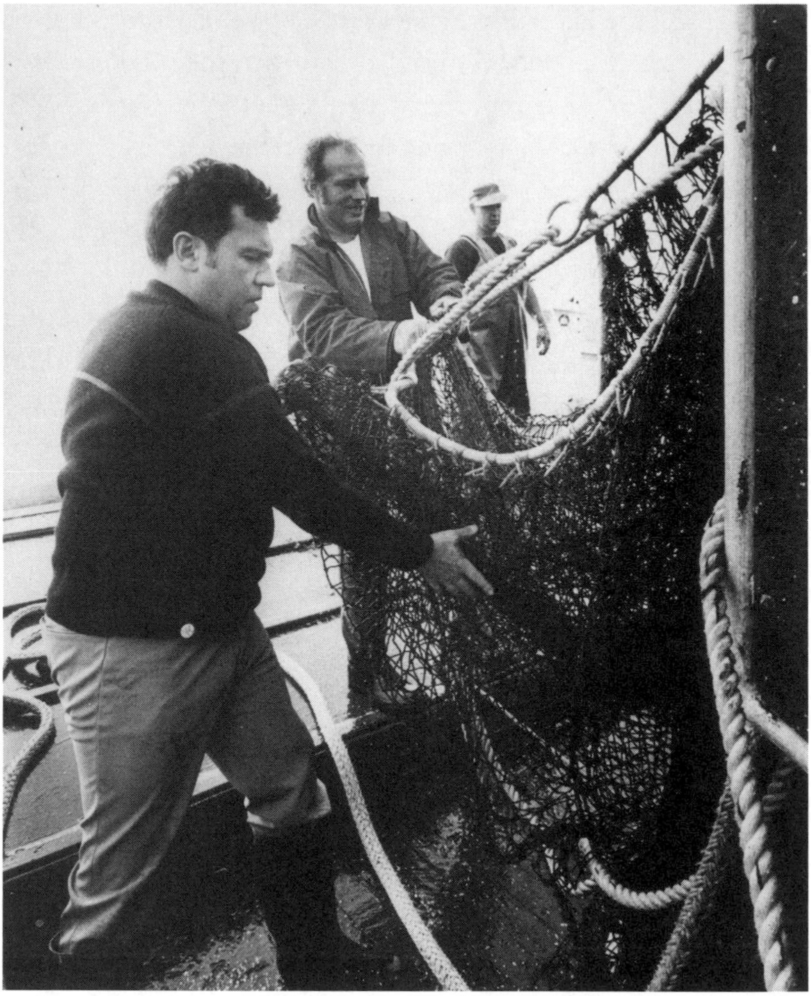

Premier Dave Barrett's initial venture to try out various work experiences took place on a commercial salmon fishing boat in the summer of 1973, dubbed a "quasi-Maoist" initiative by *Newsweek*. Barrett's first question on board: "When do we eat?" Photo by Steve Bosch, provided by the *Vancouver Sun*

pushed off his land in post-war East Prussia. "The Reds make many promises," he told *Barron's*, "but always these are broken. They only want power." Barrett laughed off the editorial, which was front-page news in the *Vancouver Sun*. "They must have got out their Joe McCarthy cut-out kit," he said, calling the writer "a refugee from Rowan and Martin's *Laugh-In*."

After reading stories he felt were unfair, Barrett loved to fire back, particularly at the *Vancouver Sun*. Once, Barrett came into the press gallery, threw a copy of the *Sun* to the floor and proceeded to jump up and down on it. On another occasion, he called a press conference in his office to harangue the *Sun* for its handling of a story filed by the paper's Washington correspondent on a brief crisis over water deliveries to Point Roberts. The *Sun* was 100 percent wrong, Barrett raged during a twenty-minute tirade. Its reporting was "inadequate, inaccurate, incompetent." It has become a badge of honour to be victimized by "incorrect" *Sun* reports, he said. Other gallery members, wondering why they were there, soon put their pens away and left. When the *Sun* reporter, by then the only journalist still standing, pointed out he had not written the story, Barrett responded, "Oh, I know. You're just one of the poor working peons for that newspaper ... inadequate, incompetent, bumbling ... " It was hard not to laugh.

But the *Sun* could be demeaning, too. A story on Barrett's historic trip to the People's Republic of China in 1974 was headlined, "Barrett in China, tired, overweight." And trivialities, such as the size of the big desk ordered by Minister of Human Resources Norm Levi, were regular fodder for ridicule. Editorials in the *Province* were forever referring to the "Socialist government," with a capital *S*; government purchases were "takeovers"; and every now and then an editorial writer would trot out the phrase, "Since the NDP seized power," as if some sort of military coup had taken place.

As a former journalist, McNelly could be driven wild with indignation. When Barrett seemed to have won federal agreement to allow an increase in the price of natural gas exports to the US—revenue that the government promised to funnel to municipalities—he was aghast that editorials advised municipalities not to appear over-eager for the extra cash. On the same story, CBC-TV reporter Ab Douglas told viewers that the government was out to "soak the Americans" without mentioning that the US domestic price was already higher than BC's charge for natural gas exports. "It's really annoying," wrote McNelly in his journal. "For years, all W.A.C. Bennett had to do was fart, and he'd get on the front pages, followed by lengthy explanations of why he did this and what he hoped to gain. Boy, are those days gone." Still, the NDP often made it easy for those in the media who were out to get them.

The government had no strategy to deal with the media. Barrett's press secretary, John Twigg, was unseasoned. His only experience had been reporting for the student *Ubyssey* newspaper and a summer or two at the *Vancouver Sun*. Reporters did not respect him, and vice versa. Twigg's *Weekly News* summary was scorned by the media, including McNelly when he was still covering the legislature for the *Province*. His article carried the headline, "Government propaganda distributed at taxpayers' expense." Several months into his new job with Barrett, McNelly described in his journal a premier groping to find ways of working better with the press. "He still fails to come up with the essential understanding, namely that the power of his office alone is sufficient for him to achieve the kind of coverage that at least makes him look like the premier," McNelly observed, acutely. "The NDP still operates on the basis of who is for them and who is against them."

The government really took it on the chin over the airwaves. In those days, hotline radio was king. Among the fleet of airwave hosts, the NDP had few friends. Pat Burns of CJOR seemed to specialize in nasty. He was on for three hours every weekday evening, regularly spewing dark threats about socialist land grabs and worse. Right-wingers Chuck Cook and Ed Murphy also manned microphones at the station. Webster was fairest of them all, and he didn't flinch from lacing into the NDP. Afterward, he liked to boast that Barrett blamed him for losing the 1975 election. With his thick Scottish burr, showmanship, unerring instinct for a story and gruff, tough interviews, Webste-r-r-r-r was one of a kind. Because he dominated the ratings, politicians lined up to be eviscerated on his show. After he jumped ship from CKNW to CJOR in 1972, former *Province* city hall reporter Gary Bannerman was given the Herculean task of hanging on to as many of Webster's former listeners as he could. Bannerman sought to raise ratings with redneck views and "investigative reports" on the government. His morning show was called *The Investigators*, laughingly referred to by reporters who didn't have much time for Bannerman or the show as "The Garburators" or "The Instigators."

In February 1974, ink on the government's Robin Hood budget was barely dry, when the government was rocked by an onslaught of tough stories. Bannerman was first off the mark. CKNW took out full-page ads touting a full-program "exposé" by the radio host. The ads showed a large, official party photo of Barrett, accompanied by the words, "Tomorrow, we're going to respectfully ask him, how it feels to be ripped off." On air, Bannerman charged that insiders made a killing with advance notice of the government's purchase of Dunhill Development Corporation for $5.8-million. The government bought the private company, including its land holdings and management team, as the foundation of a public housing program. "The news seems to get out to the privileged few, every time Barrett whispers into someone's ear," Bannerman charged. "We are free to speculate that members of Mr. Barrett's caucus were also using the privileged information ... Premier David Barrett is playing games with your money and my money. You can get it, if you are doing business with Dave Barrett, the social worker in Victoria."

Barrett was furious. Calling the allegations "malicious slander," he demanded CKNW retract Bannerman's charges with a second full-page ad in the *Sun*. He threatened to sue. Dunhill executives also strongly denied the claims of insider trading. The papers mostly stayed away from the story, and opposition demands for a royal commission, except by bombastic Peace River MLA Don Phillips, were half-hearted at best. The NDP toyed with the idea of bringing Phillips before a House committee, but eventually decided against it, while Barrett, after wrestling with the decision for several days, opted not to sue. In the meantime, Bannerman and CKNW refused to back down on anything. Several years later, as the case headed to trial, the radio station quietly apologized and coughed up an out-of-court settlement to four former Dunhill associates, who had resolutely pursued legal action to clear their names. A few days after Bannerman's attack, there was more serious trouble.

It began with an early phone call one morning in late February. Liberal leader David Anderson rolled over, groaned and looked at the clock. It was six a.m. He picked up the phone. It was someone who said he had information about Dave Barrett and the province's chicken and egg marketing boards. "Sure, great," grumbled Anderson. He hung up and went back to sleep. The person called back at nine. This time he mentioned that he had affidavits. Anderson got interested. Thus launched the notorious "Chicken and Egg War," as outwardly absurd a kerfuffle as the name implied, but one that caused the NDP, and particularly the premier himself, a huge tumble in public esteem. One could argue it was a political and personal disaster from which the Barrett government never completely recovered. And the media was front and centre. This was a saga driven almost entirely by a lone reporter's personal mission.

The roots of the "war" went back to a stormy 1972 meeting in Barrett's office, just six weeks after he and the NDP were sworn in, that included Barrett, Minister of Agriculture Dave Stupich, ministry officials and members of the BC Egg Marketing Board. They were there to discuss egg quotas and levies assessed against a Prince George egg man, Savo Kovachich, who had sold more eggs than his quota allowed. During the recently concluded election campaign, Barrett called for egg producers in the Interior and northern regions to get a fairer share of production quotas from the marketing board, which heavily favoured Fraser Valley farmers. Kovachich was known to be an NDP supporter. According to subsequent claims by board members, Barrett ordered them at the meeting to lower the fines against Kovachich, threatening to bring in legislation if they refused, and vowed to "kick the crap" out of anyone who reneged on the deal—including Kovachich. Not long afterward, penalties against the Prince George egg producer were scaled back significantly.

After that, there was not so much as a chick's peep in public about the meeting. But sixteen months later, in mid-February of 1974, *Province* reporter Malcolm Turnbull abruptly began writing about it. David Anderson, struggling to keep members of his troublesome caucus from bolting to an alternative, free enterprise option, seized on the issue. In close contact during much of the unfolding drama, it was not so surprising that Anderson and Turnbull became entwined on the story. The two men rowed together on the Canadian champion eights squad from the University of BC that won a silver medal at the 1959 Pan Am Games. Turnbull would later work briefly for Anderson after he was elected to the House of Commons in 1993. He also had an earlier connection to Social Credit. In 1966, while still on the payroll of the *Province,* Turnbull did publicity work for Dr. Howard McDiarmid, a family friend who ran successfully for the Socreds in the provincial election that year. Anderson believes it was his old rowing mate who called him early that morning with news of the affidavits, although Turnbull doesn't think so.

Turnbull's stories focused on Barrett's alleged intervention in the egg marketing board's treatment of Kovachich. Barrett denied the accusation. He said he merely told both sides to stop acting like children and settle their dispute. When Anderson asked him about the matter in the legislature, Barrett gave the same answer. The bombshell hit just before March: sworn affidavits, signed by two of those present at the meeting, surfaced in the *Province*, attesting that the premier had indeed interfered and ordered them to make a deal. Two other affidavits, also denied by Barrett, claimed the premier had interfered in a Broiler Marketing Board meeting as well, giving reporters a chicken angle to go with the eggs.

Despite the affidavits, David Anderson did not expect a big deal. The Liberal leader thought that Barrett, given the sworn affidavits, would suggest that maybe his words had been misinterpreted, or maybe his recollection was mistaken. He would make some sort of acknowledgement of the affidavits, retain his basic credibility, and the matter would die. "It was such a trivial issue," Anderson recalled in an interview. "I might have given Barrett a bit of a knuckle-rapping, but I thought it would be over in an afternoon." Instead, Barrett stuck to his guns. He continued to insist he had not said what the affidavits alleged. The recollection of those who signed them was wrong.

At once, the stakes soared. The issue became not whether Barrett had improperly injected himself in the business of the egg marketing board, but whether he was lying about it. Armed with legally sworn affidavits that disputed Barrett's version of the meeting, Anderson was off and running. The Liberal leader made the issue a personal cause. Either the marketing board representatives had perjured themselves in their affidavits, or the premier was lying, he repeated time and again. Anderson demanded a judicial inquiry to clear the air. He seemed to talk of nothing else. The drama went on relentlessly day after day. Other media began piling on.

But the Liberal leader waited until debate on the premier's spending estimates to play his trump card, designed to produce the maximum amount of publicity: eviction from the legislature. On March 5, after yet another prolonged recitation of the facts, Anderson solemnly declared, "I have no alternative but to accuse the premier ... of lying to this House." Unfortunately for Anderson, in a development worthy of a French farce, committee chair Carl Liden had either nodded off, been bored senseless or failed to grasp the gravity of the Liberal leader's accusation. Neither he nor anyone else asked Anderson to withdraw his remark. Debate continued as if nothing had happened. Puzzled and disappointed that his big moment had gone unrecognized, Anderson took his seat while the next speaker, Cariboo MLA Alex Fraser, complained about BC Rail.

Undeterred, Anderson tried again the next day. "The premier … has deliberately lied in this House," he proclaimed, once more. This time, he succeeded. Speaker Gordon Dowding was called in. He requested Anderson to withdraw his statement. Instead, the Liberal leader replied, "For the third time today, and fifth time in two days, I claim the premier has lied." Ordered to leave the legislature, Anderson formally shook hands with his four caucus members and walked out the door to a forest of microphones, in time to make the front page of the *Vancouver Sun*'s final edition. The following day, he did it again, and on the day after that.

Barrett, who had little time for Anderson, initially shrugged off the accusations as mere political showboating by the Liberal leader. He also thought the actual issue of unfair egg quotas would overshadow anything he might have said at the meeting. Barrett felt he was on the right side. But Anderson's incessant pounding took its toll. After a week or so, Barrett was on edge. Even within the NDP, there was nervousness over Barrett's persistent denials that he had threatened and intervened in the marketing board. Stupich said he didn't recall him saying what the egg men alleged, but nor could he remember much of anyone's exact words from the meeting. As the crisis began to dominate the legislature, other cabinet ministers and NDP backbenchers mostly stayed silent. It got worse.

Although Turnbull and the *Province* spearheaded the Chicken and Egg War, Marjorie Nichols was soon weighing in. In a series of hard-hitting attack columns, she questioned the premier's credibility. After two weeks of intense pressure and sensing that he was in a deep hole from which he could not escape, Barrett snapped. Spying Nichols in the legislative corridor, Barrett lit into her. At one point, he shouted, "Fuck you. Fuck you, you venomous bitch." It was one of the low moments in Barrett's topsy-turvy career. Not only was his language foul-mouthed, it was directed at a woman reporter. It could not be regarded as anything but intimidation, though Barrett, describing the incident in his autobiography, admitted that at the time it felt great. McNelly, who witnessed the incident, was taken aback. "[It was] such a tirade as I have never ever seen a politician lay on a reporter," he wrote in his journal. McNelly took Nichols for beers, hoping to calm her down sufficiently not to write about it. But she did, and the confrontation was quickly picked up by other media and the opposition. The story went across the country.

The incident shook both Barrett and Nichols. "I blew it," he told McNelly. When he got home that night, his wife, Shirley, gave him a stinging glance. "I knew without her saying anything what was going through her mind: You asshole!" a rueful Barrett confessed in his autobiography. The next day, Nichols sent Barrett a private note, asking that the matter be laid to rest. "Marj was genuinely hurt," said McNelly. He noted that she wanted to skip a big dinner that night because Barrett would also be there. McNelly concluded, "Barrett promised never to harass a reporter again. To any decent reporter, it's a bush league manoeuvre for a politician to hassle them."

But if 1974 was proving a difficult year for Barrett, it had been even more so for David Anderson. The daily melodrama of expulsion from the legislature amounted to Anderson's desperate, last-ditch effort to persuade reporters, voters and even his own party members that the Liberals, not Social Credit or the Majority Movement, were the solution to the Barrett problem. On February 5, voters in North Vancouver–Capilano headed to the polls for a by-election triggered by the resignation of incumbent Liberal David Brousson, a businessman and environmentalist who had found the workload under Barrett intolerable. (Barrett had confirmed Brousson's worst fears when he served notice that MLAs, full-time workers at last, would now receive their $16,000 salary and $8,000 expense allowance quarterly rather than by the session.)

The by-election was critical for the Tories, still reeling from Derril Warren's disastrous showing in the 1973 Kelowna by-election. A win in North Vancouver—even an outcome better than Social Credit's—was vital if they were to have any hope of survival. Scott Wallace, the new Tory leader, was hearing the same demands for unity that rang in the Liberals' ears, but as a defector from Social Credit, he was not about to rejoin his old team even if they would have him—and they wouldn't. For the Tories, it was time to produce at the polls or fold.

The vote was a life-or-death battle for Anderson's Liberals as well. Failure to hold this safe Liberal seat would be catastrophic. Since the provincial Liberal Party's golden age during the 1930s and 1940s, there had been many lean years for the little band now gathered around Anderson. The Liberals had seen their base whittled down to tiny enclaves in the well-to-do urban centres of Vancouver and Victoria, where Anderson had been elected in 1972 after a term as backbencher in the Trudeau government. A lawyer, environmentalist and former Olympic athlete, Anderson had a patrician air that placed him well outside BC's populist political mainstream, but made him appealing to the urban professionals who found Social Credit unacceptably brash and backwoods.

Anderson's colleagues were cut from the same cloth. Bluff and genial Garde Gardom, a lawyer of distinctly upper-class background and attitudes, shared the two-member Vancouver Point Grey riding with UBC professor and brain researcher Pat McGeer, who had served as party leader until an internal coup ousted him in favour of Anderson in 1972. A brilliant neurologist, McGeer had just published a savage book-length denunciation of W.A.C. Bennett—"political morality in the true sense cannot be said to exist in British Columbia today"—when party activists decided to dispense with his services. On the north side of Burrard Inlet, Brousson had held North Vancouver–Capilano while lean and hungry-looking lawyer Allan Williams represented West Vancouver, western Canada's wealthiest community.

Bill Bennett did not have the same pressures faced by the Liberals and the Conservatives. Just fifteen months after the New Democrats' sweep, Bennett had not only replaced his father and shattered the Conservatives, he was enjoying the fruits of a province-wide recruiting drive spearheaded by W.A.C. and Grace McCarthy that was generating thousands of new memberships. To his chagrin, however, the province's business and political elite continued to discount him as a viable option. Howe Street pundits believed a new "free enterprise coalition" was needed to eliminate vote-splitting by the 60 percent of the non-socialist voters.

It was this simple arithmetic that had led to the creation of the Majority Movement, which was facing its own trial by fire in the by-election. The Majority Movement's rhetoric had been unsupported by action until the fall of 1973 when activist Arnold Hean began writing to Liberal, Conservative and Social Credit MLAs urging them "to unite with other politically minded, non-socialist persons who are desirous of bringing to British Columbia a competitive, individual enterprise, social reforming government." Brousson's resignation offered the first opportunity to test the new approach in a riding where the NDP's chances of victory were slim to nil. If the opposition parties could be persuaded to unite, the way would be open to a new free enterprise party.

All three parties ignored Hean for understandable reasons. The Socreds wished to demonstrate new life. The

Conservatives hoped to return from the dead. The Liberals, desperate to show they remained a political force, could not step back from the challenge of holding one of their existing handful of seats. Anderson was most forceful in his denunciations of the Majority Movement, declaring it "fascist in content." Majority Movement leaders were ridiculed by journalists like Allan Fotheringham as "dabblers and dilettantes, short-cut artists who won't take the time and trouble to get into a legitimate political party but who want to be the anti-socialist manipulators from the outside." As the polls opened, there was no "unity" option for voters to consider.

The winner of the February 5 by-election turned out to be Liberal Gordon Gibson Jr., the thirty-five-year-old son of BC's famous "Bull of the Woods," a millionaire logger and former Liberal MLA who had built a Depression-era shingle mill into a major timber company. But Gibson eked out a surprisingly narrow fifty-seven-vote victory over the second-place Social Credit candidate Ron Andrews, mayor of the District of North Vancouver, who not only scared the wits out of the Liberals but thumped the Conservatives. This was a clear but unwelcome sign, largely unnoticed in Barrett's circle, of Social Credit's rise from its deathbed. (Bennett later expressed satisfaction at the second-place finish, which underlined how "free enterprise" vote-splitting was holding back consolidation of the opposition under Socred leadership.)

In the wake of the election, members of all three opposition parties began secret talks to achieve the same end by different means. By the time Gibson was sworn in on February 18, Victoria was absorbed in bitter partisan brawling in the legislature during the day, and seething with backroom intrigue in hotel rooms and bars at night. After all, the defection of only three Socreds to a new party that included the five Liberals and the two Conservatives would transform the new organization into a caucus that would surpass Social Credit. Talks aimed at such an outcome immediately began behind the backs of Bill Bennett and David Anderson.

Desperate to deflect attention from chickens and eggs, the New Democrats attempted to distract reporters with a real story: the feverish secret meetings that were disclosed to Peter McNelly by an informant. McNelly's source was an opposition staffer who reported that Conservative leader Scott Wallace, Liberal members Allan Williams and Gordon Gibson, and Socred Bob McClelland were in regular talks. He expected the news to break any day. Barrett and Williams seized upon the tip as a tool to disrupt the opposition and end the Chicken and Egg War. They expected the revelation that these private discussions were going on unbeknownst to their party members, and even the Social Credit and Liberal leaders, to be a bombshell.

But when Minister of Highways Graham Lea delivered the attack on March 7, the opposition at first responded with laughter. "This entire debate surrounding the premier's estimates has been a cover-up to the most vicious political game of all," shouted Lea, "and it's called 'carve up your leader.'" Pandemonium erupted as opposition members demanded that Lea "name names," but Lea overstepped himself with the claim that the conspirators had been meeting just the night before, which McClelland jumped to his feet to deny. (In fact, a meeting had been planned but no one had been able to make it.) McNelly, sitting in the gallery, watched Wallace turn "ashen-faced" as the House erupted in shouts and denials.

Media reaction was contradictory. Although the *Province* carried a detailed report, the *Sun* and BCTV decided there was no story. Lea's bombshell would have been a damp squib had Wallace not called a suppertime news conference to confirm that he had indeed been engaged with discussions on the matter with a number of MLAs, including McClelland. That forced Allan Williams to admit he had engaged in such talks, as well, on a "man to man" basis, with Anderson's knowledge. His goal, Williams said, was to accelerate the creation of a new, united opposition party, because neither coalition nor a move to merge under the banner of an existing party seemed feasible.

Barrett hoped Lea's revelations would stall the creation of the new party and, to a degree, they succeeded. As Nichols pointed out a week later, Wallace had single-handedly "succeeded in destroying any immediate opportunity for coalition" and alienated himself from his colleagues by betraying the substance of confidential negotiations. Conservative Party directors wondered how Wallace could continue as leader of a party he evidently sought to dissolve, but Wallace refused to resign. Nor could Anderson take any comfort from the revelations. Within days of the "bombshell," both Liberals and Conservatives were still meeting, again without their leaders.

The Chicken and Egg War eventually faded away, forced off the front pages by countless other legislative battles. The role of Malcolm Turnbull in the damaging affair was pivotal, and controversial. "Malcolm *was* the Chicken and Egg War," observed the *Province*'s legislative reporter at the time, Barbara McLintock. It was Turnbull who first wrote about Barrett's alleged interference long after the meeting with the egg producers had taken place. And he was the one who subsequently went to those at the meeting and suggested they swear out affidavits about what took place. Some declined, but others agreed. Further, the legal costs of the affidavits that caused Dave Barrett so much grief were paid for by Turnbull's newspaper, the *Province*. Two were registered by Michael Coleman of Duncan, a university schoolmate of both Turnbull and Anderson. Two more were affirmed by former *Sun* and *Province* reporter Ian MacAlpine, then a lawyer in Abbotsford.

Looking back, Turnbull agreed it would have been better if the board members had used their own lawyers. "But these guys didn't have a hell of a lot of money. I talked it over with [managing editor] Merv Moore, and then I told the producers that we'd like them to sign an affidavit, stating what happened. I said, 'We'll cover the costs, because you should be advised by a lawyer.'" Anderson says he had no idea at the time the *Province* paid for the affidavits.

Did Turnbull step over the line in the Chicken and Egg War, from reporter to participant? Anderson isn't sure. "I don't know. Maybe that's for a media person to answer," he said in a 2012 interview. "Malcolm was an important factor in the story. I discussed the situation with him a number of times. Heck, at the beginning, I barely knew what an egg marketing board was." But Anderson said there was a public interest at stake. "If a premier acts like this, it should be brought out." Turnbull defends his involvement. He did not report on the 1972 meeting until February of 1974, he explained, because that's when he found out about it. "I said to the board members: 'What the hell are you guys doing? Why don't you say something? If [the government is] threatening you, there's one way to stop it. You either cave in, or you go public." Turnbull insisted he didn't interfere with the news. "I didn't tell them what to do. I said, 'Look, if it was me, I might do this, or I might do that. I can't tell you what the hell to do. You're elected by your producers, and you have to answer to them, not to me.'"

A year later, BC Supreme Court Justice E.E. Hinkson weighed in on the financial levies assessed against Kovachich. His nine-page judgment barely mentioned Barrett's role. What he did say vindicated neither the premier nor the marketing board. The judge found that no agreement "with legal consequences" was entered into at the 1972 meeting, but at the same time, he concluded an eventual deal was reached because of the premier's intervention. It was a verbal saw-off, and by then, the media had tired of the story, despite attempts by Anderson and the *Province* to revive it. Most felt the judge's verdict did not prove conclusively that Barrett had lied. Nonetheless, Barrett was worried the issue would resurface. He kept asking Peter McNelly what he thought. McNelly advised him to move on, since he was never going to get "fair press" on the dispute "because, when you get right down to it, the press, even our friends, believe that you lied."

"Okay," Barrett replied. "I get the message." In the end, Barrett's blurred recollections of his "chicken and egg" intervention and his outburst at Nichols both damaged his own reputation and strengthened Social Credit. The NDP's counterattack served to abort discussions for the formation of a new party that would have again divided the "free enterprisers" into two camps, Social Credit and the others. Bill Bennett was proving to have good luck, as well as good management.

As the year from hell continued, and unfavourable stories mounted, relations with the media grew more and more antagonistic. Marc Eliesen, who had worked for the federal NDP in Ottawa and as deputy finance minister for Manitoba Premier Ed Schreyer before joining Barrett's government in 1974, was shocked by the extent of the undeclared media–government war he found going on. "In my experience, coming to BC from the east and from Manitoba, I'd never seen a more hostile media environment," Eliesen said in an interview. "There was just no respect for the position of premier ... It seemed there were different standards ... Some of the coverage was vicious, just vicious."

Eventually, the government itself decided to get into the game. Steps were taken to get its message to the public without media filtering. Despite years of reviling *BC Government News* as a Socred propaganda tool, the NDP reversed its previous opposition and resurrected the publication. Well-written in its own way and snappily laid out, *BC Government News* proved a surprising hit—in contrast to Twigg's overtly partisan, less substantive and sparsely distributed *Weekly News*. Those not on the mailing list wrote in to ask for it. Circulation rose. A new government communications branch was established in the spring of 1975. Most ministries were soon churning out their own publications and spin.

Yet, as the saying goes, it was all too little, too late. CBC cameraman Ron Thompson, a gallery fixture for years, felt the NDP did not see the value in developing a positive media strategy.

"They didn't care about explaining things. It was one reason they got defeated," he told a researcher five years later. "They rushed ahead and the public, through the media, never got the message, because things were forever unfolding, unfolding, unfolding…" Perhaps, as well, the NDP believed too much in itself, reflected Ernie Hall some years later. "Having come to this decision that our program, our ideology, is correct, and any fool can see that it is correct, it follows that anybody who interferes with the whole effect and implementation is a villain at best and a saboteur at worst."

But few were willing to be so judicious at the time. Minister of Health Dennis Cocke spoke for many in the NDP when he lashed out against a perceived alliance between the media and the "profiteering buccaneers and power brokers. The press has done a fine job in complementing the kind of personality assassination that has been going on," he said, angrily. "And they love it." Cabinet minister Bob Strachan said no government in the history of BC had been subjected to so much media misrepresentation. "There has been no balanced presentation of news in this province."

A 1975 column in the BC party's monthly tabloid *The Democrat* put it this way: "In our province today, one can find a steady drip of hate against our government on some hotline programs, much of the Interior press, the editorial columns of most major dailies, and with certain television journalists. Many people close to the press would dismiss this sort of talk as the usual paranoia of the left, but a close examination of how the press slants the news shows in many cases a consistent attempt to deny the public a straightforward rendering of the facts."

On election night, when thirty-nine months of socialist rule came to a crashing halt, Attorney General Alex Macdonald could not hold back. Staring into a row of cameras and lights, live on television, Macdonald raged against the media. No government could survive that amount of slanted coverage, he said. Then he looked into the cameras, straight at Andy Stephen. His voice quivering with emotion, Macdonald asked, "Isn't that right, Andy?"

6: The Engineer Who Made the Grade

True to their commitment the night they were sworn in, Barrett's cabinet team had been operating as if they were in office for "a good time, not a long time." While Barrett would find himself labouring in the legislature to contain media-magnified controversies or to salvage floundering legislation, other front-benchers were more than compensating for any legislative gridlock with innovative legislation that was transforming many areas of provincial life. No one was more competent or generated more change than Labour Minister Bill King. By the time his term was up, the minefield that was labour relations law in BC was forever altered, for the better. The seed that started it all first took root in King's hometown a few weeks before voting day.

Dave Barrett had been in the best of moods when he hit the historic railway town of Revelstoke on a gorgeous Friday afternoon in mid-August during the 1972 campaign. And why not? This was a summer election campaign, perfect for the casual Barrett to doff his jacket and go about in shirt sleeves. Everything was going swimmingly, and the relatively new NDP leader relished the chance to visit with "the people" in all those spectacular, scenic pockets of the province far from the hurly-burly of the Lower Mainland. Intensity had been close to zero as Barrett stuck to his masterful strategy to downplay any suggestion the NDP might actually win the election. There had been time to mainstreet in distant Stewart, time to eat some chocolate cake and speak to a dozen people gathered on folding chairs in the community hall of tiny Ymir, in the West Kootenays, and time to go for a private stroll in the sunshine with the local

Premier Dave Barrett and his toughest member of cabinet, Labour Minister Bill King, are appropriately solemn, as they field questions from reporters after introducing the NDP's sweeping back-to-work bill in the fall of 1975. Photo provided by the *Province*

NDP standard bearer Bill King, a lanky, raw-boned railroader from right there in Revelstoke.

As they talked and walked down to the banks of the Columbia River, surrounded by the towering Selkirk and Monashee mountains, Barrett put a critical question to his candidate. "Bill," asked Barrett, "do you believe in the supremacy of labour or the supremacy of the party?" King replied that he believed in the supremacy of the party. It was the answer Barrett wanted. Years later, King recalled, "That's when I first thought, if we won the election, maybe I might be minister of labour." The partnership forged that day would produce a complete reform of BC's labour laws that would set the standard nationally and internationally for a generation.

While Barrett stayed as far from planning a transition to power as possible, lest word leak out and curse the campaign, his conversation with Bill King showed that he made a quiet exception for one of BC's most intractable dilemmas: how to fix the abysmal state of labour relations in a province wracked by conflict. Well ahead of voting day, King was on Barrett's radar as the man to do it. It seemed a surprising choice. King had little experience in the legislature. He served only a brief time in Victoria after winning a by-election in 1968. He was then defeated in the Berger-led electoral disaster that followed a year later.

But Barrett and King had much in common. They were just three weeks apart in age. Both had fathers wounded in the terrible trenches of the First World War, and both had deep roots in the old CCF. Nor was King a fan of Barrett's former adversary, Tom Berger. In fact, he'd sent one of Berger's organizers packing during the 1969 election campaign. Most importantly, Bill King agreed with his leader that an NDP government should not simply toss the keys over to the trade union movement to determine how labour relations should be run in the province. Neither King nor Barrett wavered in that belief throughout the NDP's thirty-nine months in office. From the start, their resolution to steer an independent course, to create a fair playing field for both sides, rather than one tilted towards labour, clashed with BC's hardened, old school unionists. It soured their relations with the BC Federation of Labour and clouded what was undoubtedly one of the Barrett government's finest achievements: a dynamic, sweeping new labour code for the ages.

Bill King turned forty-two the day he was sworn in as minister. Until then, he'd been working on the railroad. An early school dropout, King got his first job at the tender age of fifteen as a section hand. Ten hours a day, fifty cents an hour. After that, he was a wiper. "You oiled the jackets of the locomotives and wiped them down," King explained. "You greased the rods, you cleaned fires, and you hauled a lot of coal, sand and water." After that, he spent three years shovelling coal as a fireman. You had to get the amount of steam "right on the money," or the engine wouldn't make it up the steep grades of the BC Interior. The route from Nelson to Grand Forks to Ferron high up on the Kettle Valley Line took eight tons of coal, King remembered. "It was tough work."

Eventually, he qualified to drive locomotives. King loved the switch. "You saw gorgeous scenery, wildlife, sunsets. No two trips were ever the same, and when you left the terminal, you were your own boss." When the steam era ended, King was among the mourners. Diesels, he felt, didn't have the same romance and lustre as those big, old, steam-gushing locomotives. Although never a paid union official, King was active in the Brotherhood of Locomotive Engineers, processing grievances, handling Workmen's Compensation Board cases and other non-bargaining chores. He was proud the BLE had been founded by one of his heroes, the legendary American orator, socialist and trade union organizer Eugene Debs. King treasured an edition of the *Revelstoke Review* that recounts Debs' visit there during a long-ago strike. Working for the CPR reinforced King's view that society was stacked against the working class. He read widely about social injustice. In 1967, he won a scholarship to the Labour College of Canada in Montreal.

King believed strongly in union education. As labour minister, he sponsored legislation to establish a government-supported labour college in Nanaimo. The BC Federation of Labour demanded the right to determine the college's board of directors, however, and King abandoned the project in disgust. During his years on the railroad, King also developed a loathing for the hidebound craft unionism that dominated railway running trades. "You'd have three guys in the cab, and they'd all be from different unions," he liked to gripe. King thought of them as little more than closed-door business unions. "Debs would be rolling in his grave to see how cutthroat the railway unions became to each other. I thought the NDP might be able bring them together."

The Labour Code that was to come reflected King's hopes. It included controversial powers to order craft unions into joint bargaining councils, so that one craft could not try to leapfrog over another by holding out against the same employer. Much to King's pleasure, trades on the BC Railway were among the first separatist-minded craft unions forced to work together. This anti-craft union philosophy coloured much of his overall approach to industrial relations and was yet another reason for his many quarrels with the BC Federation of Labour. The Fed, as it was widely known, would soon be led by Len Guy, a hard-as-nails printer from the backshop at Pacific Press and a long-time representative of one of North America's original craft unions, the International Typographical Union.

A navigator for bombing missions during the Second World War, the stocky, ample-bellied Guy was as tough a trade unionist as BC had. Despite a stammering speaking style that often swallowed words whole, he had no trouble delivering his message: never leave a nickel on the bargaining table, and defend union principles at all costs. His style of bargaining drove bosses crazy. Guy refused to make wage demands, forcing employers who wanted to avoid a shutdown to keep sweetening the pot until finally, he would say, "Okay." He did his best work in the backrooms, where he developed a reputation as the Fed's "hatchet man." Guy once told a reporter, "I really know how to close a deal. That's the best example of democracy I know." He didn't seem to mind a bit, when one union publication dubbed him "the meanest son of a bitch in the province." Guy was not driven by ego or personal ambition. He was from the old school. The NDP wasn't his party. The trade union movement was his party, and unions had no fiercer advocate, regardless of the government in power. Equally stubborn, Bill King clashed with Len Guy repeatedly on trade union issues. Neither liked to back down on anything they considered a matter of principle. They were like two fierce stags, butting heads for the right to determine how labour relations would be managed in the province. In time, their feud became personal.

On one night recalled by King, Guy suggested they get to know each other. It was during an intense Federation campaign to persuade the government to back off on a series of amendments to the existing Labour Code. Guy invited the minister over to his room at the Empress Hotel. When King arrived, the union leader pulled out a bottle of Scotch and poured a few drinks. As they talked and drank, however, King remained inflexible on the proposed amendments. As King tells it, Guy became increasingly belligerent. He accused Barrett and Bob Williams of forming an anti-labour conspiracy. He wondered out loud if King were a Communist, since his brother Al was a member of the Communist Party.

"He ranted and raved," King remembers. "He said that if we saw things his way, there would be labour peace. If we didn't do what he wanted, we wouldn't be re-elected." King stood up to leave. Just before walking out, he gave Len Guy some belligerent advice of his own. "We've met on a number of occasions, and you've been pretty insulting. Well, I'm not going to take it anymore," he told Guy. "The next time we meet and you're insulting,

I just want you to know that I'm going to knock your teeth so far down your throat, you won't be able to talk." That was their last meeting.

King was as working class as they come. But there was a noble air to him that brooked no nonsense. He was cut from tough cloth. When necessary, his demeanour could be as steely as the tight curly hair that topped his creased, handsome face. His iron manner was evident early on, when Dave Barrett made a minor commitment to a labour delegation that had come to see him. The nature of the promise is lost to time, but neither King nor Barrett forgot what happened afterward. When King got wind of Barrett's pledge, he strode purposefully into the Premier's office. His point was blunt: if Barrett ever again encroached on his jurisdiction without notice, he could expect his immediate resignation. "If I'm going to go down the goddamned tubes, I'm going to do it because of my decisions, not someone else's," King told the chastened premier.

Few ministers in Dave Barrett's uneven cabinet had more mastery over their portfolios than the locomotive engineer with a grade ten education. While others in the cabinet, including Barrett, dithered, King methodically cleaned house. He had read enough to know that, if you fail to renew the front lines of your bureaucracy, you are unlikely to succeed. Soon after taking office, he called ministry staff to a meeting. Change was coming, he warned. They could either embrace it, or leave. He forced some to resign after discovering minor transgressions in their expense accounts. "You had to be a bit of a bastard," said King later. "But they were cheating the public, and they were far too tired and lethargic to grasp the kind of policies I wanted to bring in." Looking back, former cabinet minister Bob Williams, no slouch himself at laying on the political lumber, called Bill King "the most tough-minded of us all."

More than twenty top labour bureaucrats departed. Among them was long-time deputy minister Bill Sands, who was shuffled sideways, then out the door. Sands' replacement, much to the dismay of the labour movement, who wanted one of their own in the job, was Jim Matkin, a young, long-haired law professor at the University of BC who specialized in labour law. By the time of his appointment, Matkin was already knee-deep in shaping the bold direction that labour relations in BC was to take under its new minister. Not even the most diehard Social Crediter could deny that something had to be done. Labour relations were a mess.

King quickly set in motion a dramatic expansion of his ministry that saw it soar within five years to more than eight hundred employees and an annual budget of $80-million, from a paltry $6-million budget and fewer than one hundred staff when he took over. As an early ministry hire in 1973, Bob Plecas had a ringside seat from which to observe King's style and relentless drive to achieve. If you were good, you were rewarded. Before Plecas had even passed his six-month probation, the young civil servant, who subsequently held numerous deputy minister posts under Social Credit, found himself presiding over the $30-million Employment Program. Plecas and other so-called "Young Turks" were able to advance rapidly in King's ministry, because promotions were now based strictly on merit. Before the NDP, according to Plecas, you had to be a member of the Masons to make it into management. Plecas also recalls a time later on when Deputy Finance Minister Gerald Bryson, in charge of Treasury Board that day, denied King a budget increase for his department. Bill King told him to get lost, picked up his budget books, walked out and over to Dave Barrett, Plecas recounted. King got his increase. "He was one of the best ministers I ever had," said Plecas, a top civil servant for more than thirty years.

BC had the most militant unions in the country, the highest percentage of unionized workers and the highest wages, while the BC Federation of Labour was as dominant and ideological a labour organization as Canada had. When the Fed talked, people listened. BC employers were no pushover, either. Many had banded together to form industry-wide collective bargaining associations and they, too, had a powerful group in the form of the influential Employers' Council of BC. The Council prospered under the resolute leadership of Bill Hamilton, who had been postmaster-general during the Diefenbaker years. He had nearly as much sway over employers as the BC Fed had over unions.

In British Columbia, class struggle was still alive. Strikes were regularly nasty, brutish and long, often illegal and occasionally violent. There was no province like it. In this volatile mix, tensions had been heightened further by Social Credit's crude, one-sided legislation to diminish union power. Passed in 1968, Bill 33 had given the government an authority to intervene in private sector labour disputes that was unsurpassed in North America. If a strike was deemed contrary to "the public interest and welfare," the government could simply order an end to the walkout and hand the dispute over to the Mediation Commission for a settlement that was binding on both sides. This was a red flag to BC's union bulls. The Fed quickly declared a boycott of the Commission, and no member went near the body during its four lonely years of existence.

Emotions really boiled over in the spring of 1972, after the Socred government ordered striking construction workers to return to their jobs and appear before the Mediation Commission. But labour disputes were everywhere that year. From a workforce of less than a million employees, nearly two and a half million workdays were lost due to strikes. "That is a ratio I have never known to be attained anywhere," observed Paul Weiler, soon to step into the maelstrom as head of the revamped BC Labour Relations Board. Confrontations were worsened by the long-standing practice of court injunctions. The regularity of companies fleeing to the courts whenever a dispute got out of hand was a festering sore for unions. Even when injunctions were obeyed, they did nothing to resolve worker grievances, prompting disrespect for the courts and an impression they were a tool of management.

Pat O'Neal, an earlier secretary-treasurer of the Federation of Labour, asked unions to send him their *ex parte* injunctions. He pasted them up in his office. Soon, they covered all four walls. The colourful O'Neal called in the press to take pictures. The stunt made all the papers. The situation was similar across the country, particularly in Quebec, where the brilliant Montreal cartoonist Aislin also weighed in on the situation. Aislin depicted a baseball umpire calling "Strike!" Simultaneously, a wig-clad judge popped up through home plate with the words, "Injunction granted."

By the time W.A.C. Bennett called an election, British Columbians yearned for labour peace. Pledges by the NDP to promote industrial relations harmony were one of the key issues that turned the tide in the party's favour. But how would they do it? Although union leaders expected a much better deal, Barrett was not their man. He had made no secret of his dislike for the close ties between unions and the NDP. Barrett believed those ties hurt the NDP in the eyes of the public. He felt they reinforced the perception that, once in power, a New Democrat government would kowtow to the so-called "union bosses." Indeed, many in the labour movement thought that's exactly what the government should do.

Relations between Barrett and leaders of the BC Fed were already icy. Three years earlier, in the hours after Tom Berger narrowly defeated Barrett for the NDP leadership, thanks to strong support from labour delegates, Barrett went to Ray Haynes, then secretary-treasurer of the Fed. According to Haynes' version of the meeting Barrett suggested that the Fed leader and Berger manufacture a fight in public. That way, said Barrett, it would not appear that unions were controlling the NDP leader. Haynes was appalled. He was a straight-talking trade unionist in his mid-forties, with strong features, a prominent brow and horn-rimmed glasses. Since taking over the Federation's top spot at a youthful thirty-eight, he had spearheaded the organization's growing involvement in pitched union battles, whether in support of individual trade unions, taking on the Social Credit government or fighting within the NDP for tighter affiliation between the party and the labour movement.

From the outset of Dave Barrett's leadership of the NDP, the two men sparred repeatedly over Barrett's drive to lessen labour's clout as an organized force in the party. A year after replacing Berger, Barrett told a closed-door political action session attended by Haynes and other union leaders that he was in control of the NDP, and he would not put up with any interference from organized labour. The NDP is not a labour party, it's a party of the people, Barrett reminded them. Not long afterward, the Federation of Labour, which shared offices with the NDP's provincial council at 517 East Broadway in Vancouver, forced the NDP out of the building by asserting its right to more space. Later, Barrett stepped in to quash Haynes' hopes of running for the NDP in 1972. The fractious relationship between Barrett and Haynes was captured in a graphic, editorial page cartoon in the Victoria *Daily Colonist*. It showed the two men dancing together, over the caption, "Fighting? Why, we're just one big happy family..." Meanwhile, each is about to plunge a blood-soaked knife into the other's back.

This animosity became known as the Berger–Barrett split within the NDP. It was deep-seated and divided the party for years, long after Berger, then even Barrett, had abandoned provincial politics. Basically, although nuances could shift with a change in the weather, the Barrett side felt labour should not play an outsized role within the party. Unions should be considered just one more element in society. They should receive a good deal, not the whole deal. Berger supporters hung their hats on the partnership role accepted by labour when union organizations joined with the CCF in 1961 to create the New Democratic Party. To them, the NDP was an instrument to enhance union clout in society and at the bargaining table.

"In a sense, people who supported Barrett were CCFers, and happy to be CCF," recalled Ron Johnson, who worked for the Fed during the Barrett years. "Berger supporters tended to be new people in the party, with a broader base." Barrett thought unions were unpopular, that they were a millstone around the neck of the NDP. "He was never happy with their affiliation to the party," said Johnson.

When the new government began to consider how to redraw labour legislation, the Fed was left on the outside. Instead of playing the pivotal role they expected, labour leaders saw King, with advice from BC Supreme Court Justice Nathan Nemetz, entrust a trio of outsiders known as "the three wise men": Noel Hall from the University of BC's Institute of Industrial Relations, Vancouver labour lawyer Ted McTaggart and Jim Matkin. They felt further burned and humiliated when their first look at the province's new Labour Code came not long before it was introduced in the legislature. The "three wise men" did most of their work behind the scenes. There were few public meetings. Deliberately, they issued no report, which they felt would give vested interests too much to shoot at. Instead, their effort went into preparing legislation. The trio spent hours thrashing out issues in King's office. Matkin emerged from the process as deputy minister. Essentially, he wrote the Code.

The fresh blueprint for industrial relations was unveiled on October 1, 1973. Totalling 153 sections, the comprehensive bill provoked gasps at its sheer, breathtaking audacity. It went where no labour code had gone before. For the first time in Canada, jurisdiction over labour disputes was removed from the courts. In their place would be an ultra-powerful Labour Relations Board, provided with broad authority never before entrusted to a labour tribunal. From now on, the lifeblood of labour disputes—negotiations, strikes and picketing—would be under the thumb of a single board, given "life and death" powers to regulate union and management behaviour.

There was much more. The Code provided a powerful stimulant to organizing. Unions could apply for certification votes with as little as 35 percent of the workforce signed up. If they had membership support from 50 percent plus one, verified by signed membership applications, they were granted certification without a vote. Onus was put on employers to prove they were not guilty of unfair labour practices during an organizing drive, while especially egregious behaviour by an employer could also result in automatic union certification. If an employer tried to thwart a new certification by refusing to bargain seriously, the labour board could exercise a unique power to impose a first contract on the parties. This innovation was prompted by King's outrage over a three-year strike at Sandringham Hospital in Victoria, where the owners simply refused to negotiate an agreement with their low-paid women employees, who had had the audacity to join CUPE.

Conditions for union organizing would never be better than they were during the Barrett years. Picketing rights, however, were not broadened. The new Code set out rules that regulated a union's right to picket beyond a strikebound employer's immediate place of business. It was permitted in some instances, but far from all. The Code had numerous other wrinkles. Individuals were given the right to opt out of their union for religious reasons. Employer groups in an industry could also be certified, and unions representing workers with similar interests, such as construction or railroads, could be ordered into joint bargaining councils. Police, firefighters and hospital workers were given the right to strike, plus the ability to opt for binding arbitration without consent from the employer. Professional strikebreakers were outlawed. There was also an imaginative section on technological change, then expanding at a rapid pace: unions could seek relief from the labour board if work practices were changed significantly in mid-contract.

The goal of the Labour Code, said King, was to replace one-sided legislation with laws that were fair to both labour and management. It was aimed at fostering industrial harmony by getting at the root causes of disputes. Both King and Barrett believed in free collective bargaining. They believed that trade unionism was a positive force in society, and they believed that the more people belonging to unions, the better. These three principles were greatly enhanced by the Code. But Bill 11 did not stack the deck in labour's favour. After twenty years of fighting the anti-union measures of W.A.C. Bennett, this even-handed approach was not what the BC Federation of Labour wanted from an NDP government. Labour leaders expected it was their turn to run the show. Instead, they felt the NDP put academics and lawyers in control, not union people.

While praise from elsewhere showered down on the legislation, the Federation angrily denounced it as "detrimental to the working people" of BC. The Fed criticized the religious exemption clause, the labour board's ability to impose a first contract, the lack of protection for "hot declarations" and above all, picketing regulations that, while erasing the power of the courts, left unions with fewer rights to picket where they chose. They also seethed over the fact that none of their recommendations for key appointments to the proposed new labour board had been accepted. "The government is proposing to place the fate of working people in the hands of a labour relations board dominated by professional and employer representatives," cried Ray Haynes, who was soon to step down in favour of Len Guy. Other union leaders called it dangerous. Some argued that it ignored the NDP's own labour policies and one even said he was sickened by the legislation.

William Stewart, a gifted labour orator with the Marine Workers and Boilermakers Union, singled out the religious exemption clause as particularly offensive. "The way we look at it, anyone who doesn't join the union is anti-union. We are going to be asked to subsidize some other form of organization, whether it's the Christian Labour Relations Association or those funnily dressed people who make strange noises outside the Bay," Stewart complained. On the eve of the bill's passage, Federation president George Johnston told its annual convention of the organization's deep unhappiness over the Labour Code. "The bright political prospects that I spoke so glowingly about a year ago have been badly tarnished," he said. "The government insists on spurning our proposed amendments to Bill 11 and using the same old worn-out phrase parroted by the employers: 'Let's give it a try.'"

Although the Federation liked many sections of the bill, those sentiments were drowned out by the force of their antagonism. Those who wondered how the Federation could be opposed to legislation that seemed so progressive overlooked how the Fed's views were shaped by the backgrounds and experiences of its leadership. Haynes, Len Guy and George Johnston, the head of the meatcutters' union whose tie clip was an upraised meat cleaver, were all from relatively small unions. The province's big industrial unions, such as the IWA and the Steelworkers, didn't need much help, but the smaller unions had to fight hard to wrest gains from powerful employers. When they went on strike, the Federation was by their side. Expanded picketing and "hot declarations," which required union workers to refuse to handle work produced behind a picket line, were key weapons in winning these disputes. Sanctity of the picket line—"Thou shall not cross"—became paramount. Regulations that curtailed the right to picket were opposed.

The Fed wanted trade union rights and not much else enshrined in the Code, recalled veteran labour lawyer Carolyn Askew, who served as research director under Haynes and Guy. Picketing should be left to common law. "Common law is basically silent on picketing," she said. "So, as long as you're not engaged in dangerous or illegal conduct or obstructing the highway, you could pretty well do what you wanted."

It was also what the Code represented that prompted much of the Fed's opposition, said Colin Gabelmann, who worked for the Federation until his squeaker election to the legislature in 1972. Though relatively minor in the overall Code, the religious exemption clause and the use of compulsory arbitration in labour disputes, even if used to help a union, violated deep-seated union principles, said Gabelmann, looking back. "They were symbols, and symbols are important." The Fed considered itself a partner of the NDP and deserving of treatment as an insider, not just another chunk of the public, he said. "That's what the fight was all about. Labour believed it should be involved and part of the process."

But the Fed's beefs were out of step with prevailing sentiment that King's bill was something special. The national head of the country's largest union, CUPE's Stan Little, called it the most progressive in the country. Federal NDP leader David Lewis, a long-time labour lawyer, made a special trip to Victoria to study the bill. He spent several hours closeted with Jim Matkin, going over every clause. At the end, Lewis could not believe how far-reaching the Code was, containing measures he could only dream of in the days when he practised labour law. He thought BC's union leaders were crazy to attack it.

Not all of them did. Prominent trade unionists Jack Munro of the IWA, Jack Gerow of the Hospital Employees' Union (HEU) and the Teamsters' Ed Lawson welcomed the legislation. On the organizing front, Sharon Yandle had been leading an aggressive but frustrating drive to unionize the province's private hospitals for the HEU. The clause giving hospital workers the right to opt unilaterally for binding arbitration shifted the winds in the union's favour. Before the Code, hospital owners faced with a union certification could merely stall at the bargaining table and dare its low-paid, female workforce to strike, as happened at Sandringham. Now, hospital workers had the right to seek a fair contract through binding arbitration, without hitting the bricks. Yandle scorned criticism of the HEU from other unions for using arbitration. "I used to say, 'It's fine for you guys. You can just get your burning barrel and sit in your three lawn chairs in front of the closed gates and wait until the strike is over,'" she recounted. "'You don't know what an essential service strike is like.'" Yandle said she would never have been able to organize women hospital workers without that right under the Code to use compulsory arbitration. She called the Fed's opposition to it "a bunch of esoterics dancing on the head of a pin."

The Federation of Labour got one last dig in at the government over the Code during the NDP's annual convention a month after Bill 11 was introduced. Following a bruising floor fight that saw many delegates jeering Bill King when he spoke, the convention voted narrowly to instruct the government to amend the labour legislation to bring it in line with "party policy." Mostly, that meant the right to picket anywhere and the right to strike during a collective agreement on issues not covered by the contract. Joyce Meissenheimer of the NDP provincial council drew loud cheers when she declared, "We did not elect a government to sit as a referee between management and labour. We elected a government to legislate on the side of labour." Federation president George Johnston said the question was clear: "Are they going to implement party policy or not?"

The answer from King and Barrett continued to be no. "We intend to carry on with Bill 11, as it is," said Barrett. King agreed, saying he was not prepared to change anything until he had seen how the Code worked. There were few divisions in the employers' community. Having feared the worst when the NDP was elected, they were relieved by what they saw in the Code. The new rules, though they strengthened many union rights, were ones they could live with. Employers' Council president Bill Hamilton told his members to give the Code a chance, before bellyaching. He became one of its strongest backers, often working privately to persuade reluctant employers to abide by rulings that favoured unions.

Bill 11 passed unanimously, although NDP backbenchers

including Colin Gabelmann and Harold Steves voted against several individual sections in committee. Dave Barrett referred to the minimal seven days required as "the first non-hysterical labour debate ever to take place in this House." As it evolved, the modernized Labour Code, and particularly the Labour Relations Board, drew intense interest from labour law specialists around the world. Most of its principles are still in place.

None of this might have happened, however, without the appointment of the singular Paul Weiler as the innovative LRB's first chairman. Choosing Weiler was one of the NDP government's most inspired decisions. He was among a flood of smart, young policy experts from across the country attracted by the openness of the Barrett administration to new ideas. They signed on, eager to work in a virtual hothouse of views on how best to serve the public good, and Weiler was the best and brightest of them all. A brilliant legal scholar with a special fondness for labour law, the Thunder Bay native was only thirty-four when Bill King rang him up in Oxford, England, and offered him the job as chairman of the yet-to-be-announced Labour Relations Board. "I gulped and said, 'Yes,'" recalled Weiler in his definitive chronicle of the five trail-blazing years he headed the board, *Reconcilable Differences*.

King made his phone call early in June of 1973, months before anyone outside the minister's inner circle knew a thing about the changes to come. But Weiler and Jim Matkin were friends, with a shared, academic passion for labour adjudication. This was their once-in-a-lifetime opportunity to put theories into practice. Matkin convinced King there was no one better than Weiler to lead the scary journey into the industrial relations unknown—without the courts, and with all aspects of collective bargaining under one administrative roof.

When Weiler assumed chairmanship of the labour board on New Year's Day 1974, no one had any idea whether it would work. In this unchartered territory, there was no road map to success. "Too often, Canadian labour law has resembled the fable of six blind men trying to deduce what an elephant is by touching just one part of its body," was the way Weiler put it in *Reconcilable Differences*. "We proposed to give a single tribunal an overview of the entire body of the law. We wanted the same board to deal with the entire life cycle of the collective bargaining relationship." This had never been done before. But Weiler seemed to do everything right. He envisioned industrial relations with common sense rules to reduce strife, while respecting free collective bargaining and the right to strike. He stressed informality from the start. Legal rulings were a last resort. Using teams of skilled officers and mediators, the board worked to get at the heart of disputes and settle them without formal hearings.

Two-thirds of all cases brought to the board were resolved by mediation. "Going to the board" quickly became a way out for parties in a jam. When decisions were necessary, they were always made public and in writing, for the first time. As the months and years passed, a legal framework took shape that all sides understood and accepted. Many of the board's rulings established labour law precedents that would eventually percolate across the country. Judgments aimed at pragmatism. Unlike judges who had a hundred other things on their plate, decision-makers at the LRB were attuned to the emotions and realities that characterized labour relations. Few decisions were appealed. Defiance of board rulings was rare.

Damaging wildcat strikes virtually disappeared as the board focused on settling issues that threatened or prompted walkouts rather than handing down arbitrary back-to-work orders that merely fanned further resentment. "There was a realization that disputes were not easily suited to resolution through a purely judicial style, by a neutral arbiter remote and above the battle, who made his ruling and let the chips fall where they may," Weiler reasoned. "Afterwards, the parties have to live with each other."

Contrary to BC Federation of Labour fears, lawyers did not dominate the LRB, plentiful though they were on the labour and management side of the table. Only two of the board's first ten appointments were lawyers, including Weiler. In a way that is hard to imagine today, the Labour Relations Board became an exciting place to be. Under Weiler's charismatic leadership, the board caught the imagination of the public. Happenings there were constantly in the news. The LRB acted as a magnet for young staff lawyers interested in the dynamics of labour relations. What began as a dramatic experiment with an uncertain future has carried on like the Energizer bunny. In an era when the impact of labour is sadly reduced, this beacon from the Barrett years still shines. Even now, no other administrative labour tribunal in Canada has as much authority over strikes and picketing as BC's Labour Relations Board.

Years later, Bill King had lost none of his admiration and appreciation for the wunderkind he hired to bring substance to his quest for a new era of industrial relations. "Our goal was to shape a mandate for the Labour Relations Board, to give it scope and authority, and get labour matters out of the courts," said King. "No one else could have established such cogent authority for the board. Paul's presence and intellect were absolutely compelling. And he wrote those beautiful decisions that were unassailable. They set so many precedents that were anathema to those used to the old days. Working with him was a privilege."

Peter Gall, now a well-known Vancouver management lawyer, was one of many labour law enthusiasts who fell under Weiler's sway. "He came in and pulled everything together. He brought all these ideas to the board, then shaped the board's jurisdiction over them," said Gall. "He was just an amazing person. It was all so exciting. Everything was new. Everyone was young. The board was so far ahead of its time. In some ways, it remains so today."

In the meantime, there were other labour chores for the NDP. Shortly after the Code was introduced, the government made good on the party's long-standing promise to grant full collective bargaining to its civil servants, including the right to strike.

Rather than a first, as the Labour Code was in so many areas, the *Public Service Labour Relations Act* was a last in Canada. Its passage ended British Columbia's status as the only province without collective bargaining for government employees. The move ended years of paternal, often vindictive, treatment of public workers that took place under the tight-fisted W.A.C. Bennett. The civil service had no say in determining their wages. Bennett decided on his own, announcing every year the pay hikes civil servants would receive for the next twelve months. When the BC Government Employees' Association briefly affiliated with the BC Federation of Labour, Bennett punished the association by forcing it to collect its own dues from members for seven years rather than deducting the dues from paycheques and remitting them in a lump sum, a practice that was virtually universal among other employers. The resulting decline in revenue nearly forced the BCGEA under.

After a brief strike by government workers in the late 1950s, University of BC law professor A.W.R. Carrothers was commissioned by Social Credit to prepare a report on collective bargaining in the public sector. However, in an episode typical of the secretive, unaccountable Bennett government, the Carrothers report was never released. For eleven years, two copies of the report gathered dust in the files of Premier Bennett and Provincial Secretary Wesley Black. Releasing the Carrothers report, which recommended enhanced but still restricted bargaining, was an early priority of the Barrett government. During debate on the *Public Service Labour Relations Act*, the premier regaled the legislature with his tale of how the matter concluded.

"Every year we'd ask, 'Where is it?' And they'd say, 'Somewhere.' [Laughter] Mr. Speaker, now it can be told. They were telling the truth. They didn't know where the report was.... We had to send out for it. Did we send out to the filing system? No, Mr. Speaker. Did we send out to the Provincial Secretary's office? No, Mr. Speaker. Did we send out to the library? No, Mr. Speaker. Was it in the vault? No, Mr. Speaker. Was it in the building. No, Mr. Speaker. Was it in town? Yes, Mr. Speaker, it was in town. It was at the home of the former Provincial Secretary [Mr. Black], stashed away, Mr. Speaker." Black complied with the new government's order to cough it up.

No longer an association, the BC Government Employees' Union became increasingly active during W.A.C. Bennett's final term, spurred by the hiring of the mercurial John Fryer as general secretary. The bearded Fryer was a thorn in Bennett's side. He cheekily sent the government's imposed wage hikes out for ratification. When Wesley Black ignored pleas to discuss bargaining, the union hired a plane to fly over the legislature, towing a banner that read, "Drop us a line, Mr. Black." Even under the NDP, however, the BCGEU didn't get all it wanted. The government agreed with its commission of inquiry that pensions should remain non-negotiable. When the union went to Provincial Secretary Ernie Hall to complain, the rotund minister leaned across his big desk and explained, "You might as well take up a sport like underwater basketball ... That extra money you want for pensions is what we use to blacktop highways at election time." To this day, Fryer doesn't know whether Hall was kidding. "But we certainly didn't win that one."

Unlike the sidelined status it had during the development of Bill King's Labour Code, labour had a big role shaping the *Public Service Labour Relations Act*. In fact, according to the Fed's Ron Johnson, the legislation was more or less drafted by him. "I stayed at the Empress Hotel," remembered Johnson, then director of research at the Federation of Labour. "I got the Saskatchewan act. I got the constitution of the BCGEU, and, with a bit of help, I produced a draft. The Fed liked it, the government liked it, and everyone was happy." Johnson said the experience showed there was an alternative to the way the Labour Code was drawn up. "Here, there were no ripples. But when we tried to talk with Bill King, you couldn't talk to him."

The BCGEU was certified to represent the government's seventeen thousand employees on International Women's Day 1974. The union's first master agreement, involving thirteen different sectors, produced the most generous wage hikes for civil servants in the province's history, plus a thirty-five-hour workweek and the right to refuse overtime. Some lower-paid clerical workers received increases of more than 50 percent. Critics called it a sweetheart deal, but Fryer defended the rich contract. "Many of our clerical had been earning less than mothers on welfare," he says. As for other raises, "We felt liquor store workers should at least get what a girl in Safeway got."

King did not limit his reforms to unionized workers. With major improvements in employment standards completed by early 1973, he turned his attention to workplace health and safety, ushering in a series of reforms that touched—even saved—the lives of countless workers. Though garnering few headlines and little coverage, the Workers' Compensation Board (WCB) has more impact on the daily lives of workers than any number of strikes and collective bargaining issues that attract all the attention. At its best, the board enforces safety in the workplace and is there to help when workers are hurt. But the WCB was not at its best under Social Credit, hamstrung by cautious managers and industrial safety officers who rarely gave injured workers the benefit of the doubt.

King was determined to make changes. He was familiar with compensation grievances from injured workers, having processed many of them as a local union official in Revelstoke. As well, his brother Al was a well-known, tireless campaigner for worker safety at the sprawling Cominco smelter in Trail. And, like all MLAs, Bill King's mail regularly contained heartfelt complaints from embittered workers who felt they had been swindled by the WCB. King promised a comprehensive review of workers' compensation. "There is absolutely nothing more frustrating or deadening for an individual than to be hurt in an industrial accident and then denied proper recompense for his injuries," he told the legislature in early 1973.

He was as good as his word. During his time as labour minister, the government enacted a series of significant amendments that overhauled many long-standing practices of the WCB. The landmark creation of independent boards of review to handle appeals of WCB decisions was the most far-reaching. Until then, appeal panels were dominated by the board's own claims officers. Not surprisingly, workers felt they rarely got a fair deal from these one-sided panels. The new review boards were appointed by the government, and they operated separately, outside the jurisdiction of the WCB. This independent appeal mechanism existed in no other province. "By divorcing the representatives of our appeal tribunal from any association with the Workmen's Compensation Board, the worker can rest assured that he is indeed receiving an impartial and independent appraisal of his case," said King. The independent boards of review were a huge hit. Both the WCB and the review board were also the first in Canada to regularly publish their decisions.

There were many other improvements. Plant safety committees and their worker representatives were given the right to accompany WCB inspectors on workplace tours. Worker and widow pensions were boosted to better reflect cost of living. Compensation for injured workers was raised. Loss of earnings was added to pensions received by workers disabled on the job, raising what they already got from the so-called, odious "meat chart" of functional disabilities setting out fixed sums for the loss of a limb, an eye, and so on. Enforcement of WCB orders was stepped up. Harsher penalties were prescribed for employers who violated them. The definition of industrial disease was broadened. More of a burden was placed on claims officers to determine why compensation should not be paid. Reducing occupational deafness was singled out as a key target of improved workplace safety. And in an important symbolic gesture, the long-time name of the board was changed from the Workmen's Compensation Board to the Workers' Compensation Board, reflecting the large number of women in the workforce.

Many of the changes were driven by the WCB's controversial chairman, Terry Ison. A lawyer and professor at Queen's University, Ison was the country's leading expert on workers' compensation. He was another of the "bright young men" whom the NDP sought out and hired to bring the province into the modern age. Like Paul Weiler, Ison was given the chance to turn his academic views into practice. Ison, however, had a more challenging time. He had none of Weiler's charm or easy rapport with stakeholders and the media. He kept a low, almost reclusive public profile, perhaps indicative of his years in academia. The first and only time Ison held a press conference as WCB chairman occurred during the dying days of the 1975 election campaign, when he denied an allegation by Social Credit mainstay Grace McCarthy that he had resigned. Business found him difficult. Employers were further upset by his bold reforms to increase safety on the job and redress for injured workers. "He was a smart guy, one hell of a smart guy," reflected Jim Matkin, deputy labour minister at the time, "but he wasn't out to be balanced." In the legislature, Provincial Secretary Ernie Hall referred to Ison as "something more than expert, and indeed, very revolutionary in some of his [views on] compensation and a full security program." A day or so after Social Credit was sworn into power after the 1975 election, Ison offered his resignation. Paul Weiler, on the other hand, stayed on to complete his term, leaving his LRB chairmanship in 1978.

Labour loved the new Workers' Compensation Board. While the BC Federation of Labour railed against Bill King on other matters, union health and safety representatives were unanimous in hailing changes to the WCB brought in by the NDP. The revamped Workers' Compensation Board was considered one of the Barrett governments great "quiet successes," policy that effectively improved the lives of British Columbians but was far from the daily frenzy of controversy regularly whipped up by media and opposition critics.

7: The Godfather and the Tank Driver

On a warm Thursday night in June 1975, the day before the legislature would at last adjourn for the summer, Peter McNelly and his wife invited Bob Williams and political aides Andrew Petter, Brian McIver and Stuart Hedley over for a beer and Monopoly marathon. They used two boards arranged in a figure eight and double the normal amount of play money. Round and round the socialists went, purchase after purchase, beer after beer, "Williams just like a kid, buying and trading and developing these properties," until four of the players were squeezed out by a Williams–Petter combine "rich enough to withstand a property assessment bill that cost $2,600."

"What a game," McNelly wrote in his journal. "As W.A.C. Bennett used to say, 'Capitalism is one of the best economic systems in the world if it's working for you and one of the worst if it's working against you.'" To business leaders, the image of Williams wheeling and dealing in the BC economy, treating the province as his game board, with the provincial treasury at his disposal, was a nightmare prospect that seemed to have become reality. Williams had launched his first big takeover within hours of the post-election breakfast at The Only. Barrett, who was more of a poker player, had joked to McNelly that Monopoly was more difficult than actual capitalism, a view Williams shared. "Seeing these guys (the Captains of Industry) first-hand and the way they handle these companies," he said, "is enough to shake your faith in free enterprise."

To the amazement of business writers, Williams' takeovers of troubled forest companies had resulted in dramatic turnarounds and substantial profitability. When Williams compared his own track record with the spotty performance of actual forest industry leaders, he could get testy. "Are you guys just out of the cast of *The Godfather*?" he is said to have asked a group of forest executives. They were about to ask him the same question. No wonder a newspaper attack ad produced in May 1974 styled Barrett and his resources minister as an unsavory joint venture with untrammelled ambitions, the headline reading, "Williams and Barrett Unlimited, Associalists."

W.A.C. Bennett and Social Credit's front bench feared and respected Barrett, but their hatred of Williams far exceeded the normal bounds of partisanship. It was fuelled by Williams' often savage attacks on them in opposition, including charges that the Bennett family had profited from real estate investments based on insider knowledge of future highway construction. Armed with his own extensive research and excellent trapline of municipal sources, Williams was relentless on the attack, combining an acid wit with a willingness to go for the jugular. Yet his contribution to the NDP in government far outstripped his role in opposition.

By 1972, the tension between the two East Enders that resulted from Williams' 1969 bid for the leadership was a distant memory. Williams had been a key figure in Barrett's transformation of the shattered Berger caucus into an effective partisan machine. He was an architect of the platform "A New Deal for People." From the day the two men met at The Only to plan the transition, Williams was a dominant personality in the administration, second only to Barrett himself. As Andrew

Petter concluded later in a review of his work, "Williams' mark can be found on almost all major initiatives undertaken by the NDP government, particularly on those related to resource policy." A couple of weeks before the Monopoly marathon, Allan Fotheringham had calculated that "Williams is 67.3 percent of this government. If he were hit on the IQ by a UFO tomorrow, the government would collapse. When all else fails, specifically Bob Strachan, Mr. Barrett throws any crisis to Mr. Williams."

Williams had a strong contempt for entitlement, class privilege and the stagnation that accompanies oligopoly, but he was never a doctrinaire class warrior. "I am a socialist who believes in free enterprise," he declared in 1964. Williams was a student of the economic theories of Henry George, who believed working people were deprived of most of the wealth they produced by being forced to pay excessive rents for land and resources. George argued that a sufficiently large single tax on the landowner would end speculation and render profitable property only to those who improved it. Williams often expressed the view that property tax should be levied only on land value, not the improvements. This perspective may not have been social democratic, but it offered an answer to the problems of a province where a handful of large corporations exploited land and resources at enormous profit while working families struggled to make ends meet.

Williams believed government intervention was necessary to liberate individual energies, not regulate them. Unlike mainstream CCF and NDP policy makers, he was not committed to nationalization. Private ownership, co-op ownership and public ownership all had a place in his ideal world. Petter considered him a pragmatist, "a decentralist calling for a break-up of the monopolies in favour of a plethora of small-scale private and co-operative enterprises."

Williams had a restless, questioning intellect and a track record of success, both in politics and land development, by the time he was elected to the legislature in 1966. More importantly, he and Barrett had formed an alliance of equals, unique on Barrett's front bench, that was rooted in the tribal realities of East Van. Both had been born and raised east of Main and each had attended Britannia High School, Williams graduating two years after Barrett. Both had worked their way through university, Williams graduating from UBC with degrees in economics and planning. But Williams, unlike Barrett, had never met his birth father. His mother, forced into a home for unwed mothers when she was pregnant, had fled with her son after his birth rather than give him up for adoption, later marrying Williams' stepfather, a carpenter. Only years later did Williams discover that his birth father had been the son of the mayor of Burnaby and grandson of William A. Pritchard, the BC Federation of Labour delegate to the 1919 Winnipeg General Strike, who served time at Stony Mountain Penitentiary on trumped-up charges of criminal sedition for his role in the upheaval.

In 1959, the year Attorney General Bonner made news by firing Barrett for election activity, Williams was generating headlines as a twenty-six-year-old municipal planner in Delta who was challenging proposals to turn farmland into serviced lots at public expense, costs that Williams calculated could never be recovered from property tax. Irritated aldermen, urged on by developers, fired him for his trouble. Williams joined the consulting practice of planner Mary Rawson, whose clients included municipalities and private developers across the province. His political interests, however, quickly led to a leadership role in the East Vancouver branch of the NDP, a seat on Vancouver city council and finally in 1966 a seat in the legislature in a two-member riding he shared with Macdonald. He was thirty-three, brimming with energy and ideas, equally at home in a boardroom, council chambers or an East Van bar.

Williams believed that the circumstances of his birth shaped his attitudes in a profound way. "The concept of legitimacy is a pervasive idea that's evil, and it's across the board. They say to the working class, 'what are you doing here? Don't you know your place?'" On his first visit to the legislature as an MLA, "I looked at the building and the marble and the sculpture and said, 'they built this great palace so you know your place and shut you up.' No way do I ever shut up." Indifferent to the animosity he might engender, Williams quickly violated unspoken boundaries of debate, criticism and personal conflict in pursuit of wrongdoers. Once seized of an issue—against Gaglardi, the Bennetts or MacMillan Bloedel CEO J.V. Clyne—Williams would never step back, using his eloquence as a sword and the privileges of the legislature as a shield. He was sued repeatedly. He felt driven by a personal mission to raise a voice for the marginalized, working families, people like his East Van neighbours, historically ignored in the legislature. Behind smiling, chubby little Dave was Williams, with what *Globe* reporter Malcolm Gray considered "a strong resemblance to the gangster overlord played by Marlon Brando in *The Godfather* ... the same fleshy good looks, softening over the collar and wispy, receding hair riding back on a high forehead." Williams was infuriatingly self-assured, incapable of being cowed, and prepared to be very nasty when circumstances required it.

After the cabinet had been sworn in on that historic evening in 1972, Williams wandered the corridors with former Provincial Secretary Lawrie Wallace to pick out his new office from the five options available among his new portfolios. The recreation and conservation offices, with their harbour views, would be nice, he mused, but Wallace thought otherwise. He handed Williams the keys to Williston's old suite overlooking the Rose Garden on the legislature's west side. "Lawrie, I want you to know this will be the last decision you'll ever make for me," Williams warned the veteran bureaucrat, but he later realized the benefits of the location, just steps from Barrett's West Annex office.

Many mornings the arriving Barrett would find Williams already waiting, coffee in hand, with Joyce Thomas, Barrett's secretary, to hash out the agenda for the day or the coming week. "He wasn't interested in the details of government to any great degree," Williams recalled. "I was, and beyond that I had a whole cadre of professionals, planners mainly, that I'd worked with through the years." Barrett had made it clear to him, Williams told a friend, "He's going to run the show." Within Williams' area of responsibility, however, he had free rein, subject to approval at the morning check-in. "I thought it was a one-term government," he reflected many years later. "That's why I worked like lightning." Unlike his colleagues, who often operated without solid policy support or strong advisors, Williams quickly placed loyal but qualified supporters in key positions across his areas of responsibility. Where specialists were required, they were hired.

Within days of the swearing in, Williams had begun assembling a team of commercial lawyers to review the purchase of Ocean Falls from Crown Zellerbach. The remote community had been struggling for years. Although he claimed later that he "agonized over that decision for months," there was little doubt Williams wanted to save the town, with its millions of dollars in public and private infrastructure, including a high school, a hospital, an airport, a hotel and homes, as well as a paper mill and the hydroelectric capacity to run it. "What really made up my mind was when I saw those residents on TV, people who had lived their whole lives there, who had grown up there. I thought I just couldn't let it happen." Although the mill lost money in 1973, it had returned to profitability in 1974 as Williams sought partners to build a sawmill and improve coastal tourism.

Within weeks of the Crown Zellerbach deal, Williams had acquired a 79 percent interest in Canadian Cellulose, the money-losing Canadian arm of Celanese Corporation of New York, with mills in Prince Rupert and Castlegar. This time Williams succeeded in acquiring three tree farm licences, a pulp mill in Prince Rupert, a lumber company near Terrace as well as a pulp and sawmill operation near Castlegar, safeguarding one thousand northern jobs and two thousand in the Kootenays. These acquisitions also proved profitable, producing net earnings of $45-million by 1974 under their new name of BC Cellulose. (Williams had recruited retired E.B. Eddy and MacMillan Bloedel executive W.C.R. "Ray" Jones to run the new company.) Then came Plateau Mills, the takeover that generated "terror tactic" headlines in the *Vancouver Sun* but net income for taxpayers of $2.7-million in 1973. Despite a small loss in 1974, Williams announced a plan to double the mill's capacity to 175-million board-feet a year, increasing the workforce to five hundred.

Once community leaders around the province realized Williams' commitment to protect regional economic development, more appeals for help rolled in. The five hundred employees of Kootenay Forest Products (KFP) in Nelson petitioned Williams for aid in 1973 when the Eddy Match Company, which owned their firm, attempted to sell out to Japanese-owned Crestbrook Forest Industries. Williams delayed the sale to await the conclusion of an environmental study, then blocked it altogether when the study showed that the large cut proposed for the area "would probably destroy the few remaining options the public has in the Kootenay region" to safeguard elk habitat and other environmental values. Early in 1974, BC Cellulose purchased KFP for $9-million, slightly more than Crestbrook had offered, but about half the value of KFP's real estate holdings alone. Williams encouraged the appointment of two worker representatives to the new KFP board, labour relations improved and the operation was returning to profitability by late 1974.

One of Williams' most powerful tools was a new secretariat he organized to support the Environment and Land Use Committee. ELUC had been created under Bennett to help develop park proposals, including federal demands to expand national parks. As chair of the committee, Williams decided to convert ELUC into a coordinating body for all decisions related to environment and resources, with a focus on supporting regional decision-making.

He built on a law, passed by Bennett for entirely different purposes, which empowered the government to override other legislation to achieve certain planning or economic objectives. Within months, Williams had planned a new secretariat for ELUC that brought together the land inventory group from the Ministry of Agriculture, a resource planning group and a special projects group. By mid-1973 a staff of twenty-two had been hired from more than one thousand applicants and Alistair Crerar, a veteran BC planner who had mentored Williams and was then heading the Atlantic Development Board, had been recruited as director. As Petter said later, Williams may not have had a single "superministry," but the ELUC secretariat effectively made him a "superminister." The land inventory group quickly became the technical arm of Williams' secretariat, mapping all the diverse ecological features of BC to support the approval process for every energy, mineral, pipeline and highway project in the province. Its data collection, painstakingly collected from scattered sources and transferred by hand to comprehensive maps of the province, became the foundation of BC's modern land management system.

Williams' 1973 response to the Throne Speech had spelled out a dramatic expansion of the province's park system. Legislation that year provided legal protection, for the first time, to seventy existing parks and created nine new ones, preserving vital landscapes and ecological zones from Naikoon, in Haida Gwaii, to Desolation Sound on the south coast, Carp Lake near Fort St. James, and Cape Scott on Vancouver Island. (Under Bennett, the number of parks had increased five-fold, but their total area had declined by 650,000 hectares.) The creation of a 32,000-hectare recreation area on the Skagit River signalled BC's determination to protect the valley from further flooding by Seattle City Light's dam south of the border. Cypress Bowl opened with two chairlifts, as well as a large network of hiking and cross-country ski trails. Barrett's park legacy was secure.

Williams was equally effective in transforming the province's urban centres. After a tour of the site for a proposed 280-metre, sixty-storey provincial courthouse complex covering three entire blocks of downtown Vancouver, Williams rushed to a phone booth to call Arthur Erickson. Already internationally renowned, Erickson had designed W.A.C. Bennett's new mountaintop Simon Fraser University. "We're not going to build that goddamn sixty-storey building," Williams told Erickson. "We want something that is right." Williams had already retained Erickson to review a wide range of provincial government properties that were candidates for development. Erickson had in turn invited Bing Thom, a rising star in BC's architectural community then teaching at UBC, to join the project. Both were soon meeting Barrett in Victoria to discuss the courthouse. "Mr. Premier, what is the budget?" Thom asked nervously. The reply: "Just make it good and fast. We may not win the next election." Erickson, Thom and their colleagues put the tower on its side to support waterfalls and an urban park that changed the heart of the city. The award-winning, three-phase complex took a decade to complete and cost $139-million, including renovation of the old courthouse to accommodate the Vancouver Art Gallery.

Williams moved equally quickly the next year to intervene in Victoria, where the province consolidated harbour lands that were threatened by a major hotel development. He was a long way from Delta land rezonings now. Barrett let him roll, calling him off only when he got a "bit bizarre." There was the time, for example, when he proposed the BC takeover of Rolls-Royce, which was then for sale. "It's up for grabs and I think it is a winner," he told Barrett in an after-dinner phone call. "What the hell has that got to do with us?" asked Barrett, for once bearing down on the details. "Don't you think your plate's a bit full right now?"

Williams was, in fact, creating a comprehensive, long-term plan for the entire northwest of the province. He had taken over

Williston's portfolios with key elements of the northwest's economy poised for shutdown. The Crown Zellerbach and Canadian Cellulose purchases had stabilized the region and moved decision-making back to British Columbia. But Williams found his first major briefing on Bennett's long-term northern economic development plans a demoralizing affair. The huge reservoirs behind Bennett's dams had not even been logged before flooding. The government faced "a massive task," Williams told the legislature, "because of the single-purpose view of a government that rarely looked ahead as it took major steps that are affecting both the economy and the environment of this province."

The route of the BC Rail extension to Dease Lake, near the Yukon border, fell midway between forest resources to the west and mineral resources to the east, but serviced neither. Neither the forest ministry nor the department of trade had been involved in selecting the route, but construction began nevertheless. A helicopter tour of the right-of-way convinced Williams a new plan would be required, one that would link the existing right of way west to the Nass and the port at Prince Rupert. It was a case, he concluded, of taking a lemon and making lemonade, provided Ottawa could be inspired to pay for the new western rail link on terms similar to investments in other provinces. Construction on the Dease Lake extension was halted as an ELUC team sat down to work.

When a draft of the ELUC secretariat's "northwest plan" was leaked to the *Sun* in March 1974, the story was drowned out by the Chicken and Egg War, but the dramatic scope of the proposal set off alarms in the north, particularly in the ranks of New Democrats. The April issue of *The Democrat* carried analysis from the Smithers office of SPEC, the Society Promoting Environmental Conservation, terming the Northwest Plan an "environmental disaster." Treating the entire scheme as a decision of government, the SPEC analysis deplored proposals to improve railways and ports, spend $500-million for new highways and create "supermills" to supply chips in place of the logs then fuelling pulp mills. Estimates that the population would double, requiring "massive immigration from foreign countries," were headed in the wrong direction, said SPEC, when BC should be planning "limits to population growth."

Determined to calm these troubled waters, Williams headed north April 26, leading a team that included MLAs Graham Lea of Prince Rupert and Alf Nunweiler of Fort George, as well as Crerar, some ELUC analysts and McNelly. After a quiet Friday meeting with the Socred-dominated Prince George city council, Williams waded into a daylong Saturday gathering of New Democrats North, an emerging force in the party that gathered eighty-strong for the day at Smitty's Pancake House. A two-hour question and answer session ended in a standing ovation, but media coverage was dominated by bitter recriminations from Frank Calder, who was angry at not being consulted on the plan, and NDP Omineca MLA Doug Kelly, who fulminated against poor communication with the backbench. Visiting Vancouver reporters quickly filed stories on Calder and Kelly.

Williams was soon back on the road, heading northeast to Mackenzie for another public meeting, this time for more than 350 in the young pulp-mill town. Monday found the team westbound once more, heading to Vanderhoof and Burns Lake, where Crerar was helping him put together a personal legacy that would become as important to him as Cypress Bowl park was for Barrett. McNelly was captivated by Burns Lake, "a hard rock cowboy town where people congregate on the sidewalks in the morning rain in boots and jackets and smoke a bit before heading out wherever they work. The town's one beer parlour is a hangout for both Indians and non-Indians alike. Everybody knows everybody else and there's a lot of country music on the jukebox." A public meeting that night drew 250 people, with the main applause going to Graham Lea, who fielded a complaint from a farmer who couldn't shoot dogs that were killing his sheep because of a law prohibiting the discharge of a firearm within a quarter mile of the highway. "Well, I'll tell you," Lea replied, "you can pass a law that stops the farmer from shooting the dog that kills his sheep, but you can't pass a law that stops the farmer from shooting the bull." Everyone adjourned to the pub.

The ELUC analysis had discovered that the Burns Lake area had unallocated timber, but no sawmill. Williams had invited bids for the wood, but reserved an equity share for four Burns Lake First Nations that constituted half the population. Barrett had favoured a 4 percent allocation, Williams offered 8 percent. Burns Lake Native leaders, notably a man named George Brown, remained unsatisfied. This visit was Williams' chance to close the deal and the two sides quickly got down to business. Williams was particularly impressed by Brown, "a giant of a guy, about six foot six, who strode in with great boots, long hair, leather hat, and a leather coat and smart, smart, smart." A one-time minor outlaw who had turned his life around to become a court outreach worker, Brown and others helped close a deal that gave the bands 12 percent of the new firm and a training program to ensure they delivered sufficient labour to the mill. The graduation ceremony for the first group of trainees was the occasion for a drunken celebration that Williams never forgot, "one of those wonderful moments in the life of politics that was a joy for everybody." Babine Forest Products was incorporated in 1974 and remained in operation until a massive explosion destroyed the mill in January 2012, killing two and injuring nineteen.

From Burns Lake, it was on to Smithers where a small branch of the Society Promoting Environmental Control (SPEC) had aroused the town to fury with its account of the Northwest Plan. Six hundred people jammed the hall where Williams, seeing the head table set up on stage, demanded that it be brought down to floor level so he could look the crowd in the eye. Then the four-hour debate began, McNelly wrote, and "the people of Smithers really put Williams through the mill. The basic message: keep your hands off our town, we like things the way they are. I was never so impressed with Williams as that night. He really stood up well." The ELUC proposal had included a single sawmill for Smithers, fed by a very modest increase in the allowable cut. By the end of the evening, McNelly concluded, Williams had "just about decided that Smithers was going to get pretty well what it wished—nothing."

As the two-car NDP cavalcade rolled west, Williams and Lea began to treat the trip as an election campaign warm-up. Things were "slipping a bit" in the north, Williams told Barrett on a Tuesday morning phone call, but the trip was turning things around. After working their way through a First Nations roadblock set up at Hazelton to demand a pedestrian overpass over the busy highway, Williams hit Terrace, where he made news by warning he would not tolerate harassment by aboriginal groups seeking redress. Workers in Kitimat urged Williams to take over the Eurocan mill, but their Prince Rupert counterparts were angry that public ownership of Canadian Cellulose had not improved labour relations at their facility. After a tough meeting with Prince Rupert Mayor Pete Lester and city councillors, including future Lieutenant-Governor Iona Campagnolo, the New Democrats boarded the ferry for the run to Port McNeill.

The trip had "calmed everybody down," the exhausted Williams concluded, but the vast Northwest Plan had to give way to new priorities: the struggle to reform the forest sector and the trench warfare of the legislature, where Williams' estimates consumed days of debate from the moment he returned to Victoria. The bitter grudge match between Williams and the Bennetts had begun a new phase in March as Barrett, Williams and others baited Bill Bennett in the House as a "Daddy's boy" struggling to talk around the silver spoon in his mouth. "At least I had a father," Bennett shot back May 22, a reference to Williams' "illegitimacy" that briefly stunned MLAs but won good reviews from the press gallery.

Bennett was slowly finding his way as leader of the opposition. When Williams rose May 7 to defend his ministerial budget, he opened with a glowing description of his northern tour, contrasting it to the "free and easy ... Cadillac caravans" of the Wacky years. Bennett was ready for battle, quoting Calder's and Kelly's attacks from news reports, styling Williams as "the super minister. This is the real premier of the province. This is the man that calls the shots in that government." If Williams believed the Ocean Falls purchase had been "the coup of the century," Bennett jeered, then the Canadian Cellulose purchase had been a double coup, making Williams a "coup-coup minister." But the opposition leader then veered into murkier waters, listing the foreign directors of the Canadian Cellulose board, people with names like Wallach, Litvine and Gross, all tied to faraway Belgian paper interests and a firm called Gottesman International, a pulp marketing firm Bennett claimed was fleecing the government on the sale of paper.

It fell to Socred MLA Harvey Schroeder of Chilliwack to connect the dots the next day. Williams was a fool to think he could play in the international business community, Schroeder said, "because you were born under the wrong star to play in that league. When they're all finished with you ... they'll kick you aside and they'll say to you, 'Sorry fella, you belong to the wrong sect. You belong to the wrong community.' Because in the international business community, you have to have a name like Wallach, you have to have a name like Berkowitz, you have to have a name like Litvine. You have to have a name like Gross. These are the boys who are the pawn movers—the pawnbrokers ... " Williams by this time was shouting, "You're sick, you're sick. Anti-Semitic speech—never heard the like of it." Schroeder, seeking to turn disaster into farce, demanded Williams withdraw the allegation of anti-Semitism. Schroeder's outburst, his subsequent "withdrawal," and Bennett's public repudiation of his comments were printed well back in the news pages.

Williams' estimates had finally passed, but there were signs all around that the tide was ebbing for Barrett, Williams and their government. Always convinced he had only one term to achieve his goals, Williams stepped up his already-gruelling pace. Amendments to the *Forest Act*, based on recommendations from a task force led by UBC professor Peter Pearse, a resource economist with impeccable Liberal credentials, increased stumpage rates on pre-1907 coastal tenures by sevenfold. Williams sought to soften the impact with a reduction in the logging tax, negotiated at a meeting with forest industry executives as the session wound to a close.

Williams had moved in the first three months of the NDP mandate to require forest companies to be responsible for their own seed collecting and replanting, duties formerly performed, if at all, by the forest service. The new rules set standards, for the first time, for the construction of logging roads, provided for green belts alongside streams and limited the size of clear-cuts to an average two hundred acres. Williams also imposed annual inventory reports to give the government its first insight into the state of the forest. In the spring of 1973, he had reformed stumpage rate appraisal rules for the Interior to base rates on the value of the log, rather than what it would produce. This removed incentives for "cheap wood" harvesters and ensured the public, not foresters, would benefit from windfall price increases. This change alone had added an estimated $30-million to the treasury.

Coast forest producers were next to feel Williams' love with a promise of new policies to end "gross underpricing" and "trim the fat" through elimination of the "former peanut pricing for the commodities the people of this province own." The "dinosaurs" of the coastal forest sector were promised "the greatest health cure some of these companies ever had." Pearse's interim report in early 1974 had begun to deliver on that pledge, proposing changes in stumpage rates that would add another $31-million annually to provincial revenues. The amendments to the *Forest Act* were passed, given royal assent, but never proclaimed by the Barrett government as Williams watched global lumber prices fall as pulp prices continued to climb. Worried about the impact on small mill owners and fresh from his own encounter with the realities of forest communities, Williams turned his attention to the small sawmill sector.

The *Timber Products Stabilization Act,* introduced in November 1974, was designed to increase the revenue small firms received for chips through the creation of a BC Forest Products Board to "improve the markets for forest products." He estimated prices paid for chips by pulp producers could triple, reviving the independent sawmill sector. When the law came into effect, the government raised prices by about 50 percent, enough to inject $90-million into the sawmill sector. Soon after, Williams lowered selected stumpage rates to help these firms even more. These interim measures set the stage for a longer study of forest tenures undertaken by Pearse in 1975. By the time Pearse was finished, the New Democrats were out of office.

While Williams worked "like lightning" to reshape resource development, Minister of Rehabilitation and Social Improvement Norm Levi was seeking to make similar progress in social services. Few British Columbians who crossed swords with W.A.C. Bennett's Social Credit were treated as harshly as welfare recipients. "Flying Phil" Gaglardi, Bennett's minister of rehabilitation and social improvement, made periodic crack-downs on "welfare fraud" a feature of his administration, enlisting a Provincial Alliance of Businessmen for Human Resources who promised to trim welfare rolls by hiring hardcore unemployable workers. When Vancouver welfare mother Toni Cowlishaw successfully appealed to the Welfare Review Board in 1972 that her social assistance was "not sufficient to pay for the necessities essential to maintain or assist in maintaining a reasonably normal and healthy existence," Gaglardi immediately overturned the board's favourable ruling, pushed a bill through the legislature eliminating the section providing for appeals, and reserved for himself the absolute discretion to set rates. Gaglardi's amendments triggered an uproar, but the minister insisted his actions were selfless. "Who am I?" he asked the legislature. "I am a rather insignificant individual trying by the grace of God to help other people ... this bill places me in control of a heavy responsibility."

"Mr. Gaglardi," replied Barrett, "you frighten me." Social worker Bridget Moran, who along with six colleagues shouted from the gallery that the bill was "inhumane and probably illegal," was promptly ejected. Six months later, Gaglardi was gone and Barrett's New Democrats were in power. Gaglardi's penny-pinching attitude to welfare was in stark contrast to his own notorious use of government planes and to the waste and overlap of welfare services. The dramatic expansion during the 1950s and 1960s of non-profit and private social services organizations with overlapping jurisdictions, conflicting mandates and a hunger for resources meant millions were wasted in administration costs while applicants trudged from one office to another to organize claims. A teenager in public custody would have one Children's Aid worker, another Children's Aid worker would manage the parents' file and income assistance would be at a third office. Vancouver's city welfare offices were like the "boiler factory of social work," a mill for the disbursement of funds on an assembly-line basis. The single men's unit, for example, would process four hundred to five hundred men a day. Despite periodic modest increases, welfare rates were far below inflation and the poverty line. Caseworkers managing the files of up to 275 families needed written approval from Victoria to approve the smallest expenditure for bedding or clothing—and social workers who spoke out were quickly terminated, even if they weren't candidates for the NDP.

Although welfare policy had been mentioned only in passing in the New Democrats' August platform, there was no doubt

Barrett had a mandate, in the words of "A New Deal for People," to implement a "humanized social policy" that included a guaranteed income to "provide everyone with the basic material resources to live a full life." So it was, as the Chicken and Egg War raged, that Barrett's legislative machinery ground out yet another law that touched the lives of hundreds of thousands of British Columbians. Bill 84, the *Community Resources Act* that received first reading March 20, mandated a revolution in the delivery of social services, integrating the province's jumble of conflicting programs into a single ministry directed more by locally elected boards—"little soviets" in the eyes of some critics—than by Victoria. Minister Norm Levi, who had built a career in social work after several years of combat experience as a tank driver in two wars, had already completed much of the groundwork before the bill reached first reading.

Perpetually rumpled, frequently long-haired, normally without a tie, often cycling to work, Levi had a relentless work ethic, a good sense of humour and an unwavering determination to shake up social services. Charges that he was unsophisticated in his personal habits were true, he told laughing MLAs during a debate on his estimates in 1973. "Bright, beautiful and capable I might be," Levi allowed, "but not sophisticated. I do enjoy fat cigars and I do very much enjoy dressing casually. I hope one day that it might be possible to walk into this House without a tie and not get thrown out."

Born and raised in Birmingham, England, the son of a Jewish tailor, Levi had been evacuated from his home to a rural village as a twelve-year-old on the outbreak of the war. Finding country life not to his taste, he returned within weeks to Birmingham where he found work as a window cleaner. In 1943, he volunteered for the British Army, became a tank driver and fought in Holland and Germany. In 1947, demobilized after a stint in the British forces in India, Levi saw an ad inviting recruits to "Join the Hebrew Legion and fight for Israel." By 1948, he was again driving tanks in combat, this time equipment seized from the British by Israeli forces during the first Arab–Israeli war. It was during one of his passages to Israel that he met his future wife, Gloria, who herself became a major figure in the BC NDP. They married and immigrated in the 1950s to Vancouver, where Levi began a career in social work. It was as a staff member of the John Howard Society that Levi met Barrett, who recruited him both as a party candidate and later as party president. Although a Barrett loyalist, Levi had remained formally neutral during the Berger challenge and his efforts to unionize social service agencies gave him good connections to labour across the deep divide that haunted the NDP after Berger's ouster of Strachan.

In a front bench that boasted some remarkable talents, Levi had few peers. He more than made up for his lack of university education with voracious reading on any and every topic, ultimately filling his house with books from floor to ceiling. He had a practical and theoretical grasp of social services policy combined with a tank driver's instincts about the shortest distance between two points. Where others, like Williams, Cocke and King, assembled teams of seasoned specialists or consulted with outside experts to generate policy direction, Levi simply acted, relying on the advice of a handful of close associates. Where others centralized power in their ministries, Levi decentralized it, actually delegating decision-making authority to scores of locally elected community resources boards.

Within weeks of his appointment, Levi began to take control of one of the hardest-fought battlegrounds in BC politics, delivering tens of thousands of Mincome cheques to BC seniors in time for Christmas. In a ministry where front-line staff had been schooled to reject all hardship claims, no matter how justifiable, Levi had the satisfaction of restoring benefits to a woman who had seen her power improperly cut off, killing all life in her two aquariums. Levi wanted his staff to use judgment; he gave unflagging support to rank and file ministry workers, even if they made mistakes, and moved ruthlessly against senior bureaucrats who proved unwilling or unable to change with the times. Yet Levi did not believe a simple change of ministerial tone could resolve the problems of the welfare system. He believed only legislation could overcome the duplication, waste and bureaucracy. Convinced he would have only a single term to achieve irreversible reforms, Levi had assembled a small, tight team of social work experts and political loyalists to carry out his agenda, which reflected the conclusions of a series of reviews and commissions right across Canada. He spelled out his plan, which he carried around in his head but never formally wrote down, in his first major speech to the legislature as minister in early 1973.

The key elements of Levi's agenda for change were integration, decentralization and citizen participation. After praising the Herculean departmental efforts required to issue the Mincome cheques, Levi began to lay out the problems he confronted. "Because of neglect on the part of the previous government," children were being apprehended at the rate of three hundred a month, leaving seven thousand in direct government care and three thousand in the care of Children's Aid Societies. From here on, he vowed, the focus would be keeping children at home. "There will be no more warehouses and no more dumping grounds." Yes, staffing and spending would increase, Levi warned, but "we will not commit ourselves to limitless purchase of service." He told MLAs of unprecedented meetings across ministries like health and education to improve coordination, and investigations already underway to determine the cost of daycare services and to eliminate waste. "In almost every community we have a multitude of services that overlap and are duplicated or are inadequate or are just plain bad," Levi said. "In some areas there is even open warfare between agencies."

Hard on the heels of Mincome, Levi had introduced Pharmacare for seniors, another campaign commitment, that provided free prescription drugs to anyone over sixty-four. These fundamental reforms were done with minimal staffing. Only sixteen were required to manage Pharmacare. Welfare rates were rationalized and increased by 20 to 40 percent and a $500 special needs grant replaced the Socreds' Emergency Health Aid program. Behind the scenes, Levi was reorganizing the ministry, moving out the old guard and bringing in his own team. An exception was Jimmy Sadler, the former assistant deputy minister whom Levi had met when he served on the John Howard Society board. Sadler became deputy minister, joining Ray Wargo, Ev Northrup of the BC Association of Social Workers and Joe Denofreo, all New Democrats with social work backgrounds, in Levi's inner circle. They and a wider circle of reformers were given free rein to implement changes all had discussed for years but never dreamed they could realize; for many, working for Levi was a peak career experience.

Despite the absence of a formal plan, Levi's team moved quickly from policy analysis to consultation and then implementation. By the time Levi rose in the House to debate his first estimates, he had already embarked on integration of services on Vancouver Island and was pledging to turn operation of those services over to regional authorities as soon as possible. What's more, he was inviting community organizations to "let us know what it is that you want us to pick up" in the form of underfunded programs. A quiet Sunday morning discussion with some friends in his office the month before had triggered the idea of "community resources centres" to manage the newly integrated services. Levi ordered Northrup to begin drafting what became the *Community Resources Act* with that concept at its core; a sketch of the new model was unveiled in March to a conference of provincial social services ministers. The new BC system, Levi declared, would be integrated, community-based and directed, but provincially financed.

Vancouver became Levi's next focus. Within ninety days of the election, Levi had invited the BC Association of Social Workers to prepare four policy papers on reform. An April 1973 report by BCASW recommended a province-wide system of comprehensive, community-based social services accountable to local boards. Weeks later, Vancouver's city social planning department recommended similar integration of all family and youth services in that city in a single agency. Both proposals became the subject of public hearings conducted by Vancouver alderman Harry Rankin and Vancouver–Burrard MLA Rosemary Brown, but no consensus emerged.

In October 1973, Levi announced his determination to create the Vancouver Resources Board to combine the operations of three Vancouver agencies in a single new organization with decentralized branches in thirteen to fifteen local areas. By the time Levi rose in the legislature on March 20 to introduce the *Community Resources Act*, an interim Vancouver Resources Board had already been in place for a month; eleven days later it assumed administrative responsibilities for all services in the city, including all their employees and union agreements. Elections for the first two community resources boards (CRB), in two south Vancouver suburbs, were completed in February. Children's Aid Society executives thought they would have two years to manage the transition, but when Vancouver's city welfare director asked Mayor Art Phillips when Victoria wanted to assume control, the answer was "tomorrow morning." The transfer from Vancouver to Victoria and then to the new Vancouver Resources Board took twenty-four hours. During the next two years, the VRB integrated services across the city, completed the election of fourteen community resources boards and managed expenditures that totalled $100-million.

Despite his commitment to grassroots democracy in the management of social services, Levi saw no need to consult with cabinet or caucus as his legislation evolved. As MLA Rosemary

Brown later noted, the proposal to elect community resources boards alarmed many caucus members, who feared with reason that boards could be controlled by partisans of other parties. The south Vancouver elections provided endless opportunities for media criticism, with CKNW open-line host Jack Webster taking particular delight in excoriating Levi's team for creating a "fourth order of government" along socialist lines. Editorialists ridiculed the idea of elections for boards that had, as yet, no status in law, suggesting that voters were being encouraged to "vote first and think later." Nonetheless, thirty-four candidates stood for ten positions and a weak 9.5 percent turnout picked a new board, rejecting a slate of NDP candidates—and any income assistance recipients—in the process.

These numbers did not disturb Levi. More than 3,500 had voted in the CRB elections, but control of very large community service agencies had previously changed hands at annual general meetings where fewer than 150 ballots were cast. Levi's interim VRB board was less controversial. Chaired by Rankin, it included Alderman Darlene Marzari, two representatives of the Federated Anti-Poverty Groups including future NDP MP Margaret Mitchell, and individual reps from the park board, the school board and United Community Services. The interim board was given twelve months to complete the job set out in the law, which passed third reading on June 20. Levi's revolution had not only begun; it was entrenched in law.

Throughout the turbulent spring of 1974, Levi had Barrett's unqualified support for Bill 84. When the legislation at last came to second reading, Barrett rose to defend his government's record and the legislation, in which "we are asking ... that the community become more and more involved in their own neighbourhood lifestyle and their own community programs." What Barrett couldn't say, because his finance officials were unable to confirm it, was that Levi's ministry was overrunning the budget, which was itself 20 percent above the previous year's spending. By July, the finance ministry was closing in on a number: $108-million more than the legislature had approved just four months before, money that had not yet been spent but would be at the current expenditure rates.

On September 19, Levi was called out of meetings in eastern Canada to take a call from Barrett. "I guess I dropped one today," Barrett confessed, telling Levi that he'd disclosed the overrun as a $100-million "clerical error" during a television interview. Barrett's revelation neutralized overnight the positive public impact of Levi's overhaul of a system that had been wasting enormous financial and human resources.

Three days after the news broke, Levi called in reporters to face the music. His assurances that the overrun was a forecast, that much of the money remained unspent, that Ottawa would take half the load based on federal–provincial cost sharing, fell on deaf ears. McNelly confided to his journal that the $100-million overrun story had validated an increasingly common media claim that the government was "on a self-destruct course." Surrey Mayor Bill Vander Zalm declared his municipality would not pay its 10 percent share of welfare costs, complaining that "this is an increase in claims because of the looseness of the system." Federal officials were equally indignant; Minister of Consumer Affairs Ron Basford demanded to review the books and an "amazed" Minister of Finance Marc Lalonde told reporters he "could not understand how you can make an error of that size." The suggestion that a finance clerk was to blame was incredible, said one reporter, but probably easier than "admitting that the budget was underestimated or overspent or worse, that Mr. Barrett as finance minister and Mr. Levi as human resources minister didn't know what they were doing." It seemed like the Daylight Savings Time method applied to welfare spending had the same destructive grassroots impact. Nurses treating McNelly for appendicitis weeks later in the Smithers hospital made sure he heard their "snide remarks" about welfare waste.

Levi was philosophical about the debacle, telling friends Barrett perhaps should have forced him to resign. He kept driving forward. A year later, as the government drifted toward a snap election, he could look back with satisfaction to scores of community resources boards across the province, all delivering integrated services under the direction of locally elected representatives. His revolution was nearly complete. Although one or two local boards were controlled by slates that opposed welfare spending altogether, most community resources boards were delivering superior services with almost no increase in administrative cost. "The concept is working," reported the chair of the Marpole–Oakridge board, one of the first created. "We're helping to maintain families and keeping kids at home with their parents ... Welfare clients are now treated with dignity." Most importantly, the volunteer boards ensured that the communities themselves "have a direct stake in ensuring that the dollars spent and the programs supplied are right for that neighbourhood." It was good—but would it endure?

8: Health, Housing and Human Rights

While Levi was driving his captured tank through what was to become Israel, Minister of Health Dennis Cocke was a Fuller Brush man selling door-to-door in Vancouver suburbs. These stark differences were reflected in their contrasting approaches to government. Each was confronted by sprawling ministries rife with waste, squabbling vested interests and political minefields. Each was committed, both by personal conviction and party policy, to undertake fundamental reforms. Each charged from the starting gate in 1972 with a determination to exploit his mandate to the full. But where Levi proceeded by frontal assault, executing an unwritten plan conceived during decades as a front-line social worker, Cocke preferred to advance in stages, after careful preparation, ready to withdraw and consolidate at the first sign of organized resistance. Where Levi operated with a small team of specialists, beginning his restructuring even before his enabling legislation was in place, Cocke spent countless hours reviewing expert opinion and meeting stakeholders. What Levi expected would be a single term in power—a window of opportunity to achieve change—Cocke believed would be a two- or three-term period of NDP government, plenty of time to get things right. Yet when Levi's changes were dismantled, Cocke's seemingly lesser legacies endured. Cocke was acknowledged on both sides of the legislature as a competent administrator and deft politician with a firm grasp of his portfolio. Cocke's colleagues, privately mocking his caution, dubbed him "Dr. Cocke" for his careful attention to the concerns of the BC Medical Association, which did him few favours by hailing him as an excellent minister. By good management—not just good luck—Cocke directed BC's largest ministry for three years without controversy, either self-inflicted or triggered by Barrett. That may have been his greatest achievement.

Born and raised in Alberta, Cocke had moved to Vancouver with his mother after his parents split up in his teens. After dropping out of school to support his family, he served for three years in the RCAF. In 1946, he married Yvonne, a Saskatchewan native and CCF disciple who introduced him to social democratic electoral politics. Cocke, however, saw no contradiction between business and the CCF. He switched from brush sales to insurance and quickly rose to branch manager of Dominion Life Assurance. A pleasant, open-faced man who combined deep social democratic values with chamber of commerce sensibilities, Cocke was a rare bridge to business among Barrett's front-benchers. Yet he was never a Barrett man.

Elected for the first time in 1969, Cocke had been a Berger loyalist. Led by Yvonne, a woman of strong feminist beliefs and formidable organizing skills, "the Cocke Machine" turned his narrow 1969 win into a 1972 landslide. The foremost survivor of the Berger faction, Cocke was outside Barrett's inner circle but never generated even a whisper of disloyalty to the new premier. He was delighted, he told reporters at his swearing in, to be taking the reins at health with its $600-million budget and four major departments, each headed by its own deputy. But as Cocke's executive assistant Clay Perry noted later, health was a second-tier ministry in terms of political power: less than 10 percent of the budget was discretionary.

Expectations were high among New Democrats that the party of Tommy Douglas, whose Saskatchewan CCF administration had pioneered medicare, would transform the province's health care system. But unlike welfare services, which had been the focus of repeated controversy under Bennett, BC's health system was so new that its shortcomings were apparent only to insiders. BC had joined the national medicare program in 1968 on a cost-shared basis with Ottawa. W.A.C. Bennett's spending priorities had favoured acute care over other elements of the system. As a result, BC's health care infrastructure had plenty of doctors and hospital beds, but was weaker on prevention, community care and public health. No matter: British Columbians believed their system was among the best in the world, thanks largely to the professionals at its head. There was no public perception of a system in crisis, nor much heart in Barrett's group for a battle with the doctors like the one that had shaken Saskatchewan.

The New Democrats' 1972 platform had, however, promised fundamental changes to ensure that comprehensive health care would be funded as a necessary public service, "not a profit-making business venture." Medical service plan premiums would be eliminated, benefits would increase, a new ambulance service would be created under public control and community health clinics would be established "emphasizing preventative care." Although the pledge to create clinics had been a fixture of NDP policy for three campaigns, voters had little idea what was intended. Bennett had fostered the growth of seventy regional health programs, funded and directed by Victoria but coordinated with local agencies that seemed to fit the bill.

Within days of his appointment, however, Cocke had swung into action, announcing that he had appointed Dr. R.G. "Dick" Foulkes as his special consultant on health policy "to present recommendations which could lead to rationalization of the health care services of the province." Foulkes, a physician who had practised in Saskatchewan, was one of the rare MDs to support

Douglas' medicare program. By the 1960s he had moved to BC as deputy superintendent of the Woodlands mental health facility and in 1966 he became executive director of New Westminster's Royal Columbian Hospital. Cocke placed complete professional and political trust in Foulkes, who was an active member of the NDP. Cocke was well aware that Foulkes lacked diplomacy and was a lightning rod for controversy, but later recalled debating health policy with him "far into the night." Unlike Dailly, who knew little about Bremer when she hired him, Cocke knew Foulkes well and considered him a friend and ally. "There's your budget," he told him. "Go to work."

Cocke then began implementing changes promised in the NDP campaign. The notorious *Sexual Sterilization Act*, which had empowered health officials to sterilize developmentally disabled adults, was repealed. Cocke introduced an organ transplant program, investigated the integration of acupuncture into approved medical treatments and later tightened community care regulations to improve standards. The government extended funding to rape relief centres, women's health collectives and shelters for battered women. Seniors received free prescription drugs, although Cocke learned only in cabinet that this program would be implemented by Levi. His focus, he told the legislature in February 1973, was much like Levi's: integration of programs, decentralization of decision-making and democratic oversight. "We have no idea of beginning this whole centralization approach," Cocke declared. "I am going to repeat it again: we feel that government should be in the financial end, supervision, setting standards and that's it." The Conservatives' Scott Wallace, a physician, was overcome: "It's like a breath of fresh air in here now."

Wallace was on his feet again a few weeks later to endorse Cocke's *Ambulance Service Act*, which empowered the government to impose standards for ambulance attendants and their vehicles. In rural areas of the province, communities had been forced to fundraise to buy their own ambulances, sometimes converted from second-hand hearses, and train their own volunteers. Incredibly, Cocke reminded the legislature, there had been no government supervision of ambulances whatsoever. "If you wished to, you could very well have used an old Model T truck or a dump truck or anything you liked." Wallace agreed that it was a "scoop and run" service. "The patient was just picked up [in] inadequate facilities and [with] completely untrained or poorly trained attendants," he added, though it was clear that the person first on the scene often saved a victim's life. "It's no good tearing out and back at sixty miles an hour if the person is dead when they get to the hospital." The bill passed unanimously amid demands that Cocke hurry up with legislation to create a single, province-wide ambulance service.

The *Emergency Health Services Act*, introduced April 1, 1974, took that final step, creating the first province-wide system with uniform standards and trained personnel. During the next six years, rural communities received access for the first time to Advanced Life Support units, Infant Transport Teams and access to an integrated air ambulance service. This, too, passed unanimously at the height of the Chicken and Egg War, during one of the most divided and rancorous sessions in provincial history. Cocke later described the creation of emergency services as "the highlight of my career." His team learned with relief, a few days after the province-wide service began, that an ambulance paramedic had successfully performed a life-saving tracheotomy on a one-year-old child. Had this procedure, one previously reserved for doctors, gone awry the integrity of the service would have been cast in doubt. A similar outcome when Liberal member Allan Williams later had a near-fatal heart attack ended remaining doubts about the service's value.

Cocke's 1973 Bill 81, the *Medical Centre of BC Act*, produced an equally enduring legacy through the acquisition of the sprawling grounds of the federal government's Shaughnessy veterans' hospital to create new capacity for research, education and a children's hospital. Cocke's plan, opposed by the Liberals' Pat McGeer because it threatened the dominance of UBC and VGH in the city's health care infrastructure, provided the space to create what would become BC Children's and Women's Hospital just a few blocks from the G.F. Strong Rehabilitation Centre and the teaching and treatment facilities at Vancouver General. "We did our homework on this," Cocke told his opposition critics. "If you vote against this, remember you're voting against the children's hospital ... You're saying, 'Okay kids, suffer on, suffer on children. Hang on.' And that's not good enough, Mr. Speaker."

While Cocke forged ahead to create the ambulance service and the medical centre, Foulkes conducted one of the most wide-ranging reviews before or since on the provincial medical system. More than sixty specific research reports were prepared as Foulkes travelled the province to gather information for his report, which was to be entitled *Health Security for British Columbians*. By early 1973, Cocke's officials were working with Levi's department to launch Community Human Resources and Health Centres, essentially community-based clinics that would provide integrated public health and medical services under one roof and with local oversight. By the end of 1973, an interdepartmental development group had identified five locations for demonstration projects to test the new model, promising the host communities they would receive full capital and operating funding as an incentive.

But Cocke was encountering significant resistance to the centres, both within his ministry and from public health officials, who still reported to municipal governments. Worse, Foulkes' own outspoken comments in the course of his review were producing an angry backlash. As Foulkes became more committed than ever to dramatic change, Cocke was beginning to see that his old ally was "causing a lot of administrative flack," in the words of one ministry official. "The gap was getting wider and wider by this point. You could see that here was Cocke on the one hand becoming more conservative as he was learning and on the other hand Foulkes was almost becoming more the opposition in reaction. He was even more determined to stick with his principles and not deviate at all." Foulkes was stunned to hear Cocke, who had "the doctors snarling at me," downgrade the "demonstration projects" to "pilot projects," experiments to be studied, not the foundation for health care reform. "It was a horror to me," Foulkes said later. "Pilot project meant something like a drogue that you towed behind an airplane and shot at, which is what happened."

Foulkes' sixteen-month review touched on virtually all aspects of the province's health care system from management and administration to diagnostic services, treatment, prevention, nutrition and the special needs of women and aboriginal people. His call for a universally accessible, public system providing a full spectrum of services tried to strike a balance between efficiency and humanity. For the next twenty years, Foulkes' work would be a touchstone for anyone interested in health policy and medicare. But convinced that he should challenge Cocke not to turn his back on health care reform, Foulkes blundered badly. The transmittal letter for *Health Security for British Columbians* contained the declaration that Foulkes' prescriptions for a massive overhaul of health services reflected the "overall philosophy of the NDP government toward health care systems" and were "in accordance with the Party's election platform on these issues."

Foulkes' efforts to force Cocke's hand had the opposite effect. Copies of the report already set for distribution were retrieved so Cocke's January 17, 1974, press statement could be pasted in the front cover. "In view of the size and complexity of this report," Cocke wrote, "it would be unwise of me to express any immediate particular reactions." Foulkes' work would be "studied for some time to come," the minister said, adding that he disagreed with Foulkes condemnation of mental health services as "the most inefficient, ineffective, outdated and discriminatory of all our existing social and medical programs." After all, Cocke said, "we have in British Columbia one of the best health care systems in the world."

Reflecting back on those events years later, Cocke was unapologetic. "The beginning identified it as an NDP piece of work and naturally, if you do that, politically it's dynamite. I had to now not disown it but I had to say, 'Well look, we're going to study this carefully and we'll take the good.'" The report was a "blueprint," worthy of study, a green paper, but not an agenda for action. Foulkes' massive sixteen-month transformational project was dead on arrival.

Clay Perry believed Cocke had approval from the top to shelve the Foulkes report, certainly from Barrett and probably from the cabinet as a whole. The BCMA leaders had made it clear they were prepared to go to war to prevent a major shift away to community health centres, especially if those centres used salaried physicians. Memories of the Saskatchewan confrontation were fresh in the minds of New Democrats. Cocke's shelving of the Foulkes report averted what many believed would have been an even larger explosion in BC. Public reaction was muted, even in the ranks of the NDP. When opposition critics tried to assail Cocke in the House, they wound up punching the air. It was all good feedback, Cocke replied blandly, grist for the mill. It may be the only example of a battle Barrett declined to join.

Could Cocke have done more? In his three years as health care critic, Cocke had developed a detailed understanding of the chaotic state of health administration, with three departments reporting to the minister and a Medical Services Plan supervised by the provincial secretary. Rationalizing this "absolutely awful" organizational structure was a major undertaking in itself, Cocke said later. Bureaucratic resistance was a daily fact of life. In the face of his staggering workload and a daily succession of brushfires Cocke developed hypertension. Fundamental changes could not emerge "out of a can of worms like we had," Cocke believed, and reorganizing the ministry was the work of a full term.

Cocke was proud of his good relationship with the fractious health care stakeholders, all the way from the Hospital Employees' Union to the BCMA, but was no patsy. "I was prepared to listen," he recalled, "not necessarily prepared to act. We used to have some screaming fights." Cocke banned extra billing by order-in-council, something the BCMA resented but dared not speak out about. Although he regretted not doing more to reform mental health, he was able to oversee the deployment of psychiatric nurses in the community, allowing a dramatic reduction in the number of institutionalized patients. Others may have been in government for "a good time, not a long time," but Cocke was one who believed a long time would be necessary to achieve real change.

As the Barrett government's political tide ebbed, Cocke added one more legislative trophy to his collection. The *Emergency Services Act* may have been the highlight of his career, he said, but the *Free Public Toilets Act* was the most fun. The bill, which passed with rare unanimity in the spring of 1975, ended the widespread practice of pay toilets throughout the province. When his private member's bill passed second reading, Cocke declared the people of the province "flushed with pride," particularly women. Denying that the government had any plans to nationalize toilets, Cocke noted that mom-and-pop businesses provided clean facilities for free; it was only the large businesses like hotels and bus lines that charged. The only positive benefit of pay toilets he had identified was a colleague who "learned to dance standing in front of a toilet door with only eight cents in his pocket." Cocke's bill passed third reading and the dancing lessons ended once and for all.

By early 1974 it was becoming clear to Barrett's team that every initiative would face some critics. However they were unprepared, after announcing renters' grants and other wide-ranging reforms to curb landlords' rights, to be condemned for inaction by the BC Tenants Organization. Under the dogged leadership of Vancouver tenant activist and Communist Party member Bruce Yorke, the dapper but rogue son of a prominent Vancouver businessman, the BCTO condemned the Barrett budget's $30 renter's grant as an "insulting" indirect subsidy to landlords. "Maybe he's right," McNelly moaned in his journal, "but god, he's boring." McNelly, unlike Yorke, was aware that Barrett had deliberately set the grant low so he could throw in an increase, Huey Long fashion, just before a provincial election. In the hothouse atmosphere of Vancouver civic politics, where citizen action had just stopped freeway construction, the destruction of Chinatown and a third crossing of Burrard Inlet, there was lots of room for Yorke out to the left of Alderman Harry Rankin and a centrist majority headed by Mayor Art Phillips, of The Electors Action Movement. If there was one issue on which the entire political spectrum agreed, it was that BC was in the grips of a housing crisis.

With vacancy rates plunging to nearly zero, tenants weren't fussy about who took up their cause, provided someone did. "Housing is a basic right," Barrett's platform had declared, "and must be provided on the basis of need rather than profit." The New Democrats had promised not only major investments in social housing, but also the extension of "bargaining rights" to certified tenants' associations, and rent review boards "composed of representatives of tenant associations and local governments" to adjudicate landlord–tenant disputes. Although the first year of the mandate had passed with little more than a review of rent controls by the Law Reform Commission, the 1974 budget had been stuffed with tens of millions of dollars in new spending to make these pledges a reality.

W.A.C. Bennett's last administration had completed the first update of landlord–tenant legislation since 1858 in 1970. For the first time, landlords were required to give notice of rent increases and tenants received basic protection. But the cancellation of key federal tax concessions the next year—essentially allowing losses on rental property to be charged to other business activities of the owner—brought new rental construction to a complete halt. About 38 percent of BC's households were renters and 149,000 families, mostly the poorest, paid more than 25 percent of their income on rent. Rental housing supply quickly tightened. By 1974, the crisis was acute for both homeowners and renters. Average MLS listings had risen $25,000 to $55,000 in the previous two years, but housing starts actually dropped sharply as construction and interest costs rose. The vacancy rate in Vancouver dropped to 1 percent in 1973 from 4.1 percent a year earlier and then to 0.3 percent in 1974.

Even boring Bruce Yorke could get tenants mobilized under these conditions. "Those who owned a house were thankful they did," concluded one 1975 study, "but they worried about whether their children would ever be able to buy." Tenants' fears were more immediate: everyone expected rents to skyrocket in the absence of new supply. When Macdonald's law commission review endorsed some kind of rent control, Barrett's cabinet got down to work, although key players like Williams were not in favour.

The housing shortage had been compounded by Bennett's ideological preference to leave all housing matters to the private sector, where single home construction was a lucrative business. Modest incentives were available for would-be homebuyers; tenants were of little interest. Even when federal money was available, Bennett's administration moved at a glacial pace to take its share. Vancouver's Raymur project was delayed six years while Victoria shuffled the paperwork. During the ten years ending in 1974, BC added only fifty-six projects with about 6,300 units, mostly for seniors. Forty percent of those units were built in 1973–1974, the first year of Barrett's administration.

In May 1973, Barrett made an evening phone call to Nelson–Creston MLA Lorne Nicolson, a former physics teacher and rookie MLA who had won election in 1972 after a bitter loss in the Berger debacle three years earlier. Barrett ordered Nicolson to load his family in the car and drive to Victoria. A math and physics teacher who enjoyed road cycling and rugby, Nicolson had no background in housing policy. It wasn't until he arrived at the legislature that he learned he was to head the first provincial ministry in Canada devoted solely to housing. Nicolson's portfolio was being carved out of Minister of Municipal Affairs Jim Lorimer's workload. There was no orientation or handover of briefing books; Nicolson simply sat down with Lorimer to see where things stood. So far, Lorimer said, his efforts had been limited to buying some land, driving the BC Housing Management Corporation to exploit federal funding opportunities, and building a relationship with the province's nascent co-op housing movement. Legislation creating the new ministry passed in October 1973.

Developers were anxious to size Nicolson up, but dinner and a baseball game with a Victoria real estate mogul went off the rails when it became clear "a very nice Asian lady" had been hired to entertain. "I realized I would need a network," Nicolson said, and he went out to find one. Lorimer had introduced him to George Chatterton, head of the housing management corporation, a political Conservative who became a trusted ally. Nicolson found useful contacts in unlikely places, securing introductions to developers and construction industry leaders from friends on his road cycling team. One particularly productive call came from the principal shareholder of Dunhill Development Corporation, a full-service development firm that was up for sale. "I discussed it with Williams," Nicolson recalled, "and he thought it might be a good idea." Accountants were secured to go over Dunhill "with a fine tooth comb." The company proved sound and the purchase offered the government instant capacity to deliver the housing program. Dunhill had developers, marketers, a land inventory, connections to the construction industry—everything, in fact,

Nicolson would need to deliver on the election commitments. "We paid $5.6-million and it was sold three years later for $21-million," Nicolson said later. "Rather than create a Crown corporation with tired civil servants, we bought a thriving company."

Within weeks of the purchase, Dunhill's managers were acquiring properties for conversion to social housing. A visit to the twenty-four-unit Norman Bethune Co-op on Gaglardi Way in Burnaby confirmed Nicolson's belief that mixed income projects at higher densities were the wave of the future, a model that was repeated all over the province. Nicolson soon secured the services of two men who would both go on to prominent careers in the housing industry. Michael Audain, later president of Polygon Homes, advised on policy; Larry Bell, who later served in a series of very senior roles both in government and the private sector, ensured that BC gained maximum advantage from CMHC funding. Nicolson was also supported on constituency matters by executive assistant Andrew Petter, a former Nelson radio broadcaster who would go on to become a professor of law, finance minister in the Glen Clark NDP government and president of Simon Fraser University.

While Nicolson supervised housing investment, Alex Macdonald took a break from "thirty-second socialism" to overhaul landlord and tenant law. The *Landlord and Tenant Act* introduced on April 9, 1974, created the office of the Rentalsman to adjudicate landlord–tenant disputes. The bill also allowed eviction only for "just cause." Most controversial, however, were provisions mandating the Rentalsman to set allowable rent increases. The *Interim Rent Stabilization Act* introduced May 2 set those increases at 8 percent for 1974, an amount later revised to 10.5 percent. Rentalsman Barrie Clark—a provincial Liberal and sometime open-line host—told Macdonald and Nicolson he could not possibly handle all the appeals that would be generated by rent controls. Worse, he would be in the untenable position of adjudicating disputes caused by his own rent rulings.

Macdonald and Nicolson appointed a blue ribbon panel chaired by Toronto housing expert Karl Jaffary to dig deeper into the rental control morass. In the meantime, Barrie Clark was off the hook. A storm of criticism had greeted Macdonald's bill; it was heavily amended in the fall session to fix a series of flaws. By Christmas, however, BC tenants were receiving their grants, watching new units get built and enjoying the security of new legal rights.

Nicolson's ministry began building housing in earnest. By accessing federal money and adding provincial resources, his team triggered a 36 percent increase in social housing stock in 1974 by adding 1,400 units. By December 1976, when the New Democrats' building surge was completed, the affordable housing stock had doubled. Nearly half a century later, those units would be one of the most enduring—though perhaps least visible—legacies of the Barrett government. Nicolson, like Levi and Cocke, was learning that the best political legacies touched people's daily lives. But perhaps none of them understood that better than Phyllis Young, Barrett's minister of consumer affairs.

An intensely private person and a political unknown when she was swept into office in the two-member riding of Vancouver–Little Mountain, Phyllis Young had been a flight attendant and full-time union official before her election. She was a feminist, a veteran of the Vancouver Status of Women. Like Nicolson, she had been taken by surprise by Barrett's May call to join cabinet as a minister without portfolio, responsible for the government's emerging consumer affairs department. Two likely reasons for her selection stuck out: consumer affairs was considered a "women's issue" and Young was not Rosemary Brown. By appointing Young, Barrett promoted a feminist—like Brown, Young had criticized the lack of a women's ministry in her response to the 1973 Throne Speech—but not his prickly critic from Vancouver–Burrard. Apart from a series of generalities in the election platform, Young had little idea where to begin, but late in November 1973 she was promoted to full minister and it was time to start.

Bill Neilson was only two weeks into his new job as deputy minister to Phyllis Young in the government's freshly hatched Ministry of Consumer Services when the Treasury Board called: "We'd like your 1974 spending estimates, please." Neilson was stunned. Not only had his fledgling department never had a budget, there was virtually no staff and barely an office. Frantically, he and his neophyte minister cobbled some figures together with the help of a borrowed government comptroller. Three days after that, Neilson was face to face with the chairman of the Treasury Board, trying to win approval for their ballpark, back-of-the-envelope sum. Oh yes, the chairman of the Treasury Board was none other than Dave Barrett, Premier of the Province. It was quite a jump from Ontario's Osgoode Hall. The brilliant young academic, considered Canada's foremost legal expert on consumer protection, had been lured west as another of the legal whiz kids who leapt at the chance to put flesh on the bone of scholarly theory by working for an actual government. Neilson's reputation cut no ice with Barrett, however. The premier looked down at the nervous deputy minister and welcomed him to the meeting with the words, "Well, so you're another one of these smart-alecky lawyers from back East." Talk about a baptism of fire. Neilson's knees buckled. He swallowed hard. Yes, he acknowledged, he was a smart-alecky lawyer from back East. But now, Neilson reminded the premier, he was in daily charge of a department that needed funds to be visible in the marketplace.

Barrett liked the response. An hour later, Neilson and Young emerged from the Treasury Board, their budget approved. Only later did Neilson realize, ruefully, that he could have asked for and received more. "We were babes in arms," he observed a few years afterward, in a speech recounting the incident to a gathering of Canadian law teachers. "We were without programs or people. We were trying to develop both, define financial figures for it all, and, in our spare time, draft legislation for the forthcoming spring session." For better or worse, that was the way business often unfolded in the Barrett administration. The goal was action. Get it done. Avoid bogging down in the mire of bureaucratic planning and crossing every *t*. Just do it.

When things worked, as they did more commonly than critics owned, the results could be remarkable. Consumer Services was a prime example. Neilson came on board in mid-November, five days after the ministry was created. "There was Phyllis Young, who had an assistant, and myself, and I had a person who did some typing," he recalled. "That was it." By the time of the

On that unforgettable election night in 1972 that brought the NDP to power for the first time, Premier-elect Dave Barrett, with a beaming Shirley Barrett by his side, is interviewed by hotline king, Jack Webster. Under Barrett, the NDP would go on to pass more legislation in a shorter time than any BC government, before or since.
Photo by Ken Oakes, provided by the *Vancouver Sun*

government's defeat two years later, British Columbia had the strongest, most activist department of consumer protection in the country, with five ministry offices across the province, 110 employees, an annual budget of $2.5-million, and twelve pieces of legislation to its credit. "They were fantastic, just excellent," Ruth Lotzkar of the Consumers' Association of Canada told the *Vancouver Sun* shortly before the election. She said the CAC was simply floored by the amount of consumer-oriented legislation passed in such a short time. On the other side of the street, Vince Forbes of the Better Business Bureau singled out the government's *Fair Trade Practices Act*. "It's the bible of merchandising in BC right now. It's outstanding."

Times were ripe for that kind of progressive push. Galvanized by Ralph Nader's bestselling exposé *Unsafe at Any Speed*, consumerism was on the move. Consumers were mad as hell at misleading advertising, shady business practices and too many shoddy goods. They were clamouring for redress, no longer prepared to take it anymore. In one of her first legislature speeches, Young ridiculed a plea for secretarial help from the plethora of male MLAs on the backbenches. "Oh boy! Do you find that you need us now?" she chortled, pointing to their hapless efforts to try and keep up with correspondence using borrowed typewriters. "They use what we in the clerical profession call the Christopher Columbus method of typing—that is, find a key and land on it."

Young had no trouble relating to consumer beefs. She had a few herself, and she was not shy about naming them or the corporate culprit. Early on in her new job, she provided the legislature with a revealing glimpse of what women shoppers can experience. "The most expensive pair of shoes I ever purchased in my life [I bought] from Eaton's ... One week later, the buckle fell off." Since she didn't have time to return them, Ms. Young said she took the other buckle off, so the $30 shoes would match. "Now that's Eaton's, for openers." Then, underwear: "I bought two slips there and the straps broke the first time I put them on. I could do a hatchet job on Eaton's any day in the week."

No consumer grievance, it seemed, was too small for MLAs to air. Doug Kelly complained about the quality of light bulbs. "You go to flick the light, and it doesn't go on." Garden hoses, too: "After a few years, there's a little leak here, and a little leak there." Don Lewis told of spending $119 to replace a part on a fuel-line pump for his tractor that cost 60¢ to manufacture. Unhappiness for Jim Gorst involved a relative's chesterfield suite that had to be returned five times before the customer was satisfied. Poorly made locks irritated Peter Rolston. "If you don't have a good quality lock on your house, you're going to be asking for trouble." In this environment, consumer protection legislation was rarely opposed.

Young was far from a dynamic minister, but she knew enough to hire the best and get out of the way. Neilson was typical of the talented academics filling policy roles in the NDP administration. With Young's approval, his overall approach was pro-active, designed to head off trouble at the pass. A *Debtor Assistance Act*, the first of its kind in Canada, set up services for budgeting advice, debt counselling and mediation to help financially beleaguered British Columbians avoid bankruptcy. The *Trade Practices Act* spelled out a broad list of "deceptive and unconscionable" business actions that required redress, rather than leaving it to the courts to determine bad behaviour. Brochures publicizing consumer rights under the *Act* were sent to every household in the province, preceded by a radio advertising campaign.

The ministry funded storefront offices in Victoria, Vancouver, Kamloops and Prince George. Each was staffed by a debt counsellor and one or two complaints officers. All were well used. Consumer complaints poured in. During the first four months of 1975, for instance, the ministry handled nearly 4,000 complaints, compared with just 801 for all of 1972, when Social

Credit provided only one officer and a secretary from the attorney general's department to process consumer grievances. Many of the complaints resulted in settlements and customer refunds, totalling $136,628 for the first ten months the *Trade Practices Act* was in effect. Young told the legislature of visiting the Vancouver storefront office one day, when a trade practices investigator "popped in and said, 'A lady just called to thank us for getting a $4,000 refund from an automobile dealer on behalf of her daughter.'"

The *Act* also pioneered what were called Agreements of Voluntary Compliance. These allowed businesses in clear violation of the act to avoid further trouble by refunding the full amount at issue, and agreeing to abide by the act in future, rather than being hauled to court. Violations were made public, sometimes with large corrective newspaper ads. Several cases involved the funeral industry. One funeral home was found to be recycling coffins, while another's promise of a brass urn to contain a deceased's ashes became a cardboard box.

The Consumer Services Ministry was also likely the best equal-opportunity employer in the entire government. Forty-five percent of its executive decision-makers were women, and special care was taken to give work to housewives, seniors and particularly the disabled. Nothing topped "the bed squad." These were a group of bedridden polio patients at the famed G.F. Strong Rehabilitation Centre in South Vancouver. Neilson had been looking for a relatively inexpensive way to monitor advertising. A doctor friend referred him to G.F. Strong. Residents embraced the task. "They had some bright polio patients," said Neilson. "They couldn't move, but they read, they thought, they argued." The group wound up monitoring eleven newspapers, eight radio stations and four TV stations for the ministry. His best Vancouver visits were always to G.F. Strong, Neilson said. "Stipends were paid. The patients were happy. Nobody complained that it wasn't enough."

Legislation was also brought in to crack down on pyramid sales schemes, tighten regulation of credit bureaus and permit the department to take companies to court on behalf of a consumer. As a final kicker, the Ministry of Consumer Services was delegated, on short notice, to police the government's ninety-day price freeze, announced by Barrett two weeks before he called the election in 1975. "We had three days to set it up, one weekend to train staff, and a few concerns about the legalities of the freeze," Neilson told the Canadian law teachers in his speech. Yet, once again, the department came through under fire. "The price freeze was obeyed," reported Neilson, even as staff handled 3,700 inquiries and more than 400 written complaints. Almost all price hikes were inadvertent and voluntarily rolled back, he said.

Neilson stayed on for one more year, persuaded to remain by Young's Social Credit replacement Rafe Mair, who left most of the measures passed under the NDP intact. Neilson spent the next twenty-seven years as a law professor at the University of Victoria, serving six years as dean. Looking back, years later, Neilson said the NDP's thrust to protect consumers produced unquestionably "the strongest and most progressive consumers' ministry in Canada. Person for person, law for law, there is no doubt about that. Absolutely no doubt at all." Like housing, consumer services was a ministry the Barrett government created from scratch to spur its drive to right society's wrongs and aid those far from the top of the economic pyramid. Strangely, the government itself also failed to pay significant attention to these achievements. On the hustings, Barrett spent his time attacking Social Credit and extolling his government's big ticket items such as ICBC, the Agricultural Land Reserve, Mincome, Pharmacare and purchases of enterprises that might otherwise have died.

Yet consumer services was a model department that accomplished everything it set out to do, propelled by a rookie minister and a thirty-four-year-old deputy minister straight out of academia. Consumers never had it better. When Phyllis

Young died suddenly in 1984, Premier Bill Bennett joined with Barrett, then on the opposition benches, in paying tribute to her public service and the respect she engendered on both sides of the House. Entrenching consumer rights was good bipartisan politics. Entrenching human rights, however, proved to be an entirely different matter.

In 1974, the *Vancouver Sun* received a small notice to run in its vast classified ad section. The proposed ad read, "Subscription to *Gay Tide*, gay lib paper. $1.00 for 6 issues. 2146 Yew St. Vancouver." At a time when gay marriages are routine and politicians of all stripes line up to be part of Gay Pride celebrations, it's hard to imagine how such an innocuous ad could have caused any controversy. But the *Sun* rejected it. The content might offend readers, explained the newspaper, which gladly ran lurid display advertisements for pornographic movies, often with a lesbian theme, at X-rated theatres across the border in Blaine, Washington.

A year or two earlier, the *Sun*'s refusal would likely have prompted no more attention than a brief outcry in the alternative press. But now, British Columbia had powerful new human rights legislation. The code brought in by the NDP was the strongest in Canada. It went beyond the traditional list of categories—race, religion, sex, age and nationality—covered by human rights laws elsewhere. For the first time, a section had been included to prohibit discrimination "without reasonable cause." The wording opened up the act to anyone discriminated against for any reason. No longer were human rights violations restricted to a finite list of categories. Enter sexual orientation.

The Gay Alliance Towards Equality (GATE) complained that the *Sun*'s refusal to publish its small classified ad contravened BC's freshly passed Human Rights Code. This was groundbreaking territory. The Human Rights Branch accepted the case, and a tribunal subsequently found that the newspaper had, indeed, discriminated against GATE. The dispute eventually wound up before the Supreme Court of Canada. It was the top court's first gay rights case. Although the Supreme Court ruled 6–3 in favour of the *Vancouver Sun*, mostly on the basis of freedom of the press, the genie was out of the bottle. In 1980, the *Sun* agreed on its own volition to finally publish GATE's fourteen-word classified ad.

None of this would have happened under Social Credit. Like labour, human rights had fallen into a dark hole during the W.A.C. Bennett administration. While civil rights activists, feminists and brave gay rights pioneers across North America were clamouring for equality, human rights protection in BC was little more than unenforced window dressing. Newspaper classified ad sections carried long columns of jobs divided into men only and women only. Union contracts often provided higher wages for men than women doing the same work. Women were specifically excluded from certain jobs, Natives could be refused service and homophobic attitudes were widely tolerated.

Complaints to the poorly staffed, poorly funded Human Rights Commission were investigated by industrial relations officers. Usually, they went nowhere. "The system was just a total farce," recalled Kathleen Ruff, who chaired the Barrett government's pioneering Human Rights Branch. "The legislation was not serious, nor was it seriously enforced. It was pretty well useless for women or any other group." The NDP wiped the slate clean; as with the Labour Code, Bill King brought in legislation ahead of anything else in Canada. Rosemary Brown praised the package as "a very tremendous bill" she was happy to support.

One measure set up a special Human Rights Commission headed by Victoria's social activist bishop, Remi de Roo, to promote human rights education and the need to curb intolerance. This proactive approach quickly proved its worth after an outbreak of youth violence against Indo-Canadian students in Surrey. Human rights staff spent the next Sunday going door-to-door in the affected neighbourhood, talking with residents about what had happened. Racial tension eased.

With full-time officers and branch offices established across BC, human rights complaints increased five-fold. Numerous boards of inquiry were appointed. Fewer complaints were dismissed. The *Human Rights Act* also toughened penalties to allow damages for a complainant's mental anguish, enshrined the principle of equal pay for work of equal value, broadened situations covered by the legislation, including protection against dismissal of employees with summary convictions, and banned provisions in union contracts that discriminated against women.

But the most critical change, as demonstrated by the *Gay Tide* case, was the "reasonable cause" provision. In effect nowhere else in the country, the clause provoked a series of landmark cases that would have gone nowhere before the NDP's beefed-up legislation. Beer parlours and restaurants that refused to serve long-haired hippies were sanctioned, a hotel that refused to provide a Native woman with a room was ordered to pay damages to the aggrieved woman, landlords were forced to rent rooms to people on welfare, an intense investigation of wage discrimination in the hospital industry resulted in significant pay hikes for women employees, and Jean Tharp, a female lab technician with the Lornex mining company, was able to pursue her long, hard campaign to win proper bunkhouse accommodation for herself among an otherwise male workforce.

Tharp's experience was a good example of how difficult it still was in the 1970s to change attitudes towards women. First, she complained that free bunkhouse accommodation and meals were available for men, but not for herself. She was forced to make a dangerous, daily commute between the nearest town and the bush. Under pressure from the Human Rights Commission, Lornex agreed to let Tharp stay in the bunkhouse. But they made no adjustment to existing facilities, requiring Tharp to use the same open showers and bathrooms as the men. The company argued that Tharp had not been that poorly treated. We could have asked her to share her two-bed bunk, too, they said. So Tharp filed another complaint. This time, the company responded by adding a separate partition for her in the bunkhouse. However, Tharp's male co-workers kept barging through the section because it was the fastest route to the dining hall. At the end, for all her trauma, Tharp was awarded an extra $250. It was proof, if any was needed, that ending discrimination would take much more than simple legislative change.

The province's employers disliked Kathleen Ruff and the enhanced human rights legislation. They may have agreed with a Hansard typographical error referring to it as the "Human Tights Act." "Even today, the employer community is not adjusted to human rights realties, so it was a big shock to them," recalled Jim Matkin, deputy labour minister for most of the NDP administration. "A lot of our time was spent with upset employers. Bill [King] was very solicitous to them, listening and trying to calm them down. Human rights was not an area where he was going to shine, but he did more in that field than anyone else has done." In the media, too, commentators such as the *Sun*'s Doug Collins kept up a constant barrage of ridicule and criticism of human rights cases. Successive Social Credit governments methodically dismantled much of the NDP's human rights protection, and Ruff's contract was not renewed. Looking back, Ruff gave high marks to the NDP: "The Barrett government brought in excellent legislation. It sent a message that everyone in the province deserves human rights protection. Whatever the form of prejudice, it's wrong."

9: Life of the Party

Most governments suffer criticism at the hands of their enemies, but the first NDP government in BC history also endured harsh attacks from its supporters. As Barrett wrestled the 1974 spring session to a close, Pierre Trudeau's minority government, propped up by David Lewis and the federal New Democrats since 1972, went to the polls in an effort to secure a renewed majority. The key issue would be the fight against inflation and the Conservatives' pledge to implement wage and price controls. The vote would not only be a referendum on the federal NDP's first brush with power at the national level; it would give voters a chance to render judgment on NDP provincial administrations then in power in Manitoba, Saskatchewan and BC.

A Toronto reporter heading into Vancouver soon after the writ dropped asked his cabbie for an assessment. "We'll be able to get rid of that fucking Barrett," said the driver. The daylight savings affair, the agricultural land issue and the obscenities shouted at Nichols had all contributed to an impression that Barrett was arrogant and a sloppy administrator. David Lewis primly declined to challenge that perception, acknowledging during one campaign swing that the local New Democrats had made some "goofs," though he welcomed Barrett's offer to campaign for the federal party in five hard-fought ridings around Hamilton, Ontario. Nichols herself concluded Barrett was a bigger issue for voters than wage and price controls, citing widespread "I can't Barrett" bumper stickers as proof.

The July 8 results were a disaster for both Barrett and Lewis, who held his ground in the rest of Canada but saw his BC caucus drop to two seats from eleven. The NDP share of the federal vote in the province plunged to 22.8 percent from 33 percent. BC pundits, including NDP provincial secretary and 1972 campaign manager Hans Brown, were quick to link Lewis' fall to Barrett's performance. In a front-page analysis in *The Democrat*, Brown calculated that one NDP voter in three had jumped ship for the federal Liberals to stop wage and price controls. "Make no mistake about it," Brown wrote. "A lot of people who work in mines, mills and factories of this province get goose pimples thinking about wage and price controls." These voters would come home to the New Democrats in the provincial vote, Brown believed, rather than vote for a "dinky outfit" like the BC Liberals when the "Blue Scare and the Bennett Bludgeon" were the likely beneficiaries. But at the same time, Brown pointed to the risk that a resurgent Social Credit Party could build on the growing Conservative vote in the province to reach "49 percent of the vote if a provincial election were held tomorrow," opening the door to a Bill Bennett majority. Even if the current backlash against the Barrett government were reversed, Brown calculated, Barrett would be lucky to eke out a minority government.

Brown's conclusion, from a senior party official writing in the party's own publication, must have made for grim reading in the Premier's Office. "Our vote has become ominously, though not irretrievably, unhinged," Brown wrote. At least half the drop "was of our own making. Our government's public relations is bad. Our good legislation is going unnoticed, unexplained and unappreciated. We are losing marginal, but critical chunks of support as a result. More important, our organization is becoming run down. In the two years since we were elected government, our membership has stagnated, our organizers have been cut back, our coffers are dry and our people are tired. The trade union movement, in the main, stands at arm's length. The middle level leadership of the party—the provincial executive, riding executives, election organizers—are being stonewalled, ignored, glad-handed but seldom involved by Victoria." Recovery was still possible, but "the initiative must come from our leadership in Victoria." As for Brown, he announced in the same issue of *The Democrat* that he was resigning to pursue new challenges.

That "leadership in Victoria," however, had been under attack from some of its supporters almost from the beginning. As early as February 1973, Barrett had been handed the kind of award no elected official would covet, a tiny golden piglet emblematic of the Male Chauvinist Pig Award for "most sexist politician" of the year. A delegation from the BC Status of Women bestowed this dubious achievement on Barrett in recognition of his refusal to create a ministry of women's equality as demanded by the NDP's post-election convention. As Barrett tried to laugh off the award in a legislature scrum, two members of his caucus briefly interrupted. "Aww, shucks, I thought I was going to be the one to present it to you," said Phyllis Young. Rosemary Brown walked by muttering "Tsk, tsk, tsk," disapprovingly. Both had, until their election the year before, been active leaders of Status of Women.

"I'm shocked and disappointed that this group [the Status of Women] would show their sexist tendencies," Barrett said in mock outrage. "I refuse to accept an overtly sexist award from a female chauvinist group." Laugh as they might, reporters could not recall a previous occasion on which a sitting premier had been ridiculed in like fashion by members of his own caucus. It was hard to argue, however, that Barrett hadn't earned the distinction. In a 1972 campaign speech in Trail, the future premier had offered the view that "women's liberation, if rational and successful, will be the saving grace of the North American male. I mean it." When the NDP convention called for a women's ministry, Barrett had made it clear he was not interested, a rejection

Rosemary Brown and Dave Barrett are all smiles in this photo from 1973. Peter McNelly, hired away from his job at the *Province* to work for Barrett, is on the left.
Photo by Glenn Baglo, provided by the *Vancouver Sun*

he emphasized a few weeks later when a women's delegation lobbied his MLAs for action.

All premiers must contend with the Official Opposition and the media. Many encounter problems within their own caucus, particularly from backbenchers who discover that their dreams of a cabinet post are not to be realized. NDP premiers, however, must contend with the additional challenge posed by an engaged and committed party membership hungry to help govern after long stretches in the political wilderness. Where members of other parties may be content to pay an annual fee and watch the news, New Democrats are movement people, absorbed in policy and process as much as in victory. They are also the human resources the NDP relies on to offset the party's perennial disadvantage in funding. Maintaining solid communications with a group of backbenchers is more difficult than it looks; keeping the channels open to a province-wide party membership can prove nearly impossible. Barrett struggled on both fronts.

Barrett's route to power had opened up after the destruction of the labour-backed Berger faction of the party in 1969. That crisis produced both a caucus and a rank-and-file that combined the pent-up demands of a long-marginalized party with the explosive energy of the new environmental and feminist movements. Barrett's environmental credentials were solid, but he was emotionally and politically unprepared for the women's movement. A populist, he was determined to resonate with the working class families he considered his base. When he was accused of sexism, part of Dave Barrett wanted to plead guilty, and another part resented the failure to acknowledge his undoubted commitment to social equality. Barrett sought to circumscribe women's equality in the catch-all category of human rights. It proved a failing strategy, drawing scorn from dynamic women's organization inside the party that was determined to bring him to heel and nearly succeeded.

Barrett's decision to keep to the "dirty dozen" for his front bench had a similar effect, putting more experienced hands on the front line but insulating his leadership from the new currents in the party. Barrett placed a huge premium on personal loyalty—he was reported to have said that "an ounce of loyalty is worth a pound of brains"—that slowed the promotion of talented backbenchers. The decision to unleash cabinet to implement the party's platform without input from caucus members emphasized the gap between cabinet and backbench that bedevils all governments. Their support taken for granted, backbenchers often learned the content of new legislation just hours before the general public. These were prescriptions for trouble and Barrett was warned on both counts.

Within days of Barrett's shoeless skid down the cabinet table in 1972, the newly elected NDP caucus had gathered at the legislature for their first meeting, a solemn affair dominated by a visit from the legendary Tommy Douglas, now Member of Parliament for Nanaimo–Cowichan–The Islands. Douglas had led the CCF to power in Saskatchewan in 1944, forming the first social democratic government in North America and winning re-election as premier four times. Seventeen years later, after pioneering achievements like medicare, public auto insurance and a provincial bill of rights, he led the federal New Democratic Party for ten years, enduring bitter personal defeats in his own ridings in two elections. The irrepressible Douglas had unequalled experience of politics' highs and lows, and he decided to share it.

"He said, 'Now, you're all on a high,'" recalled Colin Gabelmann. "'You're feeling like you can do whatever you want. Just remember, it's hard work, don't ever try to do more than you can do successfully.'" Gary Lauk, newly elected in Vancouver Centre, never forgot Douglas' admonition to "walk in lock-step with the party, and always bring the party with you, no matter what you do, because you're going to need them in the bad times." Harold Steves took away the same message: "meet with the party, work things out with the party." Common-sense advice, Lauk thought, but Barrett seemed furious at Douglas' "unwarranted intervention." When Douglas was gone, Barrett explained some realities. No one should quit his or her job, because it was hard to feed a family on an $8,000 salary and $4,000 for expenses. There would be another caucus meeting in due course, the premier said. With that, the jubilant new MLAs were sent home. Many waited weeks and months, without assignments, for their first session, only to discover that they would not see legislation until it was about to be tabled in the House. It was to be just the first of many hard lessons. Many who heard Douglas that day later believed their fate would have been different if Barrett and the cabinet had heeded his advice, particularly when it came to relations with the party.

Yet Barrett's party was far removed from the seasoned, united and deeply rooted CCF that Douglas had led to power in Saskatchewan. The BC NDP in 1972 was barely ten years old, still working out the negotiated marriage of the Co-operative Commonwealth Federation and Canadian Labour Congress' political arm that was intended to revive the social democratic movement after near-elimination in the federal election of 1958. The BC wing had replaced its leader twice since 1961, in contests that swung first toward labour-backed leaders and then away, losing three elections in the process. Many veterans like Alex Macdonald, who had served as federal CCF leader M.J. Coldwell's assistant in Ottawa during the Second World War, remained unreconciled to the merger with labour. Berger's stunning defeat in 1969 had crippled the labour wing of the BC party, effectively cutting off the government leadership from the labour movement. Inside the party, Berger's defeat had not only opened the door to Barrett's leadership, but also cleared the path for leaders of emerging social movements to take over the party machinery.

By the time volunteers began folding up the chairs at the party's 1972 convention, the BC NDP executive was firmly in the hands of this new wave of young, highly trained activists with a firm socialist outlook. Mike Lebowitz, an economist who moved to BC in 1965 to teach at Simon Fraser University, got active in the NDP in 1968 to assist in policy development for Berger. Strachan had campaigned on a series of promises that changed little from election to election, so the policy cupboard was bare. Lebowitz worked with Strachan to fashion a campaign program for Berger, drawing on a wide network of community activists, labour organizers and leaders in the women's movement who began to move into leadership positions in the organization.

The shift to the left gathered momentum at the 1971 convention, where a number of BC supporters of the Waffle Group, a left nationalist faction of the federal NDP, were elected to the executive. The Waffle Manifesto, so-called because it "waffled" on which segments of the national economy should be nationalized in an "independent socialist Canada," had been endorsed by hundreds of New Democrats including Barrett.

Although the Waffle Manifesto became a mainstay of W.A.C. Bennett's attacks on the NDP during the 1972 campaign, the national Waffle was already in retreat by 1971. The federal party's labour partners, especially key international unions like the Steelworkers, were incensed by the Ontario Waffle's attacks on their policies and demanded that David Lewis rein the group in. After a bruising federal leadership campaign that saw Waffle candidate James Laxer mount a surprisingly strong challenge, Lewis succeeded. The BC Wafflers, however, found more friends than enemies in the BC Federation of Labour, where militant leaders of smaller unions like Ray Haynes and George Johnston were in charge. A 1971 attempt by some Wafflers to challenge Barrett's leadership fizzled after an impassioned appeal from Steves, who warned that such an attack on the more left-wing Barrett would strengthen the hand of conservative labour leaders in larger international or American-based unions.

The new party leadership played a significant role in developing the 1972 platform, a moderate document that had many elements in common with party platforms in Saskatchewan and Manitoba. There was little difference between Barrett and the party leadership on these points. They parted company, however, on what power the party should exercise over government policy once the ballots had been counted. The experience of crafting a winning election platform proved exhilarating. If the party could direct the government agenda before the election, should it not direct government policy once in power? "We called on the government to follow party policy," Lebowitz recalled. "That was the tension right there. We had high hopes. There was the illusion that being a member of the party and the party being in government meant something."

More than seven hundred triumphant constituency activists rushed to Vancouver's Bayshore Hotel in November 1972 for the post-election convention, full of new proposals for government action. Only fifty of the four hundred policy resolutions made it to the floor, but two motions proposing new ministries—one for northern affairs and the other for women—won overwhelming support. When questioned about the women's portfolio, Barrett was unsympathetic. "Quite frankly," he declared, "I believe in people." Were women not people? The question remained hanging in the air.

Despite Barrett's hectic legislative agenda, the party rank and file had an unlimited supply of new initiatives to add to the government's list by the time they gathered for the 1973 convention. Membership had grown to more than 7,000 from 6,700 in 1972 and revenues rose to $81,000, enough to field six organizers. Two pre-convention issues of *The Democrat* were jammed with lengthy policy papers on the theme of "grassroots socialism." A report on the latest federal convention, the first since the complete ouster of the Waffle, sourly described the experience as a tour of "the finest political massage parlour in Canada." Hopes were higher west of the Rockies. An NDP government was bound to increase the public sector, one paper insisted, and expand public ownership of industry. "The questions the party must ask are: is this government strategy party policy? And is this socialism?" Clearly not, answered national Waffle leader Mel Watkins, in Vancouver for the convention, because Barrett had not nationalized any resource corporations. "If you're a socialist, that's what you're working towards," he told the *Sun*. "Barrett is clearly not doing anything to move people towards that, especially when he rejects the leftist direction of the party."

Among the backbenchers listening to Douglas that day in

1972 were three who epitomized the new and sometimes divergent currents in the party that had helped win the election and hoped to make change through Barrett's government. Steves, thirty-five, son of a Ladner farmer who became an activist to halt the loss of Fraser delta farmland when his family had been turned down for a permit to build a barn, had emerged as one of the most effective voices in BC's exploding environmental movement, organizing against oil port expansion at Cherry Point, Washington, and the dumping of raw sewage in the Fraser. Although a friend of the Bergers, Steves had supported Barrett for the leadership, believing him more left-wing and less controlled by labour's international unions. Gabelmann, twenty-nine, had been political action director with the BC Federation of Labour until his narrow August victory in a riding that had always been Liberal. A perfect three-way split had produced victory for the long-haired rookie in his first electoral outing. Intense, earnest and a committed activist with a broad network in the party, Gabelmann had grown up in Osoyoos, the son of a British single mother. She remarried a left-wing German orchardist who considered himself a "vegetarian communalist." A Berger supporter, Gabelmann emerged as a consistent voice for labour interests in the government, closely allied with some of the unions that gave Steves such concern.

Rosemary Brown, a social worker and television personality, was the outspoken representative of the NDP's fast-growing feminist movement. A newcomer to politics and the New Democrats, as well as the first black woman elected to any legislature in Canada, Brown had defeated a party veteran (and Berger ally) to win nomination in the two-member riding she shared with Norm Levi. Although the three MLAs would later collaborate at critical moments to oppose Barrett, each represented an emerging and different activist base in the New Democrats that Barrett ultimately could not control. The tension with labour went back to the party's founding and was a conflict Barrett knew well. The environmental movement was still in formation and the government's reforms in pollution control and park development gave it solid environmental credentials. The women's movement, however, became a daunting Barrett adversary that he understood poorly, if at all. The power struggle that resulted cost him dearly.

The call for a ministry of women's equality had been a highlight of the 1972 convention, a policy proposal fresh on the heels of the election victory that the party's women's activists believed would open the door to women's equality. The Royal Commission on the Status of Women had provided a checklist of initiatives in 1970 to achieve the task. But Barrett had made it clear that this ministry—like a similar proposal for a ministry for northern development—was a non-starter. The proposal quickly became a simple test of a New Democrat's commitment to feminism and to the party's right to determine policy, even in government. To oppose the ministry was to oppose women's equality.

Brown had used her response to the Speech from the Throne, nearly a month before Barrett's "Male Chauvinist Pig Award," to deplore Barrett's refusal to create the women's ministry. In an eloquent and wide-ranging address that marked her as a near-equal of Barrett as an orator, Brown touched on issues as diverse as urban sprawl and the flight of BC's blacks from slavery. She praised the government's early successes and then turned to her main concern. A long-promised bill of rights would be the beginning of the fight for equality, not the end, she warned. "To ensure the equality of all, Mr. Speaker, we must introduce, for a while at least, special measures to ensure the catching up of those groups in our society who have fallen behind because of the inequalities which until now have existed in it." In the long race for equality, "the inside lanes have gone to the white middle and upper class male in our society ... No human rights act, no bill of rights will ever be enough. And that is what the women—that 52 percent of our population who have been disadvantaged, discriminated against and oppressed—are saying, when they say to you, Mr. Premier, through you, Mr. Speaker, that they would like a Ministry of Women's Rights ... What better time than now, Mr. Speaker? What better government than this, to right those wrongs?"

Just four days before, the US Supreme Court had established access to abortion for women in its historic *Roe v. Wade* decision. The American women's movement had seen the Equal Rights Amendment to the Constitution—first introduced in 1923 to end discrimination between men and women—finally pass Congress in 1972 and begin the long battle for ratification. Canada's women's movement had become equally forceful, building a national campaign for abortion rights in defence of Dr. Henry Morgentaler and organizing nationally to participate in the work of the Royal Commission on the Status of Women, which issued its report in 1970. Its 167 recommendations had triggered organizing from coast to coast to win legislation implementing its program. In BC, women became active on many fronts, organizing unions, campaigning for child care, fighting for abortion rights or creating services as diverse as publishing houses, bookstores and UBC's new Women's Studies Program. For many women, advocacy turned quickly to political action and then to direct political engagement. That had been Brown's personal journey.

Only forty-two when she was sworn in, Brown had been born in Jamaica and immigrated to Canada to study at McGill in 1951. She trained as a social worker, eventually achieving a graduate degree and relocating to Vancouver, where she married psychiatrist William Brown. In 1965, her career received a dramatic boost when she was recruited to host a national television program on CTV. Brown had already been strongly influenced by left-wing and radical black leaders like Paul Robeson, Malcolm X and Angela Davis; her encounter with Betty Friedan's *The Feminine Mystique,* one of the basic texts of the women's liberation movement, marked a new turning point. As she recalled in her autobiography years later, she began reading voraciously about women's issues against the backdrop of the Royal Commission hearings, drawing lessons that pulled her toward political action and the NDP.

"Unless the women's liberation movement identifies and locks into the liberation movement of all oppressed groups, it will never achieve its goals," Brown said in 1973. "Unless it identifies with and supports the struggles of the poor, of oppressed races, of the old and of other disadvantaged groups in society, it will never achieve its goals, because to do so would be to isolate itself from the masses of women—since women make up a large segment of these groups." When Brown joined a group of women organizing to campaign for the implementation of the Royal Commission recommendations, the first project proposed was the creation of an Ombudsperson to advocate for women facing discrimination. With her media background and professional training, Brown was a natural choice. She quickly clashed with Vancouver–Little Mountain Social Credit MLA Grace McCarthy over family maintenance legislation, winning an even higher public profile.

With an election on the horizon, running for office was the obvious next step. As the BC Status of Women Council formulated a plan to endorse candidates who supported its recommendations, Brown found herself fielding proposals to run provincially from Dennis and Yvonne Cocke, then Barrett and then Marianne Gilbert, a New Democrat active in the Status of Women. Brown signed her NDP card in 1971. Although she had been courted by the Liberals, she realized that "as a democratic socialist I just would not fit into the Liberal party." Urged on by a network of feminist and left labour organizers, she finally decided to seek the nomination in Vancouver–Burrard, defeating former MLA Ray Parkinson in a jammed April nomination battle and winning election in the two-member constituency with Norm Levi just four months later. A star candidate with a high media profile and a broad base in the women's movement, she was on many lists as a potential front-bencher, likely in a portfolio that would let her drive a women's equality program. It was two weeks before Barrett called with the news she must have already surmised: her name had not been among the "dirty dozen" on Williams' brown envelope at The Only.

But why would she be, wondered many long-time New Democrats? She had been a party member little more than year, had defeated a veteran activist for the seat, had been backed by the Cockes and many of Berger's loyalists, and had a history of working with women in professional circles who carried Liberal Party cards. What's more, the idea of a women's ministry was only months old, proposed by the party's new Women's Rights Committee earlier that year and only adopted by convention after the election. The platform had dedicated two full pages to equal opportunity for women, promising to support the "drive for real equality between men and women" through measures to end discrimination on the job, in education and in pay rates. An NDP government would "work to have abortion made a matter to be determined by the woman in consultation with her doctor" and establish "free, community-controlled child care centres available twenty-four hours a day." Not a word about a women's ministry. Nonetheless, Brown's charisma and personal charm, combined with her determination to be the voice of the growing women's movement both inside and outside the party, made her the most serious challenger to Barrett's leadership inside the party.

Barrett's dismissive stand on the women's ministry, followed by the "Male Chauvinist Pig Award," locked the government into a symbolic conflict with the women's movement that dogged Barrett through to the 1975 election, overshadowing what Brown later termed the "phenomenal" gains women did make under his administration. The pig award, issued by the organization Brown had led for several years, confirmed that Barrett's judgment about Brown was sound in the minds of many New Democrats. They were content to see her on the backbench, where her main ally was Young, who also had been endorsed by Status of Women. Comox MLA Karen Sanford rose to Barrett's defence soon after Brown spoke on the Throne Speech, arguing that a women's ministry could be divisive. "The women's libbers have made women who were conditioned in our society to play an unfair and inferior role ... aware for the first time of the position they hold," Sanford acknowledged. The solution, however, was not a separate ministry but "a will to correct injustices."

The growing women's network in the NDP decided to redouble its efforts in the wake of Barrett's comments. Brown made no major decisions without consulting her circle of supporters, which now included Robin Geary, a friend she had met on the campaign trail who now served as her constituency assistant. Brown found election to government both "extremely frustrating and emotional," Geary recalled, with long weekly separations from her children, the legislative workload and the struggles within government. On the other hand "she had these thousands of letters that came in yearly from women who were supporting her, who were egging her on. She had this unbelievable appeal to women." Access to most of these planning meetings, whether of the Women's Rights Committee or Brown's circle of constituency advisors, was normally restricted to women, but not to card-carrying New Democrats. Even at convention, non-members were welcome at caucuses of the Women's Rights Committee, although they could neither speak nor vote on the floor.

Although Brown was the most visible representative of this growing movement, she was standing on the shoulders of scores of activists, mostly women, who had only recently taken up politics. These women, in turn, had countless additional connections to others outside the party: male and female, in the anti-war movement, community organizing and the wider left. This was a new power base in the NDP that party veterans had trouble understanding, never mind controlling.

Sharon Yandle, a graduate student and union organizer who was married to Lebowitz, was at the centre of this movement as chair of the Women's Rights Committee in 1972. The committee launched a newsletter called *Priorities*, a direct response to Barrett's statement that a women's ministry was "not a priority." They then began "organizing young women like crazy. We were organizing ourselves, all the women the same age, in our twenties. And we took the position that every woman is potentially a feminist—I remember that slogan—[which] meant that we would not align ourselves with any faction within the party."

In practical terms, that meant the WRC would nominate a slate for half of the positions on the party executive, in line with women's demand for parity, and invite other caucuses—labour, the Waffle, the north—to endorse those candidates. That tactic alone greatly increased the convention leverage of Women's Rights Committee activists, many of whom saw a women's ministry as an obvious tool to advance a women's agenda. To them, Barrett's refusal was a rejection of women's rights, not an administrative difference of opinion. "There were certainly men in the party, Barrett included," recalled Cynthia Flood, "who if not actively hostile were certainly disturbed by the prospect of women not only playing a supportive and indeed leading administrative role, but actually demanding, pushing for, articulating, things that had specifically to do with women."

Flood, a young mother who had come to Canada and then Vancouver when her American husband was drafted, found her way into the NDP from Trotskyist New Left politics, but quickly became engaged in *Priorities*, the WRC's new publication, and the movement for abortion rights. She and others discovered that work on the publication was a collective affair that produced new friendships and inspiration. The newsletter was run off by hand on a Gestetner, the inky stencils painstakingly typed out by volunteers who then walked round and round a large table at the party office collating each copy, stapling it and then stuffing the entire edition in envelopes for mailing. Editorial meetings were held in more comfort in someone's living room. Long distance calls to arrange regional coverage were costly and strictly rationed. The women found conventions, with their long hours, interminable caucuses and distant daycares especially exhausting, yet empowering. Flood was relieved at one conference, after a long wait to speak at the microphone, when a friend took her one-year-old daughter away "and amused her until I finished speaking." The entire convention process was draining, "but it was always very exciting to see women from other parts of the province and to discuss and share stories and feel reconnected."

The WRC experienced explosive growth, reinforced by a hired organizer who toured the province to recruit new members. By the end of 1973, the Lower Mainland committee had been joined by six other regional groups and all nine women proposed by the WRC to the provincial executive were elected, "a repudiation of the official slate, which had a few cross-endorsements but fewer women." The *Priorities* mailbag was full of letters both for and against a women's ministry. "Not that we are any less subject to sex-based discrimination than women in the Lower Mainland," wrote one northern reader, who wanted a northern ministry before a women's ministry, "but that our most crying needs in such vital fields as health care, educational opportunities and employment possibilities are the result of where we live, not what we are." Joining the drive for a women's ministry, however, were the BC Federation of Labour and a long list of other organizations.

Although Cocke eliminated pay discrimination in the hospital system in August 1973, triggering raises for thousands of women, the pace of change seemed glacially slow to a growing number of *Priorities* readers. "Despite the existence of policy sympathetic to women's rights," concluded one article, "the pattern of sexism extant in society and reflected in the government is also evident in the NDP itself." An editorial in the next issue was more optimistic: "Only through the political processes can our goals be attained and the NDP is the only party in BC committed to the concept of women's liberation." Nonetheless, more than one hundred women at a Vancouver policy conference had marched four blocks to the party's provincial office to confront Barrett personally about women's issues. As the year wore on with little additional legislation relevant to women, the committee began to lay plans for a major conference of BC women's organizations to put broader pressure on the government.

The 1973 convention came and went without action on a women's ministry. Despite a debate dominated by policy papers drafted by the left-leaning and feminist executive, including firm direction on how the Labour Code should be amended, Victoria seemed deaf to the party's directives. Hilda Thomas, a folksinger and veteran organizer from Point Grey, captured the mood in a satiric song on "little fat Dave's" approach:

> I am the man, the little fat man, who waters the policy,
> Women's rights and their long, long fight, it does not matter to me,
> Because I'm the man, the little fat man, who waters the policy.

Month after month, delegations of women would seek meetings to lobby cabinet ministers at their home ridings in Vancouver and in Victoria. Flood recalled one such meeting with Eileen Dailly, who had eliminated discrimination in the education curriculum but was otherwise quiet on women's rights. "She wasn't hostile. I would describe her more as astonished. She just found it hard to credit that there was this group of younger women in her office, saying these things. It was like she was almost bewildered." After eighteen months of NDP government, the futility of these discussions began to offend women's rights proponents. When human rights legislation failed to reflect WRC's input, the committee vented its anger in a 1974 letter to Brown. The committee's views had been presented "every way we know how—seriously, flippantly, pleasantly, unpleasantly, smiling, scowling, asking and shouting ... The only way we have not presented it is in poetry, song, interpretive dance and Gregorian chants. The sole responses we have had to our efforts have run the spectrum from absolute ridicule, contempt and hysterical outbursts at one end to, on the other end, blank uncomprehending stares that ask us: what is it you people want?" Although Brown had emerged as a hard-working and generally well-liked member of caucus, she had little to show for her efforts, either.

Even Cocke, whose wife was a strong ally of the committee, seemed to betray the cause in mid-1974 when he cautioned doctors against permitting late-term abortions. Yandle, with committee backing, slammed Cocke in a letter and a news conference outside the provincial office, not the usual stance of a party committee to its government in power. "To indicate I am not following party policy with respect to these issues is simply not true," Cocke said in a reply printed in *Priorities*. "I unequivocally support the position of our Party that abortions should be between a woman and her doctor. I also support our position that abortion should be removed from the Criminal Code."

As the 1974 convention drew closer, both the party and the premier prepared for what both knew would be a critical battle. Lebowitz advised readers of *The Democrat* that the Kamloops convention over the August long weekend would allow as much participation and decision-making by delegates as possible "rather than trying to direct it efficiently from the top down." The *Sun* picked up the theme, forecasting on the eve of the gathering that delegates would highlight "government failings in the fields of communication, labour, women's rights and ecology." Hans Brown's merciless critique of the government's treatment of the party in *The Democrat* served notice that the problem was much wider than the women's committee. The stage was set for a showdown.

On the second anniversary of Barrett's election sweep, six hundred New Democrats gathered in Kamloops for what all knew would be a decisive contest for the future of the party. A major women's conference in May had decided to propose a single resolution to the convention "containing an explanation of the situation of women, the Women's Movement, the connection between the liberation of women and socialism, and present NDP policy on women's rights ... to lay bare the real issues facing women and the real need for the government to implement women's rights policy without delay." The resulting document was eight pages single-spaced, a lengthy analysis of the fight for women's equality and its connection to the socialist movement. "A socialist government recognizes the inseparable link between women's liberation and socialism," the resolution declared, then made it clear Barrett's government had failed on all counts. "It is not socialist to alternately ignore and ridicule the demands of people who are fighting to achieve their own humanity ... A government that is sexist in its every word and deed has nothing to say to women and deserves nothing in return. Such a government is a sham and a fraud, unworthy of the support of socialists." After summarizing the policy actions that NDP conventions had approved since 1972, the resolution restated the demand for a ministry of women's rights, headed by a woman picked after "consultation with the Women's Rights Committee of the NDP."

The executive report to convention was only slightly more moderate. "The failure of the government to live up to the commitments that were made to the Executive and the continuing lack of caucus responsibility in relation to party policy is particularly saddening," the executive said. Lebowitz, who had already resigned as policy director, headed to the microphone to propose that the report be "accepted" by convention rather than "received." The chair promptly accepted the amendment and battle was joined. The hands were counted and it was clear the left had been routed. The executive report was rejected 368 to 202, the first of a series of "resounding votes of confidence in the government." Clearly, Barrett had been organizing too.

In vote after vote, pro-Barrett forces defeated his critics, sweeping the executive. Finally it was time to debate the women's resolution and both sides pulled out all the stops. "There is no magic formula," Barrett told the convention. "Words never changed anything. You must change people's attitude first." Hilda Thomas acknowledged the government's actions on human rights, workers' compensation and the minimum wage but rejected Barrett's claim that the NDP "has done more for women than any other government in North America." When at last it was time for the vote, it at first seemed too close to call. Then, the miracle: the women's rights resolution had passed by the narrowest of margins. "We had come prepared to lose," Yandle wrote later. Women delegates were ready at the back of the hall with signs saying, "This is just the beginning," to hold aloft as they stood together in defeat. But an attempt by Yvonne Cocke to refer the resolution to make amendments had been defeated, leaving an entire hour for convention delegates to talk the matter out. "A convention largely hostile to us, in which we and the government were at opposite ends of the pole, nevertheless said loudly and clearly that we are in the right and that they support us," the *Priorities* report concluded. "This is an important victory for us and strengthens our movement considerably." An unsigned article in the same issue hinted at the other undercurrents in a turning-point convention. In a party where "you are either for the government or agin it—no in-betweens allowed," the convention not only supported the women's committee but also endorsed aboriginal land claims and called, for the fourth convention in a row, for a ministry of the environment.

Although Barrett continued to reject calls for a ministry of women's rights, he did take steps to improve the government's capacity to expand women's equality. Soon after the convention,

Gene Errington, who had replaced Brown at Vancouver Status of Women, was hired as women's rights coordinator in Victoria. She was just one of many feminist activists who joined the government to implement reforms sought by the women's movement. As Brown later noted in her autobiography, Barrett's administration was the first provincial government in Canada to fund rape relief centres, transition houses and women's health collectives. Child care services fell short of the 24–7 platform commitment but the number of spaces in 1975 was more than 18,000, a far cry from the 2,500 that existed in 1971. Sexism was eliminated in textbooks. A new Human Rights Code, which prohibited discrimination on the basis of sex or marital status, was being enforced by a Human Rights Branch headed by Kathleen Ruff, who had run for the NDP and been a leader of Victoria Status of Women. None of these important gains, however, could erase the deep sense of betrayal the two-year battle over women's rights had produced in the women's movement.

There were those who saw the matter differently. "I want equality," wrote Vera Kristiansen in a post-convention letter to *The Democrat*. "I am opposed to special privileges" and opposed to a women's ministry that "would perpetuate the idea that women are unable to handle things on an equal basis. As I sit here on a windy, rainy day, writing this article, watching my five-year-old child sitting before a fireplace making popcorn ... I wonder what in the world would I rather be doing, or where I would rather be. Certainly I do not covet my husband's job at the sawmill. What a middle class idea of work some people must have." Errington, whose feminist credentials were not in doubt, later questioned the idea of a women's ministry from a practical standpoint. With a mandate that touched almost every ministry, but only a modest budget of its own, she worried a women's ministry would be reduced to begging resources and convening meetings, especially in the absence of a framework like the one provided by the Status of Women recommendations.

Despite the lingering debate over a women's ministry, the 1974 convention effectively ended the civil war in the NDP. By February 1975, Brown would launch her campaign to assume the national leadership of the NDP in the wake of David Lewis' resignation. Geary and a host of other activists across the country would turn their energies to this new crusade, carrying Brown to a final-ballot, second-place showdown with Ed Broadbent that stunned the party establishment.

In BC, however, it was clear that Barrett now controlled the party. When McNelly heard the news, he was elated. The turning point, he learned, was the defeat of Lebowitz's amendment, a floor strategy intended to "show the 'crazies,' as Barrett calls the radical wing of the party, that they were not going to be able to push the government around anymore." Eight months earlier, Barrett loyalist Harvey Beech had been deputized to take back the party, focusing on thirteen constituencies to ensure that "the right delegates went to the convention and that all understood that the party's basic goal was to get out and sell government programs, raise money and increase membership." Cabinet ministers were ordered to pay the cost of a hosted bar at a convention hospitality room and given specific assignments on the convention floor. Preparations for the executive elections were so comprehensive that eight of ten spots were filled by Barrett loyalists on the first ballot. McNelly concluded that after a year of victory celebration, of "sloppiness in the party, not caring who really ran it," Barrett had taken it over and now was poised for "one year of fighting the next election." With the party taken care of, Barrett turned his attention to government.

10: How They Forgot the Future

In the hectic hothouse of BC politics, the first week of March 1974 set a new benchmark for pandemonium. As the legislature hallways and backrooms seethed with intrigues about creating a new opposition party, Barrett was parrying Anderson's Chicken and Egg War, denouncing Nichols in obscene terms and seeking to prop up two key members of his front bench under unremitting attack by major business groups. Both Leo Nimsick, the affable mines minister, and Robert Strachan, Barrett's unsteady ally from the Berger–Barrett days, were facing corporate offensives that matched or exceeded the one endured by Stupich the year before. Barrett's success in getting the party under control, hiring skilled staff led by "the Exorcist" Marc Eliesen and drafting another positive budget brightened the NDP's hopes in 1975, but the fatigued caucus was quickly deflated again by a surprise performance by the leader of the opposition. Despite an effort to lighten the load of legislation upon cabinet, the year leading up to the election proved to be no less exhausting than any other in the term.

When Minister of Mines and Petroleum Resources Leo Nimsick finally got to his feet May 28, 1974, to begin second reading debate on Bill 31, the *Mineral Royalties Act,* he could hardly believe his good luck. Thirty-one times he had prepared to have the legislation called for debate, he told the House, and thirty times he had been disappointed as the royalty bill—already bounced from the 1973 fall session to 1974—sat stuck in the legislative gridlock created by the Chicken and Egg War, the budget filibuster and Strachan's ICBC woes. It had been three months since his bill received first reading during the opening salvoes of the Chicken and Egg War, weeks of relentless attack which Nimsick had sat out in proud silence, believing the appropriate time to reply was at second reading. Now, at last, Nimsick could defend his plan for royalties and "super-royalties" against all comers—the miners, promoters and prospectors who had been denouncing him and everything he stood for in a sustained campaign that was now more than a year old.

Despite the outcry, the NDP's planned reforms for the mining industry were modest. There was nothing like Macdonald's energy reforms, where Crown corporations were quickly established to tap new revenues, or Williams' acquisitions of forest firms, never mind the threatened government takeover of telecommunications, where the NDP platform promised a nationalization of BC Tel that was never carried out. The NDP's goals were simple: to extract reasonable royalties while securing secondary processing through construction of a copper or steel smelter. The goals were simple, but Nimsick's proposed solutions proved nearly impossible to explain.

Any royalties were offensive to BC's pampered miners, long the beneficiaries of one of the most lax regulatory regimes in North America. Reaping eye-watering profits after years of intensive investment, they were in no mood to share the wealth. Most BC ore was mined by a handful of foreign-controlled firms exporting to offshore markets. Foreign firms controlled 74 percent of copper production, most of which was destined for Japan. Kaiser Resources controlled 64 percent of coal production, while Fording, a subsidiary of Canadian Pacific, controlled almost all the rest. Cominco was on track to increase its share of lead-zinc production to 98 percent by 1975. Placer and Noranda, with their interlocking directorships, controlled 40 percent of copper production. These large companies did almost no exploration, leaving that heavy lifting to smaller firms.

Profits in BC's mining industry were among the highest in any Canadian industrial sector, generating profit as a percentage of revenue three times that of Canadian industry as a whole from 1962 to 1975. One researcher estimated Bethlehem Copper Corporation's book profits before taxes during that period "totalled an incredible 49 percent of its production revenue." Craigmont Mines was believed to have paid its $9-million in start-up costs in a single year. When the federal tax regime was factored in, mining had the lightest tax load of any industrial sector and the highest rate of profit. The multinational owners of these properties quickly retired their debts, enjoyed enormous capital gains and took hefty dividends.

Almost none of these profits flowed back to the BC treasury and never had. Taxes on the industry were so low after the Second World War that W.A.C. Bennett found himself voting with the CCF to raise them during a 1948 debate. Once premier, he hiked the mining tax to 10 percent, the maximum deductible from income tax under federal law, but further changes he attempted in 1957 resulted in a legal challenge, ultimately successful, that went all the way to the Supreme Court of Canada. The mining industry fought relentlessly to protect its virtually tax-free status. BC's open-pit ore bodies and lax environmental regulations—Social Credit allowed mining in parks, after all—boosted profits further. By 1972, the taxes that remained were declining as a share of costs and the basic regulatory structure retained its nineteenth century form intact.

But as a Cominco employee and Kootenay native, Nimsick personified the regional impact that made mining a political force. Between 1966 and 1975, the industry invested a staggering $3 billion in the province, making it the province's second-largest in capital investment. These expenditures were a big driver for small business and the service sector in the BC Interior. Mining was critical to regional centres like Trail, Prince George, Kamloops and Williams Lake and voters dependent on the industry were a significant factor in ten out of fifty-five provincial ridings. Since 1960, employment in BC's mines had more than doubled to eighteen thousand workers, especially in the booming copper sector where Japanese smelters were locking in long-term supply contracts. These jobs were not a large share of the provincial total, but where they existed they were the only game in town, a well-paid one at that. Many of the new mining communities saw entire subdivisions carved out of the wilderness, complete with community centres, rinks, new schools and hospitals.

Outside mining communities, however, there was growing anger at the industry's rapacious performance. The fact that BC's mineral wealth was extracted and exported, never refined, was offensive to many British Columbians. Nine of ten new copper mines opened since 1969 were producing for Japan, where all smelting, refining and manufacturing was centred. BC received neither royalties nor secondary manufacturing from the exploitation of its non-renewable resources. Pollution became an increasing concern. Gibraltar mine, opened in 1972, relied on such low-grade ore that only 0.5 percent of the rock became concentrate, leaving 41,790 tons of contaminated waste daily. Utah Mines, on Vancouver Island's Quatsino Inlet, was allowed to dump its waste in the ocean. Frank Richter, Social Credit mines minister in 1971, had allowed Western Mines to dump its untreated waste in Buttle Lake in Strathcona Park. When park officials expressed concern, the affected area was removed from the province's oldest class-A park.

The New Democrats had promised to tackle all these issues in the 1972 campaign platform, just as the mining boom began to slacken. A global increase in mining capacity was driving down prices and industry analysts predicted a sharp downturn in capital spending in the province until the discovery that year of a major new ore body at Afton near Kamloops. This was the situation confronting Nimsick and Hart Horn, his former campaign manager and now ministerial assistant, as they moved into the minister's Victoria offices in September. The government's mines branch, staffed largely with people outside from the industry, was a backwater even by Victoria standards, although it was responsible for all oil, natural gas and mineral production in BC. Barrett created a Resource Committee of cabinet that included Macdonald, Williams, Stupich, Hartley, Nimsick and later, Minister of Industrial Development, Trade and Commerce Gary Lauk to steer the work, but as the energy crisis intensified and the committee's strongest members focused on their own massive workloads, the work fragmented.

Cleaning up the environmental regulations fell to Williams, who announced an end to mining in parks in February 1973 and later released tougher environmental standards for other mines. Macdonald took over energy policy, implementing "thirty-second socialism." Stupich was more than preoccupied with agriculture. In the coming months, the New Democrats would split the mines branch into petroleum and mining sections, undertake dramatic changes in energy regulation, and implement sweeping changes in environmental regulations, but Nimsick was largely left to his own devices to implement the platform pledges on mining. With the arrival early in 1973 of deputy minister John McMynn, a professional mining engineer who had worked his way up from the rock face, Nimsick began to work on the issue in earnest.

The *Mineral Act*, introduced in the first 1973 session, raised alarm bells in Howe Street mining offices with its new requirement for an operations plan, including a reclamation plan and a safety plan, as a precondition to receiving a development permit. The law gave the minister the power to cancel leases not operating according to an approved plan and to take an equity position in a producing mine on behalf of taxpayers. "I do not believe that a resource that belongs to the people should be left entirely at the behest of the private sector throughout the province," Nimsick said, but more than one thousand industry employees in Vancouver expressed their violent disagreement in an emergency general meeting of the BC and Yukon Chamber of Mines. The legislation, particularly the threat of government involvement, would result in the "slow but certain death of the mining industry in British Columbia," the miners cried, dispatching Socred MLA Don Phillips back to Victoria for a four-hour marathon speech in opposition.

The government had backed up the *Mineral Act* with a *Mineral Land Tax Act* to reform the lease fees on mineral properties. Based on Social Credit legislation already in place, the bill raised the rates sharply and covered all mines, not just iron properties. Nimsick estimated the new lease fee structure would produce $15-million in 1974 and $25-million in 1975, far short of what the New Democrats believed should prevail under the royalty regime to come. With the two bills finally passed, McMynn and Horn, who had a commerce background, pulled together a staff committee to tackle royalties.

When Nimsick failed to meet his own fall 1973 deadline for royalties legislation, the business pages reported rumours of a cabinet split. Not at all, Nimsick replied lamely: "other legislation was given priority by the Queen's Printer." By February 1974, the bill was finally ready, receiving first reading in the middle of the chicken and egg controversy. A run of higher copper prices had put new wind in the industry's sails during the winter, driving profits up between 140 and 600 percent from 1972 and 1973. Less than 1 percent of total revenue was returned to the public, which owned the resource. If there was ever a time to increase royalties, this was it.

Nimsick's bill delivered, imposing a new royalty of 2.5 percent on net profit, reduced to 1 percent if the ore was smelted in BC. But he didn't stop there, adding three additional calculations on basic, net and gross value that were intended to capture revenue from internal sales among arms of the same company. Even more catastrophic in the industry's eyes was a so-called "super-royalty" designed to take 50 percent of any gain in revenue when the gross value exceeded the basic value by more than 20 percent. Even the minister himself was hard-pressed to explain the complex formula at the heart of the bill. It was "a disaster for the industry," said Mining Association President J.W. Tough. "We hadn't expected the excess profits tax. We were not consulted on this." Within days, the *Province* was headlining, "Mining Stocks Dive as Investors Bail Out."

The mining industry put the ninety-day wait between first and second reading to good use, mobilizing an outcry that touched the far reaches of the province. Investors might have been bailing out, but industry accountants remained at battle stations, churning out estimates of 1974 royalty revenue that jumped from $70-million one day to $137.7-million the next. Both Barrett and Nimsick, who met with industry leaders, firmly rejected demands that the "super-royalty" be dropped, but the miners were already shifting the debate to jobs, arguing that any royalty risked closing unnamed "marginal mines." On March 11 the Chamber of Mines held another emergency meeting, this time attended by 1,500 industry backers and representatives of all three opposition parties. A lobby to Victoria, complete with a brief describing the bill as "expropriation by taxation," was next on the agenda, followed by letter-writing campaigns, advertising and petitions. In April, the Mining Association's public relations machine began issuing a grim drumfire of announcements: cancelled exploration programs, delays in the opening of the Highland Valley copper project and threats by Newmont to shut down. The turmoil was a nightmare for NDP MLAs in mining constituencies.

By early April, the petition campaign was winning thousands

of signatures in the tiny mining towns north and east of Prince Rupert, where one miner from Granduc, who claimed to have been a Barrett supporter, warned "we didn't vote for these people to have them tax like that and find ourselves on pogey." Barrett was defiant, warning the industry that if they didn't accept the new royalty regime he was prepared to leave the ore in the ground for future generations that "have more sense."

"I would be happy to fight an election against all their ilk," the premier cried. He would get his wish.

Nimsick, a genial and no-nonsense figure, had seemed like a good choice to lead the fight for a new royalty regime. Long the party's mining critic, he had represented Cranbrook and the Kootenays as a CCF and NDP member of the legislature since 1949, working for Cominco between sessions. He soon found himself on the run, however, from an industry offensive that far exceeded anything attempted by the agricultural sector or insurance brokers. Nor did Nimsick inspire confidence in his colleagues. When Barrett used a spring recess of the legislature to squeeze in a quick trip to Japan along with Minister of Industrial Development, Trade and Commerce Gary Lauk, the prospect of a copper smelter was on the agenda, but Nimsick was left at home. He had more important things to do, he told reporters: "We can look after the copper smelter. We don't have to have Japs." The hapless minister was quickly compelled to issue an abject apology. In the battle with the mining companies, Nimsick was a lamb to the slaughter.

"The campaign that the mining industry waged against the NDP's mineral policies was one of the most powerful, sustained and effective efforts waged by an organized interest group in the recent political history of the province," wrote historian R.H. Payne. "Its major features were a very effective mobilization of a wide range of economic interest groups, a close working alliance with all three opposition political parties and a highly organized propaganda effort conducted through the province's mass media ... [a] striking illustration of the way in which economic power can be translated into political power."

The rapid-fire series of announcements gave the impression of a capital strike against the province, with billions of dollars of new investment thrown into limbo by the legislation. The size of the economic impact, as calculated in the public relations offices of the mining companies, spiralled higher and higher. First eight new mines were threatened, then fifteen new deposits were deemed at risk: $2 billion in new capital investment vanished—although it was never clear which if any of the new projects would have proceeded in any scenario. Analyses by the UBC head of mineral engineering were titled "How Bill 31 Turns Ore into Waste," and "They Forgot the Future."

Typical was the June meeting of Bethlehem Copper shareholders, who gathered one-hundred-strong in the auditorium of the firm's Ashcroft offices, overlooking one of the largest undeveloped copper ore bodies in North America. This ore would remain in the ground, said company president Patrick Reynolds, in the face of a government that had "the deliberate, sinister intention of dealing a mortal blow to the mining industry." Uncertainty created by Nimsick's bills was so acute, Reynolds said, that Bethlehem was unable to determine what its first quarter earnings were.

The province's dailies threw away all pretense of objectivity. "Kill Bill 31, keep miners on the job," shouted the headline on a full-page opinion piece in the *Vancouver Sun*; the same issue had a full-page ad from the Mining Association of BC, which predicted the bill would "wipe out jobs, payrolls ... even whole communities." Nimsick primly declined to reply to these attacks, issuing a single letter in April that was completely ignored. The disaster was compounded just before second reading when Ottawa's budget disallowed provincial royalties as an income tax deduction, effectively doubling the impact of the royalties. (The budget was defeated and the country soon went to the polls.) By the time Nimsick rose in the House on second reading, "the notion that the NDP government, through either ignorance, incompetence or ulterior ideological motives, was out to destroy the second most important segment of the provincial economy seemed almost indisputable," Payne concluded.

The legislative session, already among the longest and most acrimonious in BC's history, was once again paralyzed by an opposition filibuster. Bennett demanded the bill be suspended for six months. The corridors buzzed with rumours of a cabinet split. Gordon Gibson, fresh from his by-election win, spoke for three days. Finally Barrett rose to his feet to defend the bill in a speech that stunned the House and reaped a chorus of condemnation in the media. "The poor little mining companies," Barrett cried, rubbing his hands together as he recited the previous years' double- and triple-digit profit increases. "I can just see them in the boardroom rubbing their hands together saying 'Bring on more socialism—we've never had it so good.'" He crumpled one full-page ad from the Mining Association and tossed it over his shoulder, folded another into a paper hat that he perched on his head as he ridiculed the miners' threats to pull out of the province. The 5 percent base royalty was the same that average taxpayers paid in sales tax, Barrett said, and Nimsick "should be mildly chastised for not asking for enough ... We want a return for the people of this province." Editorialists deplored the speech, but supporters were "greatly cheered by the stuff," McNelly wrote, "and god knows they need to be cheered up." But Barrett's speech lost much of its impact when he was forced to admit some of his profit figures were wrong. Nimsick's sudden decision to bring in major clarifying amendments a few days later finally reduced uncertainty for mining companies, but came too late to blunt the impact of their offensive.

The New Democrats passed Bill 31 on June 19, virtually the

last act of the marathon spring session. In the coming months, driven in part by political objectives and in part by a new global slump in mineral prices, BC mining companies cut investment and exploration, laying off one thousand workers by year's end. Renewed efforts by Nimsick and Barrett to find a compromise would be rebuffed; the miners had dedicated themselves to the NDP's defeat. The 1974 spring session finally ended June 20 with a vote to change the procedural rules to limit debate on estimates. Bill Bennett walked out in protest.

More than one hundred pieces of legislation had been passed, most of it implementing substantive changes to government's finances and services. New laws touched every major economic sector. Social services were transformed. Every driver, tenant and injured worker enjoyed expanded protection. And despite promises of paid transportation, food and accommodation, a threatened mass protest by the Majority Movement in Victoria June 21 and 22 fizzled out, with only a few hundred demonstrators pitching tents on the legislature lawns. The New Democrats mocked the organizers, but the collapse of the Majority Movement pointed to a much more serious challenge: the remarkable revival of Social Credit. A major forest industry poll slipped to McNelly in the spring of 1974 showed that 44 percent of the electorate was undecided on how it would vote, a sign that the next few months would determine the New Democrats' fate. The New Democrats took heart from the decided vote: 33 percent for the NDP, 16 percent for Social Credit, 7 percent for the Liberals and 2 percent for the Conservatives.

After the most brutal session in recent provincial history, Barrett's team was holding its own. The bigger story, however, was the number of votes available for the party that could unite the non-NDP vote. As McNelly watched the 1974 spring session finally flicker out June 20, the empty tents sitting forlornly on the legislature lawn, he was pleased to see Ernie Hall document the session's unprecedented personal attacks, rumour-mongering and disinformation, before he finally moved to adjourn. "The campaign of fear" driven by a Majority Movement leadership that believed BC "can no longer afford the luxury of political parties" weighed on McNelly. The sense of optimism that had buoyed him earlier that day ebbed away and "I began to get very sad. I knew that the real fight was beginning and would only intensify from here on to the next election. It's not going to be very pleasant." As Barrett headed off to Japan to talk coal exports and trade, reporters noted he had lost seventeen pounds. Despite his relentless personal efforts, the New Democrats' hard work was not winning public approval. Nimsick's drubbing at the hands of the mining industry had been demoralizing. Even more disturbing for New Democrats was Bob Strachan's prolonged ordeal at the helm of Insurance Corporation of BC. The NDP's elder statesman was becoming a weak link in the front bench, the daily Question Period target of the opposition's heaviest hitters.

When the Chicken and Egg War was raging and Nimsick was preparing to finally guide Bill 31 through the House, ICBC launched public auto insurance sales a scant year after its enabling legislation was passed. On March 1, 1974, every driver in the province was required to carry Autoplan insurance. To celebrate the good news, Barrett's staff scheduled the premier for a tour of the Crown corporation's new Vancouver headquarters. But when reporters turned up to observe, Bob Strachan's executive assistant called police to have them evicted, telling them sternly that this was a "family affair" and they were there simply "to make a buck, to sell papers." Despite Barrett's intervention to welcome the media to view "the people's insurance company," the confrontation produced a harvest of negative headlines. Barrett's assessment at the end of the tour was, "Every British Columbian should be proud of this operation. When you think of what is really involved, it is amazing you don't have a thousand more mistakes than you have had."

Barrett's unfortunate phrasing distracted from the truth of his statement. Just a few months after the passage of enabling legislation in 1973, ICBC had begun selling insurance under the leadership of chief executive officer Norman Bortnick, a veteran of Saskatchewan's public insurance system. Bortnick was able to meet Barrett's aggressive March 1 deadline to implement public auto insurance. The private insurance industry, however, had fought the New Democrats every step of the way. Strachan was already confronting a BC Supreme Court challenge mounted by thirty-seven insurance companies seeking to have the new public monopoly ruled beyond the powers of the provincial government. Local insurance agents were continuing their own campaign and body-shop owners had gone to war to win the right to impose a surcharge on ICBC rates.

To make matters worse, the New Democrats could not agree on how the finances of ICBC would unfold. Strachan's January declaration promising cash refunds to anyone who could prove Autoplan rates had increased costs backfired. About 15 percent of drivers appeared to be eligible. The opposition, sensing Strachan's weakening grasp of the finances, made him a daily target. Bill Bennett had denounced the ICBC administration as "recklessly incompetent" and predicted a first-year deficit of $30-million. Strachan countered it would suffer a "nominal loss or break even." Barrett, in a radio interview, split the difference, predicting a loss of about $18-million. By the end of May, the premier was proposing to divert gas tax and licence fees to ICBC to produce flat rate premiums, regardless of the number, age, gender or home community of drivers. When ICBC cut insurance agents' commissions to 7 percent from 9, they briefly went on strike until Strachan threatened to fire them. Each week produced a new ICBC headline, often driven by leaks to *Sun* reporter Jes Odam. Drivers, however, showed their growing confidence in ICBC by increasing claims by a fantastic 25 percent over 1973 levels.

Like Levi and Dailly, Strachan had learned to his sorrow how quickly Barrett could make an announcement, such as a new rate policy or estimated annual loss, without conferring with the minister concerned. ICBC seemed to be a chronic underachiever, its rates low but not low enough, and its losses high, usually higher than Strachan had forecasted. Week after week, month after month, Strachan confronted some new crisis at ICBC from a threatened strike by insurance agents, to a lengthy shutdown by ICBC's union that lasted one hundred days. The contract ordered by an independent industrial inquiry commission in the early summer of 1975 saddled ICBC with compensation increases of 39.5 percent over twenty-eight months.

McNelly, who encountered Strachan at a house party as the spring session stumbled into June, was moved by the veteran leader's evident fatigue and reflective mood. The man who had been four times defeated by W.A.C. Bennett recalled the misery of being on the receiving end of the Socred leader's oratory, when the government backbenchers were roaring in glee and "you felt lower and lower until you knew you'd been crushed, just run over." A few days later, McNelly watched from the gallery during "an evening charged with feeling and sadness" as Bob McClelland "nearly knocked Bob Strachan's head off" with a charge that Strachan had lied to the legislature about an alleged conflict of interest on the part of an ICBC vice-president. If he had been lied to, Strachan replied, he would fire the executive, and did so the next day; that crisis passed, but others, often driven by plain brown envelopes passed to interested reporters, quickly took its place. In some respects Strachan's achievements at ICBC were to prove even more durable than the ALR, but by the summer of 1975 the Nanaimo carpenter who had emigrated from Glasgow forty years before was a spent force.

After a year of relentlessly negative media coverage, it seemed like the New Democrats' luck had finally turned in the early days of 1975. As the legislature sleep-walked through debate on the Throne Speech, the CBC broadcast a sensational Sunday-night documentary called *The Reckoning* that disclosed the existence of a secret committee set up at BC Hydro during W.A.C. Bennett's administration to cover up massive cost overruns on the Columbia River dam projects. The CBC alleged that this committee, which included some of W.A.C. Bennett's most trusted advisors, had reported directly to the premier. Its task was to hide damning evidence about the true cost of his most cherished initiative by reallocating spending to other Hydro projects or even other government departments. The Columbia River project had to remain "on budget"—and did.

In the wake of Watergate, allegations of a cover-up on the Columbia River Treaty, a pet Bennett initiative that had dominated BC politics during the 1960s, had explosive political potential. The story took the New Democrats by surprise. While Williams parried Question Period probes by Liberal Pat McGeer, who had his own reasons for minimizing the damage the revelations could inflict on Bill Bennett's Socreds, government officials ransacked Victoria's files for a smoking gun. Within forty-eight hours there was a discovery: an entire book, marked confidential, containing reports of the committee, which had been chaired by BC Hydro co-chair Hugh Keenleyside. Among those involved was Einar Gunderson, W.A.C.'s former finance minister, key fundraiser and a Hydro director.

Barrett's team was on a high as the premier paged through the book, gleefully reading damning passages aloud. The confidential documents left no doubt that "reallocation" had been recommended. Here, at last, was a chance to play offence, to remind voters about Social Credit's mishandling of what many British Columbians believed was a sell-out of the province's energy future at the expense of hundreds of kilometres of flooded valleys. But had the cover-up scheme really been implemented? Williams, who dramatically released the documents at a Friday news conference, could not be sure. He dispatched Stuart Hedley, a trusted aide, to Vancouver to dig deeper. Hedley quickly called for backup. Barrett, then just days from tabling his budget, called Peter McNelly and ordered him to fly to join Hedley. As a seasoned journalist, McNelly knew that some would call the Socreds' "reallocation" a reasonable strategy if it could be argued that these related projects benefited from the Columbia scheme. "Others would call it a blueprint for lying to the public."

Hedley, a reputed "hatchet man" unafraid to play hard ball, tried to brief McNelly as the two men drove directly to BC Hydro's elegant glass and turquoise tower at the top of Burrard Street, where the secret committee's records were ready for review. Based on what Hedley had told him, McNelly believed the files could contain information that would finish the Bennetts and Social Credit as a political force. He had an assignment any journalist would envy: direct access to the province's most sensitive files with a mandate to report back to Barrett and Williams by Monday morning. Spread out on a Hydro boardroom table were the corporation's board minutes and ten reels of microfilm containing the entire record of Columbia Treaty spending. They explained their assignment in careful, non-partisan terms to a nervous Hydro official and sat down to work.

The first reel of microfilm took McNelly into the deepest secrets of Hydro's short history. Canada had sold the Columbia's vast energy potential in 1964 for a single lump sum payment to BC of $273-million that Bennett claimed would pay for the cost of two major dams and half of the cost of the massive Mica Dam. This cash was the sole return BC would receive for thirty years of the "downstream benefits" American utilities would reap in the form of extra power generation capacity. Yet within a year of the treaty, according to the microfilm, the shortfall on construction costs was already $180-million over and above the inflation pressures Bennett instructed Hydro to absorb. "I was incredibly excited that night as I learned for the first time everything Keenleyside learned and the order he had learned it," McNelly wrote. "I felt I was entering his private past, getting to know how his mind worked, uncovering the secrets he had never revealed to anyone but a select few." McNelly learned later that Keenleyside was at work that same day drafting his own response to the CBC piece with private coaching from *Province* publisher Paddy Sherman, who went so far as to insert Keenleyside quotes into a story filed by Victoria legislative reporter Barb McLintock. At his Sunday news conference, Keenleyside categorically denied any wrongdoing and launched a bitter personal attack on Williams.

But the memos, marked "secret," "confidential" or even "strictly private, personal and confidential," were piling up on McNelly's desk. One letter to Bennett from Keenleyside disclosed "the deficit and [attached] a secret memorandum showing how all this developed." With Keenleyside's help, Bennett had weathered a 1966 election debate on the treaty, ordering Keenleyside to ignore inflation in his cost estimates, to delay construction of the Mica Dam, and to shift costs to other accounts to keep the Columbia overruns secret. All of Keenleyside's attention was focused on managing the massive dam projects, driving forward expropriation of countless homes in the flood zone, tallying the environmental costs and in McNelly's words, treating "even the human beings in the Arrow Lakes area as just another administrative problem."

McNelly and Hedley worked through the weekend, sleeping just two and a half hours on Sunday night before flying back to Victoria, their files bulging with more than two thousand documents. Barrett, who had been "rubbing his hands" in elation at the CBC revelations, now "cautioned us against any early release of things," turning the files over to John Wood, his executive assistant, and cabinet members Macdonald, Lauk, Lorimer and Williams for study. The days turned to weeks and then months, despite Williams' initial pledge of a full public inquiry. By early

April, Marjorie Nichols was speculating that Williams "has now had time to sift through BC Hydro's files and has emerged empty-handed." The real explanation was more complex. There was plenty of ammunition in the files, but an attack that might have been devastating in 1973, when W.A.C. was still on the scene, had less impact on his son. More importantly, Barrett's administration was shifting, at last, from chaotic headlong charges to longer-term strategy. Barrett was seeking to control events rather than react to them. A now more seasoned and risk-averse government was turning away from old battles to prepare for new ones, particularly an election that Social Credit firmly believed would come within months.

Recruiting McNelly had been Barrett's first response to the sense of crisis that had begun to engulf his administration at the end of his first year in office. McNelly proved an adept problem-solver, turning a controversy over property assessments into a long-term win for New Democrats. By the end of 1974, McNelly had added the new promotional publication *BC Government News* to his responsibilities. Soon after hiring McNelly, Barrett had moved to take control of the party organization. Beech's lockdown of the party executive at the 1974 convention was the result. By December 1974, *The Democrat* had been transformed from a laundry list of government shortcomings to a cheerful update on developments in Victoria.

Barrett's next target was caucus, where loyalist Brian McIver was installed as executive assistant to the caucus executive. A delegation headed to Saskatchewan to see how caucus and government communicated there. The delegation, which included Steves and Port Alberni MLA Bob Skelly, was amazed to see backbenchers working on legislation with ministers well before the drafting stage. They urged similar procedures in BC. Tensions in caucus were eased as well by Rosemary Brown's decision to seek the leadership of the federal NDP, recently vacated by David Lewis. When Oshawa MP Ed Broadbent declared he would not run, Brown met with Barrett and secured a lukewarm endorsement as BC's "favourite daughter," but Barrett reserved the right to endorse his old rival Stu Leggatt, now in Parliament, if he came forward.

When Leggatt bowed out and Broadbent suddenly jumped back into the race, Barrett quickly switched his support to Broadbent, prompting Allan Fotheringham to conclude that Brown "is so forceful in her feminism that the premier walks in a great circle around her for fear some girl germs might get on him." Brown made up for the slight by repeating her call for a ministry of women's equality, acidly telling reporters "the premier is a rational person. However, some people think more slowly than others." The breach with Brown could not be healed, but the federal race, in which she ran a surprisingly strong second to Broadbent, effectively took her off the provincial scene.

With the party subdued and the caucus on a tighter leash, Barrett had turned his attention to government itself, recruiting an experienced "policy advisor" from the NDP administration of Manitoba Premier Ed Schreyer to impose order on the budget and legislative agenda. Marc Eliesen, a commerce and economics graduate, had worked for the federal finance ministry until Tommy Douglas recruited him to be research director for the federal NDP in 1968. Schreyer had soon appointed him deputy minister of finance and then planning advisor to his cabinet. Barrett tried to recruit Eliesen in 1973, but the man who became known as "the Rabbi" or even "the Exorcist" to his BC colleagues refused to move until Schreyer was re-elected later that year. When he landed at last in Victoria in the summer of 1974, Eliesen discovered that Barrett had not warned anyone he was coming. He quickly acquired offices, hired people and "started to provide some systematic order with regard to how things came before cabinet, what came before cabinet, decisions recorded."

"I hope he's as good as he's cracked up to be," McNelly wrote, "because there can't be any more bullshitting around. It's all for real." Eliesen was impressed by the strength of Barrett's front bench, Barrett's political will and the breadth of the government's achievements. He quickly forged a close personal and professional friendship with Barrett, within weeks supplanting finance deputy Gerald Bryson and even Williams as one of Barrett's closest advisors. He took control of budgeting and reined in spending. Eliesen's stops in Ottawa and Winnipeg had given him a national network without peer in Victoria. He was adept at "consultation, the exchange of rumours, the bluffs, the calculated disclosures that are not disclosures at all, the subtle trading on status and influence," McNelly recorded. "Marc is good. He's tough. He's a power person."

There was a camaraderie on Barrett's team Eliesen had not experienced before, a lighthearted, informal atmosphere that contrasted with the deep sense of mission, purpose and commitment that drove most of cabinet. Then there was the distinctive BC NDP culture—some cabinet ministers still called each other "comrade"—that took Eliesen by surprise. Even more astonishing was Barrett's insistence on handling all the government's media relations. "I told him, 'look, you should only be associated with good news. If there is some negative news that has to be articulated, you've got cabinet ministers, you've got bureaucrats." Barrett listened, nodded, and ignored him.

Eliesen made more headway on other fronts, convincing Barrett he should hire Vancouver Status of Women organizer Gene Errington to lead a special policy unit on women's issues. The 1975 Throne Speech, largely written in Eliesen's office, included a commitment to ensure appropriate celebrations of International Women's Year. One by one, the government's deputy ministers learned it was no longer possible to drive new spending programs through Barrett's Treasury Board. The growing resentment of Eliesen around Barrett's cabinet table was proof of his impact.

The new sense of calm invigorated the Barrett team. "There is no doubt that a mood of aggression, confidence, happiness and plain good times is back," McNelly wrote. Ever since a July vacation had ended the stream of misery that dominated the first half of 1974, Barrett had been operating with growing confidence. A fall trip to China with business and labour leaders from the forest sector had generated a sheaf of positive clippings. Another forest industry poll conducted at the end of the year showed the NDP with 32 percent of decided support compared to 24 percent for Social Credit and 23 percent for the Liberals. Barrett quickly worked up a list of Social Credit MLAs he hoped to defeat in an election he thought might come in twenty months.

It was not all clear sailing. Eileen Dailly's sudden January 17 dismissal of Stanley Knight, the education commissioner hired to replace Bremer, provoked derision among government critics and dismay among New Democrats. Declaring that Knight had failed his probation, Dailly gave Knight four hours to clean out his office and then approved the dismissal of Knight's entire policy group. "Dailly problems in education," joked an anti-NDP billboard on the Island Highway, but no one was laughing among the thousands of teachers who had supported the party in 1972 and now saw the prospect of systemic reforms evaporating. Barrett had fired Bremer on television without notice; now Dailly followed up with Knight's termination. What was Dailly's answer if asked what her education policies were? McNelly asked Barrett. "I'd respect her a lot more if she'd just say 'none of your goddam business,'" the exasperated premier shot back. The media coverage quickly died away, but the controversy overshadowed Barrett's successful effort to turn back a federal proposal to impose a tax on BC's natural gas exports.

The Throne Speech February 18 was a lacklustre affair, a quick review of the New Democrats' 1974 achievements with modest commitments for improvements. The legislative agenda would include election finance reform, amendments to various existing laws and little else. The press gallery, which had been joined for the occasion by luminaries like Fotheringham and Nichols, quickly filed and adjourned to the Empress Hotel's Bengal Room to drink the night away. The mood was very different from two years earlier, when the New Democrats were blowing the cobwebs off the legislature and business was booming.

It was clear the global economy had stalled. Double-digit inflation was undermining real earnings and unemployment began to rise. Despite his 1974 campaign rejection of wage and price controls, Prime Minister Pierre Trudeau was under increasing pressure to impose a solution to inflation. Real economic growth in Canada was stagnating at the lowest level in twenty years. In British Columbia, where employment growth continued, unemployment grew even faster. Wages, however, continued to rise as quickly as inflation. By the end of 1975, average weekly wages in Canada would be 13.4 percent higher than they were in January, as were prices. It was against these realities that Eliesen had to craft Barrett's third budget.

Barrett's Treasury Board, which included Williams, Strachan and Ernie Hall, had begun curbing spending in a series of meetings late in 1974. The goal was to eliminate a looming deficit before the 1975–1976 budget. Revenue had exceeded expectations but spending was up even more. In January, Barrett ordered a spending freeze, halting new hiring and cutting discretionary spending. This new, prudent mood was belied, however, by the New Democrats' third record-breaking budget, a "job security" budget forecasting a year-end surplus in 1976 despite another record total expenditure of $3.2 billion. Annual provincial spending was now $1 billion higher than it had been when Barrett took office, a remarkable jump that mirrored similar but less dramatic increases in other provinces. Barrett's 1975 program was seeking to achieve "great economic equality and social justice." School taxes were reduced, renters' tax credits increased to $100, small business taxes were cut and municipalities promised a share of growing natural gas revenue.

Gas taxes were raised to keep transit fares down. Large business did not fare as well. The corporation capital tax exemption was raised but the rate of tax on utilized capital was doubled.

Bennett quickly rose to denounce the budget as "the most politically expedient and most irresponsible and dangerous budget which has ever been laid before the people of British Columbia in recent years." With commodity prices headed down and resource revenues following, Bennett predicted a deficit at the end of the budget year. His attack was lost in the continuing coverage of the Columbia River affair, then ended altogether. Chastened by the length of the1974 session, Barrett had imposed new rules that limited debate on estimates to 135 hours in all and forty-five sessions, still one of the longest such allocations in a provincial legislature. (The British Parliament in Westminster allowed only twenty-nine sessions for estimates, despite its 625 members.) With no major legislation coming forward, reporters had little to report beyond the droning questions and answers of budget estimates. By the end of March, McNelly found things "very calm now ... The hysteria of last spring seems to be entirely gone. No longer does it appear that we are making mistakes every day. Instead, we have the offensive on some major issues." Opposition attacks, in one case based on a forged letter, had blown up in Social Credit's hands. Polling showed the Socreds falling back to a tie with the Liberals. Worst of all, Bennett's own plodding performance was gaining unwelcome attention.

A razor-sharp mid-February profile of the "Young Bennett" by *Globe and Mail* writer Christina Newman classed the forty-two-year-old Socred leader as "good-looking in the manner of a television actor who gets small parts on *The Waltons* or *Little House on the Prairie*, well-dressed with a healthy tan and puzzled hazel eyes. But there is something eminently forgettable about him. Five minutes after a two-hour face-to-face conversation, it's impossible to be sure you would recognize him in the Hotel

Vancouver's Timber Club dining room among the lunchtime middle managers."

A businessman interviewed by Newman confirmed that "Bennett could have any amount of money from big business that he needed without having to beg a dime." But then, sitting back in his leather chair overlooking Vancouver Harbour, he conceded he was not sure money would be enough. "Dave Barrett has a hold on the imagination of the people in this province despite what the papers say and despite all the hot water he's been into. He's warm. Shrewd. And my God, he's funny. Bill Bennett's so scared of that he doesn't even like to go into the legislature. If you get the two of them on a platform in a campaign, it will be like putting a boy with a peashooter up against a man who's been firing a howitzer for all his long hard life."

McNelly found it easy to agree. Day after day, Barrett was dominating the House, a performance his aide found "pure art, the spontaneous creation of a political reality." Strachan, who knew more about opposition than anyone on either side of the House, said "he has never seen the collapse of the opposition such as we have seen during the premier's estimates." The New Democrats underestimated Bennett. If he was losing the debate in the House, he would have to leave the legislature to find a more favourable battleground. But how to leave? Bennett's strategy showed that the Social Credit leader had studied Barrett as closely as Barrett had studied his father.

The estimates debate smouldered on like the fuse on a time bomb through March, then April, finally sputtering to an end at the forty-five-session mark on the evening of May 13. With the subsequent explosion, McNelly wrote, "everything is changed." Barrett was put on the defensive, the Liberal Party was destroyed and Bill Bennett emerged as the undisputed leader of the free enterprise coalition, escaping the House to a round of massive rallies electrified by his calls for "freedom." All sides had been watching the clock run out. Tension rose as the 135-hour mark came and went. Debate could not end until that point or forty-five sittings, whichever came later. The forty-fifth sitting concluded as the House adjourned for the weekend May 9. Liberal leader David Anderson demanded clarification of Standing Order 45 (3), which required the remainder of the estimates to be approved "forthwith." The rule should be suspended, Anderson suggested, but Speaker Gordon Dowding disagreed. The stage was set for closure when estimates resumed the following Tuesday evening.

The intervening weeks in the House had not been good ones for Bennett. Barrett so effortlessly brushed off the Socred leader's challenges to his estimates that Fotheringham styled him a political version of hockey legend Gordie Howe. The opposition no longer had the ability to "filibuster in debate," Barrett said testily. He then imposed a schedule limiting the hours of debate for each ministry. If the public was outraged by these manoeuvres, there was no sign of it. Clearly Bennett needed a strategy to end the debate on his terms. Closure offered him an opening.

There was no sign of the coming storm during a sleepy afternoon of debate May 13. The House adjourned for dinner in good humour after approving a bill to eliminate discrimination against women in a host of statutes, though Minister of Mines and Petroleum Resources Nimsick had been uncertain about his own ministry's proposal to allow women to work underground. "There's no place in the mine, really, down underground—except maybe in certain instances—where women can compete," Nimsick had argued to growing laughter. "They're not physically built the same as men. And thank God for that!" When the House resumed in committee for estimates more than two hours later, the tone had changed. Chairman Hartley Dent briskly read Standing Order 45 (3) and then passed two votes in less than a minute despite shouted objections and points of order from the Social Credit benches. Bennett and Phillips refused to take their seats. "You can't afford to tell the truth," Bennett shouted. "You want to deny democracy by the clock." Speaker Gordon

Dowding hurried to the chair to restore order, ordering Bennett and Phillips to withdraw. When first Phillips and then Bennett refused, Dowding ordered the sergeant-at-arms to expel them.

Bennett walked out into a media scrum, free at last. He would leave the legislature, he declared, where democracy was being throttled, to tour the province. "Until the government relents and allows free discussion of estimates, I will take the estimates to the people." A Socred rally the next day drew six hundred; one in Kelowna soon after more than one thousand. He would never "freely or willingly" surrender the legislature's right to control the public purse, Bennett vowed. "This government has a history of overspending unparalleled in this country. All we want is time to debate the $2.3 billion in spending." Barrett was seeking authorization to spend $6,000 a second, Bennett calculated. His battle cry: "Not a dime without debate."

The Socreds' decision to force a confrontation over an obscure procedural issue had been taken over the dinner hour that fateful Tuesday evening, Fotheringham wrote later. "It's a brilliant gamble if it works. Bennett sprinting off on what he feels is an issue that will grab the public while the government is still tied down in an incomprehensible procedural wrangle that it has not yet been able to explain. If the gamble works and the bushfire catches, it's game over." There was demoralization on the NDP front bench. The government had been boxed in, McNelly observed glumly, and the Socreds rejected a belated government attempt at compromise two days later. In a late-night pub session, he found Harold Steves, Port Alberni MLA Bob Skelly and a couple of reporters "elated, absolutely manic" about the collapse of the compromise plan, convinced like Barrett that voters would punish Bennett for his "anarchic" behaviour. Really? That evening's session had ended with bitter shouting matches between NDP and Social Credit MLAs in the legislature hallways, but there was no doubt, McNelly concluded, that "the rules debate has been resolved in favour of the opposition."

The "not a dime without debate" confrontation gave Bennett crucial momentum and stalled Barrett's efforts to regain the initiative. Both parties now focused only on the coming election, which all knew now could not be more than eighteen months away. With his legislative strategy in ruins, Barrett and his caucus headed to Vancouver for the NDP's annual convention, where the main newsworthy development was the failure of Barrett's slate to sweep every provincial council spot. Despite a bomb scare and a procedural battle to allow aboriginal leader George Watts to give a lengthy unscheduled speech from the floor, the seven hundred delegates at UBC's Thunderbird Gym were "pulling together," according to *The Democrat*. The convention program contained messages from Barrett and others summarizing the party's history and the government's achievements. "It was not until 1972 that the interests of the ordinary people became stronger politically than the interests of the owner-elite," the booklet said. "It has been a long and bitter struggle for that victory here in British Columbia and we must not let it slip away back in to the hands of big business interests."

"Socialists who may not like Barrett or his style now have a good reason to work hard for the NDP rather than sitting out the campaign," wrote *Sun* reporter Neale Adams. "The NDP remains the 'people's' party, not Dave Barrett's." To underline the point, the convention picked Yvonne Cocke over Barrett's preference for party president. Clearly exhausted, Barrett had left the convention for the day soon after his keynote address, not stopping to mingle with delegates. He was soon back on the road for another two weeks, travelling to New York, Kelowna, chamber of commerce meetings, anywhere he could find an audience. His speech to a large crowd soon after the convention showed how much the dramatic shifts in BC's political landscape were undermining his confidence.

"We're not that super great as government," he said, "we're not that fantastic, we're not that unbelievable. All we've done as government is a few things that inside of us we all know should have been done a long time ago, but were never done by any other government. But we've done things that I dreamed about doing when I was a boy growing up in Vancouver. I dreamed that someday we would have government in British Columbia with the guts to do things that were right, not just expedient." For the first time, he seemed to confront the possibility that his dream could slip away.

11: Back to Work

The relentless battering the New Democrats had received in the legislature and the news pages had taken its toll. The 1975 legislative agenda had been as heavy as the previous year's but lacked the blockbuster, "legislation by thunderbolt" impact. In the wake of the "not a dime without debate" furor, the New Democrats began backing away from fights—betraying what McNelly termed "overextended psyches and burned-out intellects"—dropping the *Emergency Programme Act* and deferring the *Election Expenses Act* to a planned autumn session. Nor was Barrett able to turn public attention to the emerging successes of his government.

Few were aware, for example, that by 1975 the massive job of designating BC's farmland was largely complete. A dedicated team at the Agricultural Land Commission had taken over a cramped and narrow office in Burnaby—they dubbed it the "Yellow Submarine"—during the summer of 1973 and covered its walls with maps and charts. Using the $25-million fund set aside for the purpose, the ALC had acquired eight thousand acres of farmland intended to provide viable farms for young farmers. In contrast to other provinces, where farmland continued to disappear under suburbs and pavement, BC's agricultural lands slowly began to grow. Public opinion was swinging in the ALR's favour, a factor which did much to restore Stupich's reputation as a policy-maker. Barrett's 1973 forecast that the ALR would prove irreversible was coming true.

The exhausted New Democrats of 1975 also managed to hark back to the hard-driving crew of two years earlier by recommissioning the *Princess Marguerite II,* a vintage luxury liner built by the CPR in the 1940s for service between Victoria and Seattle. When the CPR shut down the service in 1974, Victoria's tourism sector was dealt a hammer blow. In April, Williams rode to the rescue with the $2.5-million purchase of more than eight acres of Victoria waterfront and the *Marguerite* from the CPR. Just sixty days after the purchase, fresh from a full refit, the *Marguerite* sailed once more for Seattle, packed with tourists, dignitaries and a beaming Barrett front and centre. It was the kind of public relations coup—like the inauguration of the Vancouver-to-Squamish Royal Hudson excursion train—that Barrett loved. The premier had become obsessively distracted, however, by the shifting political sands. In the increasingly rare moments McNelly was able to spend with him, Barrett was absorbed in election strategy. "We have to start it all over again, Harvey," he told the ever-present Beech. "Just like we did in 1972."

But after a Saturday night poker game in early June, his first night off at home in seven weeks, Barrett told McNelly he was putting his worries aside. "I've got my head straight and I know the only way we're going to win the next election is if I get out there and talk to people myself. I've got to be smiling Dave, chubby smiling Dave, take off my jacket and tie, start cracking jokes, get them laughing. If I ever act like I'm worried, that all this stuff is getting to me, we're dead. We wouldn't last a minute if people thought I was worried." The collapse of the provincial Liberals, inconceivable to New Democrats just a year earlier, was accelerating. The vote splits crucial to Barrett's success were slowly but surely overcome by Bennett's resurgent Social Credit.

The disintegration of the Majority Movement and the NDP's dismal federal election performance the previous summer had

One of the NDP's most popular moves was to buy and refurbish the storied Royal Hudson steam locomotive, which had been languishing in storage, and use it for regular runs between North Vancouver and Squamish. Tourists and BC residents alike flocked to make the trip. The train was also a photo op no self-styled people's premier could pass up.
Photo by Glenn Baglo, provided by the *Vancouver Sun*

strengthened Bennett's hand. He had remained carefully neutral in the federal campaign to avoid ruffling feathers among Liberals or Conservatives. When Allan Williams announced on July 9 that

The CPR was about to let its popular ferry service between Victoria and Seattle aboard the *Princess Marguerite* come to an end. Spearheaded by Resources Minister Bob Williams, the government bought the ship, kept it running and acquired a large chunk of Victoria's harbourfront, as well. Williams looks out from the bridge as the service resumes in June 1975.
Photo by Steve Bosch, provided by the *Vancouver Sun*

a unity party would be formed in thirty days, Bennett ignored him, as did everyone else. His patience was quickly rewarded with the defection of Peter Hyndman, the defeated Conservative candidate in Capilano, to Social Credit. Saanich Conservative MLA Hugh Curtis was next, effectively cutting the Conservative caucus in half and leaving Wallace to carry on alone. Then Liberal Bill Vander Zalm, who had challenged Anderson for the Liberal leadership in 1972, took out his Social Credit card. The nursery business owner who had sought support during the leadership race with a promise to "whip-lash drug pushers, cut off welfare deadbeats, update education, crack down on wife deserters and provide government-financed dental care" seemed to fit right in.

Vander Zalm and the others soon discovered that Bill Bennett's Social Credit had little in common with W.A.C.'s party. There was no "permanent coalition" inside the new organization, as the elder Bennett had styled it, but a single provincial machine with an updated structure stripped of references to the Christian faith or any other potential obstacle to membership. Bill Bennett exploited the shake-out precipitated by the 1972 rout to tap a wealth of young, new talent that had been shut out by the stagnation of his father's last years in power. His days were filled with breakfasts, lunches and banquets with potential supporters and candidates. As the organization began to grow, each new high-profile recruit was hailed in a news release or even a news conference to foster a sense of momentum. Would-be candidates, with the possible exception of current MLAs, were not guaranteed a nomination or a cabinet post. The result was a burst of nomination activity in competitive seats that increased Social Credit's reach across the province.

The end of the Majority Movement had unlocked a steady flow of corporate contributions to Social Credit. Federal Liberal fundraisers reportedly threatened some businesses with repercussions in Ottawa if they failed to provide some support to the provincial party. They were ignored. Pressure was building within the Liberal Party to expel Williams and McGeer from caucus, but new pledges of loyalty from Williams, McGeer and Gardom stabilized the situation until the legislature reconvened early in

1975. Early polls that year were encouraging for the Liberals, but none believed they could mount an effective campaign in the face of the Social Credit juggernaut.

Despite their partisan differences, Liberal leader Anderson and Tory leader Scott Wallace were agreed on one point: neither could stand Bill Bennett. "I had a really tough time waiting to see if Bill Bennett was liberal," Anderson said in late February. "But now we know he isn't. Look at the people around him. It's the Grace McCarthys and the Agnes Krippses, the old faces." Wallace was even more direct, winning desk-thumping applause from the New Democrats for a sneering attack on Bennett's interest in a return to preferential balloting, "another ploy by a second-generation political neophyte to latch on to a vehicle which, once it has carried its driver into the halls of power, can be discarded." Barrett said, "If there wasn't an NDP in BC, I'd vote Tory. I'll tell you that right now."

On April 22, 1975, with the legislature still droning through estimates, Anderson and his caucus squeezed into the elevator of Victoria's Harbour Towers Hotel for a secret dinner with Bill Bennett in his ocean-view suite. With the hockey game on in the background, the six men got down to business. Bennett's offer was straightforward: front-bench responsibilities for Williams, Gardom, McGeer and Gibson if they crossed the floor. There was no room for Anderson. Bennett urged him to stay at the head of the Liberal caucus, finally united by its reduction to a single member. Anderson's humiliation was complete when he read a detailed account of the discussion in Fotheringham's Saturday column four days later. Any Liberal who wanted to merge with the Socreds could "get the hell out," Anderson told reporters. "There is no hope in hell of beating [Barrett] with a unity party or a Social Credit Party under the leadership of Bill Bennett. Barrett will only be beaten when someone takes away the moderate votes he got last election and that someone can only be a party of moderates." The dissidents made it clear they were quite prepared to leave. Lea's "carve up your leader" charge had come true a year late.

Anderson had sought support in unlikely quarters for his response to his three defectors, checking with McNelly to ask how Barrett would react if he called on the dissidents to quit. McGeer, he said, was the type of person who could tell you you had cancer, smile and tell you not to worry, you still had three weeks to live. McNelly consulted with Barrett, who proposed a news conference by Liberal Party officials to denounce the dissidents. The suggestion was passed back through Anderson's assistant Gerry Kristianson and the press conference led the evening news.

On May 9, Williams and McGeer resigned to sit as independents. Gardom followed May 20. All three praised Anderson's leadership but implied they were making a personal sacrifice for the good of the province. "The need for a free enterprise grouping capable of replacing the present government is no longer merely desirable," said Williams, "it is an absolute necessity." McGeer declared that the crisis faced by the province "requires that people put the overall good of the province ahead of party politics," adding more pragmatically that "I don't want to spend another Parliament in opposition." Although it was obvious the three defectors would wind up eventually on the Social Credit benches, Bennett's operatives kept that move in reserve.

In a matter of days, the political landscape had been transformed. The Liberals, whose continued strength was critical to the New Democrats' survival, had crumbled to two seats from five. Wallace was the sole surviving Conservative. Bennett had left the legislature to roam the province, speaking to packed houses. From their side of the House, the New Democrats could see the new opposition emerging before their eyes as legislature staff shuffled the ex-Liberals' seats to a new section. The free enterprise coalition was coming together at last.

As summer turned to fall, matters did not improve for the NDP. Battered by a strengthened and consolidating opposition, a sputtering economy and its own indecisiveness, the government was on the ropes of public opinion. Unemployment was high and inflation even higher. By late September the province was in crisis, beset by a wave of damaging strikes that showed no signs of ending. Most of the vital forest industry—BC's major economic engine—had been shut down for nearly three months. Pickets ringed 125 Lower Mainland supermarkets. At BC Rail, operations were hampered by on-again, off-again job action, and a walkout by Teamster propane-truck drivers had left senior care homes on Vancouver Island without heat. The NDP's euphoric victory thirty-seven months earlier seemed years away.

What's more, Barrett and many of his colleagues were unable to suppress the suspicion that sinister forces outside the province could be contributing to the turmoil. When McNelly reported hearing "two strong clicking noises" on the line in 1974 as he relayed information to Barrett about Turnbull's role in the Chicken and Egg War, he discovered that many in the premier's circle, and Barrett himself, had already calmly accepted that someone might be listening in. For most of their thirty-nine months in power, many in the NDP government believed that no less than the US State Department and the Central Intelligence Agency were closely monitoring their socialist agenda and were not above direct interference to hasten their downfall. Those feelings took flight with the violent, 1973 overthrow and death of Chile's socialist president Salvador Allende.

Barrett had been deeply affected by Allende's fate, widely believed to have been facilitated by the CIA. He ordered flags outside the legislative buildings to be flown at half-staff. When the Trudeau government in Ottawa recognized the Pinochet dictatorship a month later, Barrett heatedly denounced the decision. "Barrett was very upset about Allende's overthrow," McNelly recalled. "It brought home how governments could internally manipulate events in other countries. If the CIA could murder Allende, what would they do here?" The NDP leader had also not forgotten the extremist article on his government in *Barron's* earlier that year, which ran under the headline, "Chile of the North?" He became fatalistic about the possibility he might be assassinated. McNelly's journal outlines a macabre conversation early in 1975, when Barrett discussed—in serious tones—who should take over as leader if someone took him out. "If they want to get me, they will," he said.

The United States was furious at the Barrett government's decision to raise the price of natural gas exports, and there was shock and concern over its entry into the marketplace to buy up companies and nationalize auto insurance. Were their investment dollars safe in BC? Was this Communism? In February, columnist Allan Fotheringham cited a US news story quoting a source in the State Department. The source said they were interested in the Barrett government "because it's the kind of government that doesn't exist elsewhere in Canada." When they read that, according to McNelly's journal, everybody in the government "quietly lit up." Around the same time, a muckraking magazine identified Robert Funseth of the State Department as "probably a CIA agent." That name rang a bell for McNelly. He remembered having lunch with Funseth in Victoria, after the 1974 federal election. During their talk, Funseth focused on energy issues, particularly the government's natural gas policies. Two years after that Victoria lunch, Funseth, a veteran of the State Department regularly assigned to world trouble spots, emerged as a spokesman for the department under Secretary of State Henry Kissinger.

That summer, nationalist gadfly Mel Hurtig, head of the Committee for an Independent Canada, rocked the government with allegations that Social Credit had asked the CIA in 1973 to investigate Barrett, Alex Macdonald and Frank Calder. Although Hurtig would not identify his source, Barrett took his assertions seriously. "To this day, I don't know if Hurtig's story was true," he wrote in his autobiography, "but he certainly provided enough details to make the story interesting." Back in March, Provincial Secretary Ernie Hall had voiced publicly what his cabinet colleagues were thinking. "The CIA is everywhere else. Why not here?" he suggested to a *Victoria Daily Times* reporter. "I wouldn't be surprised at all, if we are being supervised." Hall may have had in mind the curious case of the suspect employee at BC Petroleum Corporation. The RCMP tipped BCPC chairman Jim Rhodes that one of his employees might be a CIA informant. On further investigation, the man's impressive credentials were found to be false. Rhodes fired him. Minister of Labour Bill King shared concerns that US operatives were at work and sniffing around. Years after the long, hot, strike-plagued summer of 1975, King still suspected "dark forces" were involved in the resolute stand by the companies, many of them multinational corporations, against BC's forest unions. "We have significant investment from the United States in our province, and we delude ourselves to think that it's always benign," he said.

As he struggled with his response to the strike wave and the decision of when to call an election, Barrett worried about the Hurtig and BCPC revelations. Did they portend even more sinister "outside influences" coming into play? He acknowledged in his autobiography that they helped spur him to action sooner rather than later. Against a veritable sea of troubles, it was time to remind the public what real leadership was all about—that a strong, decisive helmsman was still in charge and on their side. The strikes had gone on long enough. What transpired October 7, 1975, was one of the boldest—if not the boldest—of all the earth-shaking moves made by his radical government. With a single, swift bill that caught the entire province off guard, Barrett and the NDP brought in the most sweeping back-to-work legislation in Canadian history. More than fifty thousand union members—all in the private sector—were ordered to return to their jobs.

For an NDP government, such a course of action should have

been unthinkable. This, after all, was a party formed in partnership with the labour movement, an alliance that lined NDP coffers with money from Canadian unions. But Barrett's uneasy relationship with his province's labour leaders was well known and long-lasting. He was convinced this was the right thing to do, economically and politically. He felt he needed to do something to recapture momentum, and this was it. He also had a tough labour minister on his side who was not someone to be trifled with. Bill King was a minister unafraid to roll up his sleeves, summon parties in a strike to his offices in Victoria and plunge into the midst of a difficult labour dispute to try to get a settlement. And in critical disruptions, when his personal mediation didn't work, King did not shy from using legislation.

In August 1974, King had had the legislature summoned for an emergency session to order striking firefighters in four Vancouver suburbs back to work, shoehorn them into a joint bargaining council and force them to accept a new contract similar to one accepted earlier by firefighters in Vancouver. He acted after the firefighters refused to guarantee they would down picket lines and respond to house fires during their strike. The *Essential Services Continuation Act* also provided King with new powers to intervene in other labour disputes that threatened "the life and safety" of the public. During the regular fall session a few months later, King ended a two-year dispute that had disrupted tens of millions of dollars' worth of construction by imposing a contract on elevator contractors. It was one of the few times a government has ever legislated a settlement against the employers' side of the bargaining table. King defended the move, lashing out at the contractors for acting in a "very prima donna fashion" and trying to force BC workers to accept the same deal that was reached in Ontario.

On a more minor issue earlier that spring, the government had also used legislation to force striking municipal workers in Kamloops to repair riverbank dikes needed to hold back the fast-rising Thompson River. Lecturing both sides in the dispute for failing to act like "responsible citizens," King—though of course he didn't know it at the time—heralded the astonishing back-to-work legislation that was to come in October. "If people refuse to accept responsibility in this case, or any other, then the legislature of this province is the appropriate agency to make that determination, show a higher sense of responsibility and deal expeditiously with it," he told the House.

When the October 7, 1975, emergency session began, the purpose of the back-to-work bill was identified only in vague terms, with no details. The legislature was then adjourned for thirty minutes to allow the dumbfounded opposition to study the dramatic measures that were actually in the bill. This time, although Bill King fronted and agreed absolutely with the bill, it was the premier's show. As he made his way out through the chamber's creaking, revolving door, Barrett was pumped. Peter McNelly watched him emerge. "His eyes were shining, hard and bright. His muscles like a cat waiting to spring," McNelly recorded in his journal. "He took my arm and whispered in my ear, 'We just legislated the whole fucking lot back to work. The whole shitload.'"

For the moment, Barrett was king of the hill. While union leaders fumed, support for the back-to-work legislation was almost universal, from the public to the government's harshest media critics to Social Credit leader Bill Bennett himself. Bennett spoke for many when he said he was proud to endorse the bill, terming it one of the government's finest displays of leadership. Headline huzzahs resounded. "A gutsy move," said one. "Everyone back to work," hailed the *Victoria Daily Times*. A delighted McNelly gushed the next day, "The province is still reeling. You can see it on people's faces. You can feel it in your veins. By tomorrow, the descent into reality will have begun, but for the moment, at least, it's like being on the first great rush of the roller-coaster."

Amid the euphoria, however, there was no denying that

Bill 146 was yet another blow to the already-tattered relations between the government and its erstwhile labour allies. For those still smarting that all their support for the party over the years had not paid off with an administration responsive to labour wishes, this seemed the deepest cut of all. For many union members and NDP activists, the stunning, sledgehammer scope of the back-to-work order cast a demoralizing pall over the election that was to come little more than a month later. They would vote for the NDP, maybe even drop them a dollar or two. But they would not expend nearly the same energy for a party they now believed had abandoned its long support for hallowed labour principles.

The build-up to Bill 146 had been agonizing for the government. In fact, the harbinger for the coming denouement went back to June, when Bill King introduced the *Labour Code Amendment Act*. On the surface, there appeared little in Bill 84 to provoke more than a whisper of rancour. It was full of technical, housekeeping changes to the existing Labour Code, already winning plaudits as maybe the most progressive industrial relations legislation in the world. The amendments had been sought by Paul Weiler. The estimable chairman of the province's landmark Labour Relations Board had presided over the board for eighteen months. He decided there were matters that needed tinkering. Bill 84 enhanced the LRB's already substantial powers and further reduced the role of the courts, but mostly in the hardly hot-button realm of grievance and arbitration procedures. Jurisdiction over arbitration appeals was taken from the courts and handed to the labour board, which also assumed power to settle between-contract disputes by getting at their root cause, rather than relying on the precise language of the pertinent collective agreement. Bill 84 also gave domestic, agricultural and professional workers the right to unionize for the first time.

Yet leaders of the BC Federation of Labour were enraged. To them, Bill 84 fanned the flames of what they hated about the initial Labour Code even higher. More tribunals, more legal arguments, more lawyers, more outside interference in the trenches of labour relations, where they wanted as few fetters as possible to fight the boss. NDP backbenchers Colin Gabelmann, Harold Steves and Rosemary Brown, who had distanced themselves from some sections of the 1973 Labour Code, also spoke out against the bill. Gabelmann's opposition was particularly heartfelt. His clearly expressed criticisms, answered just as impressively by Bill King, produced that rarity of events in the legislature, a real debate. There was none of the posturing, hectoring or bombastic partisanship that normally consumed the spoken business of the House. Neither man was intent on scoring political points. Instead, they sparred philosophically over the proper role of government in labour relations.

This was so refreshing, some reporters actually left their cluttered cubicles to sit in the public galleries and just listen. They relished the chance to hear two members of the same party disagree—respectfully and articulately—on a matter of principle. King argued that regulations and a strong administrative tribunal are essential to ensure a fair playing field for management as well as labour. "We can't transfer from the courts the authority to regulate and to oversee problems in industrial relations, and then simply leave the authority in a vacuum, in an unregulated way," he told Gabelmann. "We cannot have an unregulated morass which, in my view, neither the trade union movement nor the public would want in this province, because it would certainly lead to chaos."

Not so, responded Gabelmann. It simply isn't true, he argued, that labour and management are equals, needing only a referee. "In fact, the relationship between capital and labour in North America is very much like sending a flyweight up against a heavyweight," he contended. "You don't have a referee in that kind of boxing match." The parties should be left to settle matters on their own, without a powerful third force on the sidelines always ready to butt in, said Gabelmann. "That's the position our party took for years when we were in opposition." Their fundamental difference of opinion played out for a full week during clause-by-clause study of the bill. As debate went on, the heavyset leaders of the BC Federation of Labour glowered powerlessly from the gallery, angry and frustrated that not a single point they advanced made a bit of difference to Bill King.

When Bill 84 passed, the Fed used none of the legislative niceties that Gabelmann, Steves and Brown had observed. Len Guy and Fed president George Johnston strode into the press gallery. In a few short, clipped sentences, while puzzled reporters wondered what the fuss was about, Guy and Johnston declared that it was all over between organized labour and the NDP. The BC Fed had lost confidence in the labour minister. Bill King must resign or be fired, they declared. The breach between the government and the NDP's perennial union allies was complete. And there were even harder trials around the corner. The trite, overused phrase "long, hot summer" was about to become a reality.

Despite a multitude of sophisticated mechanisms to promote industrial peace, a superb chairman of the LRB and a wealth of skilled mediators and labour arbitrators, nothing could be done about the terrible scourge of inflation that was sweeping across Canada and British Columbia. The cost of living had soared more than 12 percent in 1974. It was on the same debilitating path in 1975. In response, bargaining had gone mad. Unions were demanding, and winning, off-the-chart pay hikes both to catch up and to guard against future inflation. The province's average annual wage increase in 1974 was 16.2 percent. Settlements were running even higher as 1975 progressed. Employers who didn't cough up were soon surrounded by picket signs, the government among them. Nearly two thousand ICBC employees had launched what became a long, crippling strike. The year-old Crown corporation had offered a substantial 34-percent wage hike over twenty-seven months. Fred Trotter, the diminutive, red-nosed president of Local 378 of the Office and Technical Employees' Union, scorned the proposal. He wanted 43 percent. The price for municipal peace was also high. CUPE members were winning annual wage increases of 21 percent, while public transit drivers had just snared a two-year deal, hiking their salaries by 40 percent.

In this wild environment of escalating wage increases, the province's key employers, grouped together in the powerful Employers' Council of BC, decided to take a stand. Labour expectations had to be cooled off. They forged a loose pact to take the unions on. First up was the forest industry, responsible for fifty cents of every economic dollar generated in the province. Master agreements for the vast coastal membership of the International Woodworkers of America and the two pulp unions—Canadian Paperworkers Union (CPU) and Pulp, Paper and Woodworkers of Canada (PPWC)—expired within two weeks of each other, in June, setting the scene for one of the biggest bargaining showdowns in Canada's most unionized province.

The IWA had nine locals at the negotiating table, representing thirty thousand workers. They faced off against Forest Industrial Relations, formidable negotiators for more than a hundred unionized logging operations in and around the coast. On the pulp side, the Pulp and Paper Industrial Relations Bureau bargained for all of the province's twenty paper mills. Workers at a dozen mills were represented by the CPU. Eight had the PPWC, an independent Canadian union with a well-honed tradition of almost anarchic ultra-militancy. Over the years, the three unions had negotiated their way to the highest forest industry wages in the world. For these negotiations, the rival pulp unions had agreed for the first time to form a common front. Communication channels had also been opened up to the IWA.

The forest companies, however, were undeterred. They were ready to stand firm against their unions, and conditions for that could not have been better. The industry was in a severe, cyclical decline. Close to ten thousand IWA members were already laid off across the province because of slumping lumber sales. There was also a glut of pulp and paper on the market, causing a significant drop in price. At the bargaining table, despite the sky-high wage increases all around them, BC's three forest industry unions were stunned when the companies offered them nothing more than a year's extension of their current contract with only a cost-of-living adjustment tacked on at the end. There would be no formal wage increase at all. The industry called this their "definitive end position." But it was really a declaration of war.

The war of the woods that followed was as nasty and debilitating a labour dispute as BC—no stranger to lengthy, bitter strikes—had ever experienced. Much of the fighting took place between unions. The IWA, which chose not to go on strike, clashed openly with striking pulp unions for picketing sawmills where IWA members were still at work. The three unions were also at odds, almost from the beginning, over bargaining tactics. There was particular bad blood between the domineering regional president of the IWA, Jack Munro, and the CPU's prickly western regional president, Art Gruntman. While PPWC leader Reg Ginn was rather genial and down to earth, Gruntman seemed unbending, humourless and resentful of all the attention showered on the salty-tongued, burly Munro, who was loved by the media for his colourful quotes. The two feuded for years.

Bill King tried everything to head off a strike. At a closed-door meeting with more than fifty company and union negotiators in early July, he told them an industry shutdown would amount to a general strike. It could bring the province to its economic knees. No one blinked. No one budged from their position. Did anyone even listen, or care? King's offer to appoint an industrial inquiry commissioner was rebuffed by the pulp unions. They also spurned the minister's plea to stay on the job, while a special mediator, BC Supreme Court Justice Henry Hutcheon, looked into the dispute.

At midnight, July 14, the strike was on. Close to thirteen thousand pulp-mill workers walked out into the teeth of a weakening pulp market and a group of hardened employers determined not to offer a penny more. A month later, Judge Hutcheon recommended an across-the-board wage increase of $1.55 an hour spread over two years and a complex COLA (cost-of-living-adjustment) clause that might provide a few cents in the pact's second year. This was a hefty improvement over the companies' "definitive end position." But the pulp unions rejected it with nary a by-your-leave. They proceeded to up the ante, vowing to expand their picket lines to IWA sawmills. The IWA itself was split. The executive recommended acceptance of the Hutcheon report. Five local presidents urged a "no" vote. In the end, a razor-thin majority of 51.2 percent rejected the report. That was far from enough to wage battle, and IWA negotiators kept their picket signs in storage. They opted to reach a deal peacefully, across the bargaining table.

While Apollo astronauts and Soyuz cosmonauts neared their historic rendezvous far above in outer space, on the ground in BC, union solidarity shattered. Jack Munro blasted "super militants" in the pulp unions for seeking to "spread their mess around" by picketing IWA operations. When the pulp unions criticized the IWA for being less than strong trade unionists, Munro said he was sick and tired of their mudslinging. At a picketing conference called by the BC Fed, an angry IWA voice boomed out from behind closed doors, "I'm not about to take that crap from some two-bit union." Asked about pulp-union demands for a one-year increase of $1.50 an hour, veteran IWA leader Syd Thompson snorted, "I thought only God was up in the clouds, but it's obvious the pulp unions are as well." IWA members at Takla Forest Products in Fort St. James simply ripped up PPWC picket signs outside their mill and went into work.

But the pulp unions were bleeding internally, too. As the strike went on, hundreds of pulp workers applied for welfare to feed their families in mill towns such as Powell River, Crofton, Campbell River, Castlegar and Kamloops. Several local presidents broke with their leaders and privately urged the government to intervene. "Negotiations are like two giants sitting across the table, using all the weapons in the world," said a distraught Al McDonald, president of the PPWC's Kamloops local. He thought it was wrong for his union to throw working IWA members off the job. During debate on Bill 146, Bill King tore a strip off both sides for allowing a situation that forced workers onto welfare. They must be close to starvation, he told the legislature, anger in his voice. "That is an indictment of both management and labour, when they are prepared to stand idly by and see their employees and members of their unions affected in such an extreme and adverse way."

The pulp unions seemed oblivious to their precarious plight. Continuing dismal market conditions meant it was nigh impossible to put economic pressure on the companies, hence their desperate but divisive ploy to picket working sawmills. Noting pulp and paper products piling up in Europe, Bob Williams observed with exasperation that the pulp unions "make their decisions, but by God, where they get their advice is a good question." The companies simply sat back, hanging their hat on the Hutcheon report, which they had accepted "reluctantly," though by no means unanimously. And why not? Not only did a prolonged shutdown cause the big forest corporations little financial damage, but it was also likely to seriously diminish union wage expectations in the future and hurt the bottom line of a government they didn't care for. By the time the strike entered its third month, in addition to the pulp-mill shutdowns, more than 90 percent of the coastal forest industry was idle. About twenty thousand IWA members were laid off while another seven thousand had been picketed out by the pulp unions.

The breadth of the work stoppage was unprecedented, with no resolution in sight.

However, this was not the only labour impasse in the province. Yes, the bitter ICBC strike had finally been put to bed after fourteen weeks, when workers agreed to an exceedingly generous wage increase of 39.5 percent over twenty-eight months. But disgruntled trainmen on BC Rail were staging rotating strikes, and scores of supermarkets were shut down by a strike/lockout over aggressive demands by union bakers, meatcutters and clerks for annual wage increases of up to 50 percent. The large pay hikes sought by the three food unions caught the eye of no less than the oft-lampooned head of the Food Prices Review Board in Ottawa, Beryl Plumptre. She demanded the BC government do something about it. Dave Barrett and Bill King laughed her off.

Meanwhile, a little-noticed strike by 180 propane-truck drivers belonging to the Teamsters Union was starting to make news. After weeks on strike, the drivers began picketing the Canadian Pacific barge ferry that carried propane rail cars to Vancouver Island. Canadian Pacific agreed to halt the shipments, leaving hundreds of residences and business establishments in Nanaimo, including senior care homes, without heat. Although the situation had yet to make the front page of the major dailies, Bill King unexpectedly announced an emergency session of the legislature to order an end to the propane dispute. "Many elderly citizens are without an adequate supply of heat. We can't let this go on," he told the media. It was a subterfuge. Behind the scenes, the government was preparing its big move: an end to all strikes, not just the walkout by the relatively few folks who deliver propane.

The legislative guillotine had been set in motion during an evening visit to Barrett's house not long before by King and Deputy Minister of Labour Jim Matkin. The two made a strong pitch to the premier for action. He was of the same mind. Talks were going nowhere in any of the disputes. It was a crazy, damaging situation that could not continue. "We'd been getting feedback from a lot of pulp workers that they had to be rescued, and the employers were creating a real problem for the government by being so hard-nosed with the unions," Matkin recalled. "Both Bill and I made the point: let's not do this halfway, let's go the whole way." Barrett, then Williams, agreed. Not a hint of the government's plan leaked out. When King announced on Sunday, October 5, that the House would meet in two days to end the propane strike, the opposition, the media and the labour movement mostly yawned. One outsider, however, was in on the secret. It was Jack Munro.

Munro was everything the pulp union leaders were not. Moderate, and an unwavering supporter of the NDP government through all its scraps with the BC Federation of Labour, he had not called his members out on strike. In fact, the IWA was still at the table that very week, closing in on a new contract. Even as government drafters were preparing the back-to-work bill, Munro was canvassed for his opinion. The government felt his support or, at least his lack of resistance to the move, was critical. So, although he denied it for years, Munro knew the bill was coming. He even had a key section changed. Originally, the legislation was to kick in twenty-four hours after receiving royal assent. Munro desperately wanted a deal before the bill became law. He thought twenty-four hours would not be enough. The government agreed to double the deadline to forty-eight hours. "Barrett really liked the IWA," Munro explained in an interview. "He didn't want us to be legislated back to work, so he changed the bill." The extension worked. Almost to the minute, forty-eight hours after the bill was enacted, Forest Industrial Relations and the IWA shook hands on a new agreement.

The NDP caucus, on the other hand, did not get the news until shortly before Bill 146 was unveiled in the House. Members were taken aback. Barrett laid his leadership on the line. Either they supported his decision, or he would walk. Only three members—Gabelmann, Steves and Brown, yet again—declared they would vote against it. In the legislature, with a lump in his throat and tears in his eyes, Gabelmann said it was "morally wrong" for the government to be stampeded by public opinion. "I will not be part of that." He continued, "As is obvious by my emotionalism in this debate, I'm very unhappy about the legislation. I do not intend to support it. I'm very unhappy that I have to do that, but I don't believe there to be a threat to life in any of these current disputes." Gabelmann's fellow backbencher Gerry Anderson, the union pipefitter from Kamloops who had defeated Phil Gaglardi, retorted that no one had a monopoly on principle. Strikers in his riding will be glad to go back to work, he said. Minister of Economic Development Gary Lauk gave a financial damage report. Work stoppages and the industry downturn were likely to reduce stumpage and royalty revenue by as much as 70 percent from the previous fiscal year, he said, dropping from $190-million to $50-million. "This is bound to affect the treasury."

Bill 146 hit labour leaders like a thunderbolt. They were struck nearly dumb with rage. "My first reaction is one of disbelief," sputtered Len Guy. "It's utter strike-breaking," said an embittered Art Gruntman of the CPU. "It's disgusting, unbelievable, repugnant." The talk was of defiance. Barrett's lecturing words to the media further riled union emotions: "We are fed up with the situation. We are saying to the disputants: 'grow up.' The province comes before management. The province comes before labour. We are saying to both sides, through legislation, get on with it. Get your heads together." The legislation did not impose settlements on anyone. Rather, it proclaimed a ninety-day cooling-off period for the parties to negotiate agreements while picket lines were down. There was no cooling off Len Guy, however.

That night, accompanied by George Johnston, Guy journeyed to the storied IWA building on Commercial Drive to preach resistance in a dramatic appearance before a rafters-full meeting of the Vancouver and District Labour Council. His message to the

Barrett government was as blunt as any message Guy delivered across the table to the company men at Pacific Press. "Bill 146 represents a complete betrayal of the principles and policies of the NDP and a complete betrayal of the working people who helped elect this government," he told the Labour Council. "Rarely in modern times has a government in Canada interfered so brutally in free collective bargaining, or has a government engaged in strikebreaking on such a massive scale." To thunderous applause, the Federation secretary-treasurer issued a call to action, urging all "genuine trade unionists" to fight against Bill 146 and in defence of free collective bargaining. Hugh Comber, the usually soft-spoken president of the bakery workers union, told the agitated crowd, "I understand the premier said it was time we all grew up. Well, I think I grew up today. I had been childish enough to believe that there was a government over there on my behalf." When Comber said he wasn't sure whether he could order his members to comply with the bill, delegates responded with a loud, spontaneous ovation.

But far from Commercial Drive, far from the strategy rooms of the striking unions, something was happening that no militant bluster could roll back. Across the province, thousands of ordinary union members, the rank and file, were not waiting for their leaders' instructions. They began streaming back to work, their will to continue a seemingly unwinnable battle sapped. "You'd better get away from the gates, Art," Jack Munro jibed at Gruntman. "You'll be trampled by your own people returning to work." CPU representatives called off their strike. Too many members wanted to return, Gruntman admitted. The PPWC went back, too. The same was true for the three supermarket unions. When a reporter suggested to George Johnston that defiance of Bill 146 was doomed by lack of support from the rank and file, the Fed president and head of the meatcutters' union didn't disagree. "Quite frankly, that's a true statement," Johnston replied.

Dave Barrett and Bill King, on the outs with leaders of the BC trade union movement almost from the moment they took office, won a clear victory. Their gamble that they knew the feelings of ordinary workers better than the heads of their unions paid off. Each had received scores of private letters from striking mill employees, pleading for an end to the impasse. Writing in his journal during the first flush of enthusiasm for Bill 146, few described more vividly the predicament the government had been facing than Peter McNelly. "In a situation where major industries had been shut down for months, where the wage demands read—in percentage terms—like horror stories, and where the industries could sit on their inventories and laugh at our principles while the votes oozed away, Barrett had no choice," McNelly wrote. On a prearranged northern tour, Barrett was warmly received. The mayor of Burns Lake, describing himself as "an old Socred," was lavish in his praise. "At last, we have found a government with the guts to go in and do something." In Smithers, on a radio call-in show, Barrett did not mince words. "We are not a labour party," he reiterated. "Our CCF–NDP roots are in the working people, but we are not a trade union party."

Back in Vancouver, the oomph went out of an emergency meeting of BC union reps. The Fed tried to put the best face possible on what had happened. "We have lost a battle, but the war has just begun," the organization vowed in a statement. One day, the Barrett government will be replaced by "a true NDP government, true to the honourable traditions of J.S. Woodsworth, Angus MacInnis and Tommy Douglas," said the Fed. That tub-thumping cry also fell flat, as Grace MacInnis, daughter of J.S. Woodsworth and widow of Angus MacInnis, said both men would have supported Bill 146. "They believed it was important for powerful groups to realize that the whole community is more important than any one section in it." Then came the unkindest of all the squelches. The revered Tommy Douglas himself came out in favour of the bill. Douglas, who served seventeen years as premier of Saskatchewan, said there can come a time when the negotiating process breaks down and government needs to step in. "If you accept the responsibility of government, you have to do what has to be done..."

There were many who thought Barrett would call an election right away, riding the winds of his rediscovered leadership. But it took another month before Barrett pulled the pin. His first public appearance on the campaign trail was at the annual convention of the BC Federation of Labour. Most delegates put aside their differences, greeting the NDP leader with applause and a standing, albeit restrained, ovation. But some remained in their seats, and the CPU's thirty delegates walked out. "It would be hypocritical of us to forgive and forget," said Art Gruntman. More than a few unions, including the CPU, restricted their support in cash and volunteers to the three MLAs who voted against Bill 146: Steves, Brown and Colin Gabelmann. It didn't help. Gabelmann's North Vancouver–Seymour riding was one of only two in the province where the NDP outspent Social Credit. He was crushed, as was Steves. Rosemary Brown, however, managed to retain her seat in Vancouver Burrard.

Looking back years later, Bill King said he had no regrets over the massive back-to-work order. "There was a general, economic threat to the province. That's how we perceived it," said King. He added darkly that the shutdowns may have been orchestrated by employers on purpose, to hurt the NDP. "I have no proof, but was there ever another occasion in the labour history of this province where that kind of general, widespread work stoppage threatened the economic underpinning of the province? It never happened under Social Credit," King said. He agreed that the move hurt the NDP in the year-end election that soon followed. "You bet it did," said King. "There's no doubt we didn't get the labour support we would have otherwise received. But you know, that's a penalty you pay for doing what you think is necessary."

As a postscript, it's interesting to note that Bill 146 came into effect just before the federal government introduced wage and price controls. Trapped by the controls, supermarket workers wound up with wage increases well below the pay hikes they had been offered before going out on strike. The militant pulp unions, on the other hand, fared better. In a bittersweet twist, their bacon was saved by none other than their hated rivals, the IWA. The IWA's new contract exceeded wage control guidelines. But Munro's frantic drive to settle before Bill 146 came into effect paid off, since the deal was sealed a week before controls were imposed. The pulp unions were thus able to secure the same wage increase won by the IWA, despite the federal wage-control program, because it was determined they had a historic wage relationship with Jack Munro's union. Needless to say, Munro received no thanks from either of the two pulp unions.

12: And Good Luck to Us All

In the dark December days of 1975, the newsroom of the *Victoria Daily Times* was a small, but relatively happy spot in the world. The paper had weathered a seemingly interminable six-month strike the year before, an experience leavened for its mostly-young staff by putting out a regular strike newspaper. Bright reporters on their way up, lifers, ex-Brits and old hacks provided a mix that kept life interesting for those on staff, not to mention covering the news and putting out the paper itself. The editor of the *Daily Times*, George Oake, fit right in. He was a youthful thirty-five, the youngest editor in the formidable cross-country chain of FP Publications. When he took the job, Oake's vow was to shake up Victoria, a city he considered lost in another century, and shift the paper's editorial stance leftward to small-l liberal.

As the provincial election campaign entered its final lap, Oake made a remarkable decision, one that set him apart from all editorial writers in British Columbia. He wanted the *Daily Times* to endorse Dave Barrett and the NDP. Fearing the worst, Oake took his radical resolve to Stuart Underhill, a former Reuters correspondent and the paper's publisher. Much to Oake's surprise, Underhill said, "Fine. Go ahead and write it." Oake went back to his classic Underwood typewriter in the small cubicle that served as his office and pounded out a draft. It took him just a few hours. He'd been working it out in his head for days. "I passed it to the publisher, holding my breath," he recalled years later. "I was young and arrogant enough in those days that if he hadn't approved what I wrote, I would have quit." Underhill suggested only one small change. He asked for the decision to be termed "reluctant." Oake agreed: "I thought that was reasonable. I only wanted to say the NDP was the better party."

When readers unfolded their newspapers the next day, they found an editorial decrying Bill Bennett's Social Credit Party as "an amorphous new lump of prattling jingoists [who offer] nothing more than a blind loyalty to cowboy capitalism, the kind of rip and tear the rest of the country discarded years ago." The *Times* criticized the Barrett government for its financial policies, pointing to spending habits akin to "a small kid in a candy store" and some private industry purchases that were "foolish, pathetic salutes to ideology." But the paper praised the NDP administration for its "new emphasis on people," its many social measures and having the guts to bring in its recent back-to-work legislation. In the last paragraph, the *Times* concluded, "Premier Barrett is an exceptional leader, in our view, a compassionate man with strong feelings for BC and the parliamentary system he serves. The *Times* believes the NDP deserves a second mandate from the people of this province."

Reaction was immediate, and it wasn't pretty. The *Times* was deluged with hostile calls. Scores of readers cancelled their subscriptions. Local advertisers began pulling their ads from the paper. And Oakes received personal calls from angry readers at home. One threatened to kill him. Another vowed to ensure that Oakes moved back to Russia, while his wife, Lorraine, was told she had not raised their children properly, and that she was "dirty." Garbage was dumped on their lawn. Oakes heard later that his job was on the line, too. Only the calming intervention of the *Vancouver Sun*'s legendary editorial director, Bruce Hutchison, saved him from being fired the next day by the head of FP Publications, Richard Malone. Oakes was taken aback.

He had expected some criticism for his rogue editorial but was stunned by the extent of the backlash. "It was so violent," said Oakes. "Until I wrote that editorial, I didn't realize or understand the depth of hatred out there towards the NDP."

The virulent animosity evoked by Oakes' editorial was a fitting capper to what was undoubtedly the darkest, most unsavoury election campaign in the province since the wave of anti-Chinese fear-mongering in the 1930s. The normal business of electioneering was effectively overshadowed by a frenzy of right-wing, free enterprise hysteria that the socialists might claim another term in office. Over its thirty-seven days, documents were stolen, outlandish allegations tossed about, Liberal and Conservative candidates threatened for endangering the "free enterprise" vote, hecklers beaten up and all-candidates meetings disrupted by organized jeering. Large newspaper ads from shadowy sources warned voters their choice was "Freedom of Individual rights or Socialism." On the eve of voting day, *Vancouver Sun* columnist Jack Wasserman, who had also been threatened, wrote, "There is something Hitlerian about the atmosphere in which the election campaign is being carried out."

At the end, there had been too many threats on Barrett's life for police to ignore. The premier of the province and his family waited out the returns under guard by four members of the RCMP in a depressing Coquitlam motel room. The blinds were drawn, the windows covered over by aluminum foil to discourage snipers. Politics in BC had always been deeply polarized between left and right, but never like this. The ideological gulf in this searing, volatile and at times frightening campaign was wider than in any previous election battle. The mainstream middle was basically silenced. The Dave Barrett who called the election was a changed man from the relaxed, freewheeling, jovial campaigner of 1972. Thirty-nine months in office under constant attack from media and the business community, an attack augmented by the government's own mistakes, had left their scars.

For his surprise, Monday-afternoon election announcement on November 3, Barrett had worn a statesmanlike, dark blue business suit with matching striped blue tie. He read from a prepared text. He seemed tense. After all his government had done during its relatively short tenure, the premier told the people he needed a fresh mandate to fight the forces of ... wait for it ... inflation. Barrett referred to recent "difficult but necessary" decisions to send strikers back to work and impose a price freeze on food and other essential goods. Now, he said, there may be even more difficult decisions in the months and years ahead "to win the struggle against inflation." Barrett concluded, "I am determined to help make the fight against inflation work. But for the next years, I can only hope to make it work if I have the necessary support to fight to make it fair, with equal sacrifices for all and favours to none." As a reason to go early to the polls, during the foul weather months of November and December, with twenty months remaining in the government's mandate, it was far from convincing. But Barrett had to trot out something to justify his decision. Once on the hustings, he barely mentioned inflation. This election would be fought on the government's record. The issue was straightforward: Did the NDP deserve a second term, or not?

Barrett had been wrestling for weeks with calling a snap election. After unions obeyed the government's back-to-work legislation and Prime Minister Trudeau came in with federal wage and price controls, however, he hesitated. In the meantime, he shuffled his cabinet, handing over his finance responsibilities to Dave Stupich, rewarding Bob Strachan with a plum posting to London as the province's agent general, demoting over-matched Minister of Mines and Petroleum Resources Leo Nimsick to Tourism and promoting Gary Lauk to Nimsick's former job. Lauk's first move was to implement a complete review of mining taxation. As Barrett mulled what to do, gales of early election rumours swept the province, from the corridors of power to constituency offices to late-night palaver in the beer parlours.

Within the NDP, tension became unbearable. Nobody could get any work done. "Everyone was on a two-week coffee jag," Peter McNelly wrote in his journal. "People were phoning each other, talking, guessing, psyching each other up for the event." Then in late October Barrett announced sweeping price controls for the province. Everyone relaxed. The election seemed to be off.

A week later, following a restless night of tossing and turning, Barrett declared it was on. The decision to risk it all after a tad more than three years in office, rather than governing at least into 1976, remains controversial even today. Why chance ceding the reins of power ahead of time? A later election would have given the NDP an opportunity to smooth over its rough edges, while bringing in numerous measures cabinet ministers were still working on. But Barrett could see a strengthening of the free enterprise legions gathering against him. A unified anti-NDP coalition, which spelled potential doom for his government mathematically, needed only a few more planks. A worsening economy was another harbinger of more trouble ahead. And private polls, while hardly rosy, indicated the NDP at least had a chance.

Still riding a leadership high from ordering all those unions back to work maybe, Barrett thought, he could catch Social Credit and its inexperienced leader Bill Bennett with their pants down, unprepared for a province-wide battle. If defeat were in the cards regardless, waiting might result in even fewer NDP seats, as the right solidified and Bennett improved. "There was a strong possibility that the Socreds, with their unlimited access to funds and a supportive media, could build even greater opposition to our government," Barrett wrote twenty years later in his autobiography. More darkly, he suggested there were elements in the United States prepared to pitch in to get rid of the NDP. "Could some form of US intervention be far off?"

Cabinet and caucus were divided. But powerful ministers Bob Williams and Bill King were election hawks. "If we had gone later, we might have been decimated," Williams recalled. King agreed: "I felt there were forces at work that would coalesce when they had a more precise time frame for the election. Those forces would intensify and we would have a very difficult time. We had a difficult time anyway, but that was my thinking." Provincial Secretary Ernie Hall, however, was aghast. John Fryer of the BCGEU was a neighbour of Hall's at the time. He was home recuperating from a serious automobile accident. He remembers Hall pounding on his door. "Bang, bang, bang. In came Ernie, visibly agitated," recounted Fryer. Hall burst out, "I think we've just screwed ourselves. Williams stampeded Dave into an election. Williams, with all these statistics that the economy was going into a nosedive. It's absolutely the wrong decision." Most party officials, including Cliff Scotton, newly-appointed campaign manager, were opposed as well. They would have liked much more time to marshal resources and map out a campaign strategy to preserve BC's first socialist government.

Barrett's timing was also a blow to electoral reform. The NDP had promised to impose limits on election campaign spending seemingly forever. They hadn't done it. Given the well-heeled corporate backers of Social Credit, that failure hurt no one but the NDP. As *Vancouver Sun* reporter Bill Bachop observed when the election gun went off, "The NDP government faces the most concerted, big-money campaign that any sitting provincial administration in Canada has had to cope with ... The dollars will flow like water." The first late fall election in more than half a century also left untouched and unread a comprehensive report on electoral redistribution that had just been submitted by Thomas Norris, a former BC Court of Appeal Judge and the fearless arbiter who conducted the 1960s inquiry into union racketeer Hal Banks. And the voters' list was stale, unrevised since 1972.

Barrett once again insisted the NDP was the underdog. Party president Yvonne Cocke didn't seem to get the message, however. On day one, she ventured that the NDP would lose seats, but retain a majority. Barrett and others were furious at Cocke, both for making a public prediction for an NDP government and for having it include a loss of seats, too. The word went out: only elected politicians were to speak about the campaign. "I don't care if Yvonne thinks she's got enough balls to be premier," Bob Williams muttered to McNelly. More early stumbles were in store.

Nisga'a elder Frank Calder, embittered by his humiliating, forced departure from the Barrett cabinet, exacted his revenge, winning banner newspaper headlines by joining and running for Social Credit. He accused Barrett of being anti-Indian, anti-labour and anti-north. Several days later, radio station owner Joe Chesney, a first-time candidate for the NDP in suburban Langley, embarrassed the party with some horribly inappropriate "humour." After referring to Bennett as "Buffalo and the Three Stooges," Chesney took a shot at Frank Calder. "It looks like the act has now been joined by Tonto," he said, drawing gasps and even boos from the pro-NDP crowd. Ad agency head Manny Dunsky didn't help, either. Arriving hastily from Montreal to prepare the NDP's election advertising, he told the media he had a secret slogan to propel the party to victory. Accompanied by pictures of Dunsky with cigarette in hand, coverage of his remarks enhanced a public perception that backroom outsiders from away were flocking to BC to man the good ship NDP.

The Socreds meanwhile, as Barrett had hoped, were caught by surprise. Just emerging from their annual convention, by all accounts a dreary affair, they had only one candidate in place and an organization not close to election readiness. All that changed in a heartbeat. Bill Bennett was so startled and excited by the news, he slipped off a curb trying to cross a street in Kelowna and twisted his ankle. Soon, limp and all, he was off on the campaign trail, drawing big crowds, condemning the government for financial mismanagement and vowing "to clean up the mess." No one but the media minded that for the first three weeks Bennett stuck mostly to the same tired speech he gave at Social Credit's recent convention. Not his fault, Bennett explained, as there simply wasn't time to write a fresh one.

Barrett was right about Social Credit's lack of political polish. Bennett was raw, unsure of his political instincts and a dull orator with little of the natural, public warmth the premier exuded in spades. With a posse of bumbling researchers, the Social Credit campaign careered from gaffe to gaffe. More often than not, accusations levelled against the NDP produced embarrassing retractions. In one dreadful example, Bennett was rebuked by no less than the eminent Thomas Norris for his charge that the NDP had had an advance look at Norris' report on redrawing electoral boundaries. Norris called Bennett's assertion "totally irresponsible." There was "no chance in the world" of anyone getting a peek at his report "unless we are all liars," retorted the ex-judge of the BC Court of Appeal. Extreme statements from Socred candidates were also a problem. North Vancouver District Mayor Ron Andrews topped the charts with his allegation that an NDP victory would put British Columbians at risk of losing their land and homes to the government. The biblical fervour of Victoria Social Credit hopeful Ian Randle was close behind. "When the righteous are in authority, the people rejoice. But when the wicked are in power, the people mourn," Mr. Randle reminded his followers.

Driven by a thirst to evict the hated socialists and taste power themselves, many Socred nominating meetings were unruly, overcrowded and bitterly contested. The best man did not always win. Little-known Vancouver businessman Alan Lau snatched one of the party's two nominations in Vancouver Centre by busing in 182 mostly elderly, signed-up members from Chinatown, after treating them to dinner at Ming's. When Lau's purported academic credentials were found to be wanting, his running mate, the flamboyant Herb Capozzi, taped over Lau's name on their election signs and campaigned on his own.

Former minister without portfolio Agnes Kripps, whose name still resounds in the annals of old Socred wackery with her desire to relabel sex education as BOLT (Biology of Living for Today), was infuriated by her failure to re-secure a nomination in her former riding of Vancouver South. Kripps charged that her bid was sabotaged by monied interests backing rivals Gerry Strongman and Stephen Rogers. "If big business is going to move in and run the show and people no longer matter, I am concerned," she told the *Vancouver Sun*.

Bennett steered carefully away from these mini-dustups. But he was front and centre in the campaign's biggest controversy: the stolen BC Rail telex, or as entitled by the witty Alex Macdonald, "The Case of the Purloined Letter and the Jubilant Delinquent." The telex was an eight-page classified document from federal Minister of Transportation Otto Lang, confirming Ottawa's approval and financial support for a northern extension of BC Rail. A copy was in the briefcase of consultant John de Wolf, the former provincial Conservative leader who had been assisting the government with rail negotiations. Someone lifted the briefcase from de Wolf's parked car, then returned it under mysterious circumstances three or four days later. But a photocopy of the telex wound up in the hands of Social Credit. At an evening rally in Merritt, just ahead of Barrett's planned announcement of the extension, Bennett triumphantly held high a copy of the telex, stamped with the premier's official mark. The Social Credit leader demanded the government back off on the deal until after the election.

When it came out that the telex had been stolen, Bennett—rather than being embarrassed—had the chutzpah to demand a judicial inquiry into the theft. He accused the government of sloppiness, with no understanding of confidentiality. That was a bit much for many to swallow and Bennett's handling of the matter, which was front-page news for days, was roundly criticized. Trying to make political hay out of a document that had been stolen did not look good. The telex turned out to have been removed from de Wolf's briefcase, photocopied and handed over to Social Credit campaign chairman Dan Campbell by Kenneth Tyson, a West Vancouver businessman. He had been asked by an office building commissionaire to help find the owner of the briefcase, which had been dropped off in the lobby. "Certainly, I wanted the Opposition to have that document," said Tyson. "I was aghast at what was in the briefcase. I thought it was dynamite."

Bennett also took a big public relations hit when he refused to take part in a televised leadership debate agreed to by Barrett and the other two party leaders.

But nothing derailed the momentum of Social Credit's campaign train. Despite his leaden delivery, large, boisterous crowds turned out wherever Bennett spoke. In many places, he outdrew Barrett, the best political performer of his generation. It was the message supporters came to hear, not verbal fireworks. The loudest ovation always greeted Bennett's vow to end welfare abuse and restore authority to the classroom. At the same time, Bennett pledged to keep so many specific NDP programs—Mincome, Pharmacare, rent controls and almost everything else—that a frustrated Barrett wondered out loud why Bennett was running against him.

Behind the scenes, Social Credit quickly became far more organized than many realized. With an astonishing membership base of sixty thousand and no shortage of cash, the tireless "Amazing Grace" McCarthy, when she wasn't issuing ludicrous warnings about a sinister NDP plan to form a secret police force, spearheaded efforts to build an efficient election machine. There were well-briefed captains and large phalanxes of volunteers for every poll in the province. The goal was to out-organize the vaunted NDP, handicapped by lingering union and activist disenchantment. Social Credit may have done it. The money flowed in. At Bennett's nomination meeting in Kelowna, not one but two rock bands were hired to entertain the crowd, and each of the thousand or so hometown boosters who filled the hall was given a boater hat to wear. For Bennett's last big rally, the party rented no less than the Pacific Coliseum, home of the Vancouver Canucks, packed it with more than twelve thousand of the raucous faithful, and for good measure, paraded in an elephant with jowly Langley MLA Bob McLelland riding on top.

All told, Social Credit spent nearly twice as much as the NDP: $1.7-million to $940,000. That didn't count the outpouring of anti-NDP ads from interest groups and self-proclaimed freedom fighters that flooded the province. Does money talk? Not always, but in the thirteen ridings that Social Credit won by fewer than 1,300 votes, they outspent the NDP more than two to one. In the meantime, cash virtually dried up for the Liberals and Conservatives, whose 29 percent of the vote had played such a prominent role in the 1972 campaign. Although analysis showed the NDP would have won regardless of the split vote, their margin of victory would have been as thin as a cat's whisker. This time, free enterprise forces were desperate to ensure that anti-NDP voters streamed towards Social Credit. Day after day, they hammered home the message: a vote for the Liberals or Conservatives is a vote for the NDP. Halfway through the campaign, Conservative Party president Tony Saunders acknowledged its success. "The corporate doors are closed," Saunders sighed.

Then, the threats began. Gus Boersma was an alderman in the picturesque Rocky Mountain community of Fernie. He ran a local life insurance business. Shortly after he announced his intention to run for the Conservatives, Boersma began receiving worrisome phone calls. The callers, a dozen businessmen and clients, all said the same thing: Boersma's business would suffer if his vote helped defeat the local Social Credit candidate. He withdrew. "There's a fear campaign going on," Boersma said. Another Conservative candidate in Prince George, Alan Anderton, said he had received telephone threats from "right-wing extremists," telling him to quit. Tory leader Scott Wallace could barely contain his rage. "Those people on the right screaming about the socialists taking away individual freedom seem to be doing a pretty good job of it themselves, when they have the vindictiveness to blackmail you in the survival of your business," Wallace told reporters. From forty-nine candidates in 1972, the Conservatives were able to muster only twenty-nine standard-bearers in the 1975 race. Supporters had been paralyzed by fear, Wallace charged bitterly. He said he couldn't count the number of people who told him to hang in there, but "ducked out" out of publicly pitching in to help. Lack of funds meant that Wallace was essentially an asterisk on the campaign trail, confined mostly to his own riding of Oak Bay.

There were threats and anger on the Liberal side, too. Kamloops candidate Don Carter reported that Social Credit supporters warned him his travel agency would suffer economic pressure if he didn't drop out. He stayed on the ballot, eventually earning a respectable 15 percent of the vote. Other prospective Liberal candidates, however, had been intimidated from running by similar scare tactics, according to party president Patrick Graham. "Horrible calls are coming in," he told the *Vancouver Sun*. "We're being called Commie bastards, and worse. I've never seen anything like this. Not in Canada."

This campaign, the heckling tables were turned on the NDP. Most of the catcalls at public meetings, though certainly not all, came from those opposed to the New Democrats. The few anti-Socreds who braved the almost religious-revival delirium of Bill Bennett rallies did not have an easy time. As voting day neared, emotions escalated. In Victoria, government employee Adam Ustik was punched and hustled out the door by several enforcers when he tried to yell questions at Bill Bennett. A telephoned bomb threat cancelled a meeting in Nanaimo. In the fishing community of Steveston, a raucous, all-candidates gathering was cut short after a jeering mob occupied the front rows of seats and shouted down candidates from the NDP, Liberals and

Conservatives. Social Credit's Jim Nielsen was not interrupted. "It was not just that the speakers were shouted down," Ernie Novakowski, campaign manager for NDP incumbent Harold Steves, said afterward. "It was the way they were shouted down. They were standing on chairs, threatening, screaming."

The NDP campaign was centred on one man: the premier. Manny Dunsky's secret slogan was revealed as, "BC has strong leadership. Let's keep it that way." The words were emblazoned on billboards over a lovely, professional picture of Barrett. There was no mention of the NDP. While Bennett often barnstormed by bus with glad-handlers galore, Barrett stuck to cars and planes, accompanied only by his son Dan and closest political friend Harvey Beech. "It was really on the fly," Dan recalled. "Going from town to town. Harvey or I would drive. We'd stop to pick up some sandwiches for lunch. One-hour martinizing to get rid of any spots you had on your clothes. Living out of a suitcase. The weather was often crappy. Cold, too." Once the small group arrived, there was time for Barrett to do some local media interviews, meet the NDP candidate to ask what the government could promise the riding, scribble a few notes on a napkin, bring the house down with a barnburner of a speech, and maybe have a late-night beer or two with the few reporters along. "It was a lot different from the way campaigns are today," said Dan.

Barrett was a master campaigner. No one in the province could deliver a political speech like he could—equal parts passion, humour and full-throttle attack against "Bill Bennett and gang." Meeting after meeting, arms pumping up and down, he pounded away: "Don't let them take it away from you." He rarely failed to mention a meeting, likely mythical, with a Victoria businessman who thanked him for keeping the *Princess Marguerite* ferry run to Seattle in service. The businessman went on to admit liking a number of other moves by the government. "I just don't like this socialism" was Barrett's inevitably popular punchline. Wherever he went the premier was the best show in town, never failing to attract sizeable audiences. While Social Credit rallies emphasized hoopla with bands, streamers, balloons and the unavoidable boater hats, Barrett would appear on stage with no razzle-dazzle, no whipped-up fanfare except for applause from those on hand. There was never a prepared text, just a glass of water to fortify the NDP leader for the next hour. "My speeches come from my head and my heart, not from an advertising agency," Barrett would say. At the end of each speech, the premier took questions, giving time for large collection buckets to be passed around and filled with donations to fuel the good fight.

Barrett began hitting his stride midway through the campaign. By the time he reached the resource-based, counterculture town of Nelson in late November, he simply caught fire. Before a foot-stomping, enthusiastic crowd of 1,100 people who had ventured through a heavy snowfall to crowd the gym at Notre Dame University, the premier responded with his most rousing speech of the campaign. Feeding off the crowd's exuberance, Barrett waved his arms and shouted "Whoopee!" every time he dished out a good line. There were many. "I finally figured out what free enterprisers mean when they talk about socialism," Barrett proclaimed, his voice rising in great, mocking tones. "When it's a matter of saving a businessman's skin, it's a grant. When it's a matter of giving aid to someone else, it's socialism. From now on, when we talk about people, it's going to be grants, and when we talk about companies, we're going to call it welfare." The place went nuts. Whoopee! Lacing into Social Credit and their supporters, dialing up the polarization level, Barrett said the election was a battle: "It's the people against the big, vested interests, those great big saviours of freedom." In full rhetorical flight, he lambasted Social Crediters as "that conglomerate bunch of back-sliders, boat jumpers, high divers and half benders." He did not elaborate. A wowed Allan Fotheringham, who was there, said Barrett's speech that night "ranks with the ones they talk about."

No one could rouse an audience like Dave Barrett, perhaps the finest political orator in the province's history. For sheer political theatre, when he was fired up, Barrett's unique mixture of humour, compassion, fury and love was not to be missed.
Photo by Ralph Bower, provided by the *Vancouver Sun*

Barrett always felt good when he was campaigning and talking to folks outside the Lower Mainland, his *g*'s droppin' like flies. As he barnstormed the province, he was rockin' and rollin' at the top of his game. But deep down, he could hardly have been confident. With those who had fought for years against Social Credit now flocking to join the party, and the Liberals and Conservatives in disarray, it couldn't help but be a tough slog. Barrett had run a faultless campaign, Socred hiccups abounded, and an ugly atmosphere was afoot in the province. Yet would that translate into enough NDP votes to hang on as government? In his journal, Peter McNelly expressed what many in the NDP camp, including its leader, must have felt: "Our canvassers remain enthusiastic. People seem to be turning to us. But there's this creepy feeling that we're going to lose. It just won't go away." Like most faced with an uncertain future, Barrett lived in hope, ready to clutch at any sign of salvation.

McNelly describes a Saturday evening of poker in mid-November at Barrett's house in Victoria. It was also municipal election night in the Lower Mainland. A number of pro-NDP candidates were in the running. Barrett had one ear on the radio. When a positive result came in from his home base in Coquitlam, he was ecstatic, McNelly said. "He was jumping up and down in little hops, whooping, punching the air with a half uppercut in quick jabs from his side. Grinning and grinning." There was similar good news from Burnaby. "Barrett couldn't control himself. He just couldn't slow down," wrote McNelly. "A wave of hysterical delight pushed through us. We were all laughing wildly, at almost nothing. Nobody concentrated on the poker. Dave kept jumping up and turning the radio on." In the Greater Vancouver suburbs where the NDP had done well in 1972, there was no sign of a swing to the right. That was the consensus of Harvey Beech, Barrett's chief grassroots watcher. Pro-Socred candidates were mostly doing poorly, and "NDP stooges" were winning, Beech told Barrett, during a long telephone conversation about the results. "Dave came back from the phone with tears in his eyes. Literally," said McNelly. "He was that happy."

The final few days, however, were not good. Provincial Secretary Ernie Hall was roasted for sending letters on government letterhead to workers at publicly owned Panco Poultry, warning their jobs might be in jeopardy if the NDP lost. Front-page banner headlines heralded statements by MacMillan Bloedel president Denis Timmis to the Royal Commission on

Forest Resources. Timmis said the climate of investment uncertainty in BC was unmatched in the province's history. He alluded to "a sense of confrontation and distrust between government and the forest industry." Timmis was the second major forest executive to skewer the NDP during the election campaign, but this attack hurt more, since he had accompanied Barrett on his trip to China and was not considered a corporate hawk. In the last day or so, newspapers were full of extremist ads warning of the perils of socialism. "A Group of Concerned Citizens" bought space for a prominent, three-column ad that contained just eleven words, in big black letters: "Thursday the election is Freedom of Individual rights or Socialism."

"Interested and concerned British Columbians" paid for an ad targeting Bob Williams. "[He] has said seven years will be time enough in which to impose full socialist economic theory on BC. He has already had three years and look where we are now! ... Do not fail to vote!" The Canadian League of Rights chimed in with its clarion call for British Columbians to "Wake Up!" The NDP's "state socialism" is out to impose public ownership on all major industries in the province, the League warned. "Is your business ... your place of work [next]?" Social Credit's East Vancouver constituency got into the act with its own big, bold ad headlined, "IS BRITISH COLUMBIA HEADED FOR THE FATE OF SWEDEN?" The East Van Socreds, seeming to accept that Dave Barrett came across better than their man, informed readers that the choice was not about leadership personalities, but "state control of British Columbia versus individual enterprise." Less hysterical but hard-hitting were a series of full-page advertisements paid for by "private insurance companies" that ripped ICBC and "the fun of dealing with a government bureaucracy" with no consumer choice. "Thanks for the memories," the ads said.

Barrett did get one last blaze of publicity. Using language unthinkable in today's era of diplomatic niceties and verbal caution, the premier tore into high-profile Washington State Senator Warren Magnuson, who had demanded a stop to BC's "gouging" of the US on its export natural gas price. "You mind your own business about our politics, and we'll mind our business about yours," Barrett lectured the absent Magnuson, before a roaring crowd at an overflow rally in the Fraser Valley. "I'll tell you, Mr. Senator, that same old giveaway gang is not going to get back in and give away gas again ... We are going to demand a fair price, regardless of what some American politicians say." Barrett had been set off by Magnuson's remarks at a luncheon in Washington, DC. Referring to BC's successful efforts to increase its export price, the senator said, "Put a burnoose around the head of Mr. Barrett and those people up there, and they're just the same [as oil producers in the Middle East]." The NDP had worked hard to get Ottawa's approval to boost the price from below a dollar per thousand cubic feet when they took office to $1.60, but this was still below the $2.25 charged US customers by Texas. "Mr. Senator, as long as Texas charges $2.25, that's what we want, and if you want to get our price down, you go fight Texas first," said the stoked premier.

Barrett ended his campaign with a fist-pumping rally in his old stomping grounds, Coquitlam. At his populist best, he bellowed, "Social Credit just wants power—raw, naked power for the same old gang, the big business establishment in downtown Vancouver." He concluded, "I have one last message. This land is your land ... We must never go back." On voting day, as long lines formed outside polling stations, a front-page story in the *Vancouver Sun* informed readers that the RCMP had placed Barrett under police guard after several threats against his life. That night, Barrett sat in shirt sleeves with his family in a charmless room at the Squire Motor Inn in Coquitlam to wait for the voters' verdict, along with a few aides and invited reporters. Four plainclothes Mounties kept watch from across the corridor.

It was not a cliffhanger. At 8:35, Barrett looked over at Shirley, giving a thumbs-down gesture. "We're getting wiped," he murmured. Their fourteen-year-old daughter, Jane, got a laugh when she said, "If they bring back the strap, I'm quitting school." A few minutes later, Barrett changed into a grey suit, light blue shirt and dark striped tie. "Okay, let's go," he said. A small cavalcade of cars with an unmarked RCMP vehicle in the middle began making its desultory rounds. At the party's Port Moody committee room, Barrett told sombre volunteers there was nothing for the party to be ashamed of. "We have brought BC further ahead than any other government in the country. Our programs will be copied and emulated throughout Canada."

Headquarters in New Westminster were practically deserted when Barrett arrived. He stayed to have a cup of coffee with Shirley as the television showed little-known car dealer George Kerster with a narrow lead in Barrett's own riding. Later that night, in keeping with the tone of much of the campaign, a bunch of Kerster scrutineers who were angered at what they thought were counting irregularities charged into one of the returning-officer rooms and demanded to put their own seals on the ballot boxes. Then they stormed out, leaving behind overturned tables, broken glass and beer bottles. The next day, chief electoral returning officer Ken Morton said that Coquitlam returning officer Anne Richardson had been harassed and "brow-beaten" by Social Credit scrutineers. The returning officer in Burnaby North, where there was another close race, had also been harassed on election night by an unruly group of Socreds, Morton said. "It makes me boiling mad."

As the NDP went down in flames, no one in the province could have been happier than the old man in Kelowna, W.A.C. Bennett. Not only were the socialist hordes back outside the gates, the seventy-five-year old patriarch would soon see his son Bill installed as premier, the first filial succession in BC history. The large front-page picture in the *Vancouver Sun* on December 12 was not of a grinning Bill Bennett, with wife Audrey. It showed father and son, together. The elder Bennett had his arm around Bill's shoulder, smiling that great Wacky smile, undiminished by age. Bennett Sr., who holidayed in Florida during the campaign, said the province could relax now that a free enterprise government had been returned to power. "I said in the past that people needed to put their finger on the hot stove of socialism," he exclaimed, eyes brimming with tears of joy. "They've felt it, and now they've taken their finger away." Frank Calder's elation was not far behind W.A.C. Bennett's. He chortled to a reporter, "If you happen to see Little Davey the comedian, tell him that the Little Chief laughed and laughed and laughed, all the way back to Victoria."

At the Bayshore Hotel in Vancouver, where Social Crediters were already well into their wild celebrations, pandemonium broke out when Kerster's victory over Barrett was confirmed. "Good riddance!" screamed one man in a boater hat. "It was like living in Russia with him as premier." Barrett's mother, Rose, was born in Russia. She had few words for reporters on election night. "What should I say? What can I say? He didn't fight dirty. If he was dirty, he would have won." At the Louis Brier Home for the Aged in Vancouver, Dave's father, Sam, who had lost his sight from the lingering impact of being gassed at Passchendaele, sat in the dark on the edge of his bed and listened to the results on his small radio. He didn't listen for long. After a while, as described by *Sun* journalist Lisa Hobbs, Sam Barrett switched off the radio and nodded, "as if in acknowledgement to a voice within him: 'I accept it. I accept it.'"

Headquarters for the NDP was a far from posh entertainment hall in Burnaby, likened by one wag to a groovy California funeral parlour. On the outside, it was identified as "The Gai Paree," which hardly matched the mood on the inside. The sting of defeat had worn off somewhat by the time Barrett showed up. Relaxed and smiling, he even cracked a few jokes. Talking to party members for the last time as premier, however, Barrett was sombre. He reminded them of all their government had accomplished.

"One temporary setback based on fear does not stop the goodness in man marching forward ... The war for a more mature, loving and human society goes on," he said. "Our commitment to building a better society is why we came together in the CCF in the first place, and what we arrived for in government, now and in the future."

Someone in the crowd shouted, "It's just money." Barrett did not rise to the bait. "Well, look, relax," he said. "We have a proud history, a proud present and an even prouder future. All I have to add, it's, it's ..." His voice faltered for the first time that terrible evening. "It's nothing, this temporary setback. Good luck to the new government. And good luck to us all." Barrett collected his family, walked out to the cold, dark parking lot and headed back to the Squire Motor Inn. It was time to be alone with the people he loved. It was over.

The final results were crushing for the NDP. Social Credit claimed thirty-five seats, while the New Democrats' seat count dropped from thirty-eight to eighteen. "It was horrible," McNelly wrote in his journal the next day. "I felt like we had witnessed a mass public hanging. Only I was part of it. Dave Stupich's face looked like he'd been punched out in a beer parlour brawl." The toughest loss of all came in Barrett's home riding of Coquitlam where he fell by eighteen votes to Kerster, the nondescript car dealer. That personal defeat, delivered by constituents who had always supported him with solid majorities, hurt Barrett deeply. A moral victory for the NDP was that despite its tumultuous, progressive program of change, the party maintained its share of the popular vote from the 1972 election, at slightly more than 39 percent. But an avalanche of former Liberal and Conservative votes swept Social Credit to power. In total, the two smaller parties lost 18 percent of their 1972 popular vote. The Socreds went up 18 percent. Overall, Social Credit recorded its highest ever share of the popular vote, a tad under 50 percent. Never before had so many voted to keep the NDP out.

In a trenchant post-election column on what he termed "the night of the car dealers," Allan Fotheringham quoted a prominent Vancouver businessman who had never before voted Social Credit. He had planned to do so on December 11 after a lifetime of supporting the provincial Liberals. The unnamed businessman told Fotheringham, "I am going to get up in the morning, and drink about half a bottle of gin. Then I'm going down to the polling booth and vote Socred. I'm then going to come home and wash my hands for about an hour. Then I plan to drink the rest of the gin and get drunk."

Peter McNelly had left a promising career in journalism, where he rose quickly, to join the Barrett team. He saw its flaws up close, but he believed in the government's programs, in their quest to redress society's ills and enhance the public good. McNelly took the NDP's defeat hard. "I had this weird feeling that the event was only taking place on television. It all seemed so abstract," he reflected in his evocative journal. "The weeping people with their eyes shot red, and the public works department types down from the legislative buildings nursing their beers seemed more real. You could at least hold their hands and look into their eyes and know that those people outside the room called 'the electorate' had just wiped you out." The Monday after the election, the painful task of leaving power began. "It was like the first day of dismantling a home," wrote McNelly. "The files being carted from place to place. Endless people walking up and down hallways, pausing. Secretaries standing around like jilted brides. The press hanging around like wolves with electronic aids to make them seem almost human."

Not all was gloom and doom. Highways Minister Graham Lea walked into Barrett's office with a big smile and declared, "Well, we sure got 'em this time. They still haven't figured out the global strategy." Barrett burst out laughing. Gary Lauk cracked that the Socreds' first order of business would allow used car dealers to turn back odometers. And McNelly offered that the NDP were victims of Grace McCarthyism. After meeting for the last time with the NDP caucus, Barrett was asked by reporters if he had anything to say about his leadership. "Yes, I support it," he quipped.

As W.A.C. Bennett had done, Barrett, with Minister of Finance Dave Stupich beside him, released a final accounting of the current books of the province, before leaving office. They reported a modest deficit of $40-million, which they said could be erased by continuing NDP cuts that had already saved $143-million during the first eight months of the fiscal year. At the same time, the government's many interventions in the marketplace had boosted the value of Crown corporations from $3.8 billion to $5.7 billion during the NDP's three years. Since the election, Barrett had been inwardly seething at the fate these accumulated assets might face under Social Credit. His fears prompted a last, passionate plea to the people of the province, before handing over power to Bill Bennett. "You own these assets, and they are worth every cent," Barrett told British Columbians. "Don't sell them to some fast-talking huckster, who tells you they are Socialist. These assets will make your lives easier. Do not allow any government, ever, to sell them off." In his autobiography, Barrett wrote bitterly, "My warning, tragically, went unheeded."

Conclusion

There can be little quarrel that the Barrett years were the most tumultuous three years in the long, colourful political history of British Columbia. They were a non-stop roller coaster that the government rode right to the end. By the time voters finally flicked the "off" switch, the province was exhausted, perhaps no one more so than Dave Barrett himself. For thirty-nine months, he had been front and centre of a raw, untried administration that tried to change society in almost every facet. There never seemed to be a down day. During its relatively brief time in office, the Barrett government set a legislative pace unmatched before or since, averaging more than two bills a week, enacting in total 367 pieces of legislation. Few were piecemeal changes. Some were breathtaking, some were radical, and many remain with us today. Democratic reforms aimed at giving the opposition a fairer shake were seized upon to prolong sessions to record lengths. It was legislation by opposition-induced exhaustion.

Barrett was also a tour de force outside the legislature. He was forever railing away at the elite, targeting the mining moguls, the big money boys on Howe Street, the banks, the fat-cat corporations and the hostile owners of newspapers with his fiery, well-honed denunciations. Most would rank Tommy Douglas and Barrett one and two as Canada's most socialist premiers. But Douglas never made news like Barrett. The all-encompassing age of media was just beginning, and Barrett basked in the attention, good and bad. When it was bad, he was like a moth drawn to a flame. When it was good, he was a bear gorging himself on honey. Either way, he was hooked. He couldn't stop himself. Speeches by Barrett, when he was in the mood, could lift people out of their seats like no one else. He was in constant demand across the country.

Just prior to calling the 1975 election, he delivered a scorching address to the NDP convention in Alberta. Before a rapturous, overflow crowd of more than a thousand delegates in the heart of oil country, Barrett was interrupted forty-one times by applause, four times by standing ovations, as he ripped into a project that is still making headlines nearly four decades later: the Alberta oil sands. This was a time when Syncrude and other oil companies were demanding government aid to develop the project. No way, declared Barrett. "If those price-gouging oil companies want an answer before January [on their demand], I've got an answer for them," he thundered. "Get out! Get out!" The delegates roared. He travelled—to Britain, to Europe, to Japan, to China, to Seattle, to Washington, DC, to New York City, innumerable times to Ottawa, even all the way to the Maritimes to talk to the NDP there. Barrett's drive to change society for the better was relentless. He had a deep, burning hunger to right wrongs, to root out injustice and to deliver a society that lived up to the old labour slogan, "What we desire for ourselves, we desire for all."

Through all this, still in his early forties, Barrett's energy at times seemed inexhaustible. It wasn't. Notwithstanding a raucous, election-night wake with Norm Levi and a few aides, full of dark, alcohol-enhanced hilarity that carried on into the wee small hours, Barrett was a mental and physical wreck when the ride finally came to an end. His government shattered, his own political future uncertain after a humiliating loss to an obscure car dealer in his own riding, he had to get away. He dutifully reported on the province's finances, turned government over to his successor, and then for two weeks while the province pondered what life would be like under the mirthless Bill Bennett, Dave and Shirley Barrett escaped to Manzanillo, Mexico, to think about their own future.

There he decompressed, overcame his depression from the election, and relaxed. He came back rejuvenated. When the caucus decided they wanted him to carry on as leader, Barrett was ready. Bob Williams resigned his seat in Vancouver East, and Barrett went back to his childhood roots to seek re-election to the legislature in a by-election. After a relaxed campaign full of nostalgia, Italian homemade wine and too much offered food, he won an overwhelming 70 percent of the vote. A *Sun* photographer captured the moment when Barrett strode back into the legislature in June 1976, a broad smile on his face and a spring in his step, Bill King escorting him on the right and Alex Macdonald on the left. There is no hint of "loser" in his exuberant expression. This was a consummate politician, for whom losses and wins were just waypoints on a long journey, returning to his natural habitat. Debate and oratory were Barrett's vocations and he excelled at both; he was never comfortable carrying a protest sign and uneasy around picket lines. What some called extra-parliamentary politics, he deemed a distraction from the main task, which is to win elections and make change. He belonged in the legislature.

The big smile, the strong ethical standards of his administration and his incessant calls for "love" all go a long way to explaining both Barrett's enduring impact on the life of the province and the remarkable resilience of his popularity. Voters might disagree with Barrett's ideology but few believed his motives were improper or his aspirations self-centred. In fact, Barrett radiated hope for a better world and a conviction that human beings were capable of creating it. When he saw that breaking down, he was never reluctant to lash out. There was no better example of that than late in his term when he accepted a

Back in the legislature after his landslide victory on June 3, 1976, Barrett is all smiles as he is escorted to his seat by former cabinet mates, Bill King (left) and Alex Macdonald.
Photo provided by the *Vancouver Sun*

routine invitation to address a Young Presidents' gathering at the upscale Bayshore Hotel. As he arrived, Barrett happened to hear a presenter from the FBI warn the conservative business leaders about future kidnappings by revolutionary groups. According to the *Vancouver Sun*'s account, he was also in time to watch a karate expert demonstrating self-defence techniques. Aghast at what he had witnessed, Barrett decided to let his audience of conservative, mostly American, business leaders have it. "Here you are: a happy upper middle-class in North America," he began. "What the hell kind of a world are we living in? What have we been doing to ourselves in North America?"

The audience sat in stunned silence as Barrett wondered aloud at what had become of the land where he spent "eight beautiful years" in his youth. "Never in my wildest dreams did I think I would [now see] a country of paranoia, violence and greed. For God's sake, what are you doing?" If blacks and Chicanos continued to be starved of basic services, he warned, they would rise up and get rid of white middle-class Americans, and "all that training in judo isn't going to save you." He challenged the Young Presidents to change. "[You lack] even a basic Christian responsibility to other human beings ... You've made your bucks. Now, it's time to give something back."

At the same time, his unbounded confidence in the ability of working people to lead, to govern and to make change was what many voters liked about him the most. He had more confidence in them than they had in themselves and it allowed them to forgive him for his miscues, slip-ups and setbacks, especially when they considered what he had achieved.

Although Barrett, of course, never got another crack at running a government with lessons learned, scars healed and the political wisdom to make it a "long time" in office, he came close. In 1979 Barrett nearly caught the unprepared Bill Bennett off guard, with another sly, understated campaign that earned the NDP their highest-ever popular vote, a shade under 46 percent. The 7-percent increase in the party's vote and eight new seats were a clear indication that many British Columbians, in the wake of the anti-NDP hysteria of 1975, had reflected on the Barrett record and decided he deserved a second chance. Unfortunately for Barrett, the right-wing coalition forged by Bennett held together just enough to deliver him four more years as premier with a narrow 31–26 majority in the legislature.

In 1983, Barrett appeared on his way to victory. He was on a roll, packing public meetings as part of a rollicking campaign that completely overshadowed Bill Bennett's stumbling tour of the province. But with less than two weeks to ago, Barrett made an ill-advised pledge to scrap Social Credit's public sector wage controls, which were popular. Bennett's response on BCTV's evening news turned the campaign around. Although the NDP's share of the popular vote dropped only slightly, and Social Credit's went up by an equally small margin, the changes were enough to deliver a 35–22 advantage in seats for Bill Bennett's party.

In both elections, Barrett and the NDP had been done in by the very polarization and right-wing unity they had done so much, inadvertently, to spawn during their years in government. He later judged the "coalition of the right and the centre one of the worst things that's happened in BC. There is no rational debate." In the wake of his 1983 victory, with the provincial economy mired in recession, Bennett unleashed his massive "restraint program," a legislative blitzkrieg of twenty-two bills designed to eliminate the Barrett legacy once and for all. Hailed by Milton Friedman as a model of neo-conservative political strategy, the restraint program ignited the kind of popular mobilization Barrett had never enjoyed as leader, either in government or opposition. The province was brought to a standstill by an escalating general strike that ended with a negotiated agreement concluded by Jack Munro in Bennett's Kelowna living room called the Kelowna Accord. Bennett's program survived largely intact, but his own political career was crippled and he followed Barrett into retirement from provincial politics.

Barrett's opponents, particularly in the business sector, feared his re-election with such intensity that they completely reshaped their approach to public policy, creating a new think tank to advance their values that had a global impact. Appalled by what he believed was the Waffle Manifesto's influence on NDP thinking, MacMillan Bloedel vice-president Patrick Boyle mobilized J.V. Clyne's fundraising skills to create a counterweight to the "incorrect ideas" at its root. The Fraser Institute, basing its analysis on the theories of Friedrich Hayek and Milton Friedman, sought to "re-establish the dominance of free enterprise ideas, the values of the market and property rights." The Adam Smith Institute of London later declared that "ideas which started with the Fraser Institute have been eagerly taken up in other countries and spread ... around the world." The institute's policy prescriptions were at the core of Bennett's restraint program in 1983.

Social movements that had been decisive in 1972 but demoralized and demobilized by 1975 found reasons to revise their first impressions. Teacher Ken Novakowski, fired in Dailly's purge of the education ministry's research unit and angry at the collapse of the New Democrats' promises of education reform, recalled the post-Barrett years as a "golden age" in the classroom because of the improvements in teacher-student ratios. Author and college instructor Stan Persky, then a story producer at the CBC and a volunteer at a Vancouver newspaper "of working class struggle," took a post at an NDP-created community college in Terrace just as Barrett started his 1975 march to an election. The college's board was completely purged only weeks after the election, but the college itself survived, as did three others intended to bring higher education to the hinterland. "The revolution was over, but not the college," Persky wrote many years later. "A lot of small, good things happened."

Rosemary Brown later acknowledged the New Democrats' achievements for women as "phenomenal," with breakthrough investments in rape relief centres, women's health collectives, daycare, Mincome and the *Human Rights Act*. Women's equality remained a touchstone for New Democrats and Mike Harcourt, the next NDP premier, made sure to create a Ministry of Women's Equality. Even the labour movement, while never forgiving the back-to-work legislation, overcame its criticism of the Labour Code, ultimately treating its original draft and Weiler's early decisions as sacred text.

Historians have also taken another look. Early reviews of the Barrett government were not kind, fastening on its many flubs and mistakes, its onslaught against the province's so-called free enterprise forces, and the chaos that often obscured its achievements. One of the foremost critics was political historian David Mitchell, who wrote the definitive chronicle of W.A.C. Bennett and his impact on British Columbia, followed by a book on Bennett's Social Credit successors. Mitchell, once a Liberal turned independent MLA in the early nineties, was dismissive of Barrett's achievements, referring to the NDP leader at one point as a "clown prince" who "poisoned politics in the province," adding that "in the field of winners and losers, history will judge Dave Barrett a loser." Much later Mitchell acknowledged that the Barrett years had left a tremendous legacy. "In the aftermath of the Barrett years, there was a lot of navel-gazing, soul-searching, back-biting recriminations and blame going on among political observers and partisans," he explained in an interview. "Now that things have cooled off and we've had some perspective, I think we can now see that this juncture in the political life of British Columbia was very, very significant. It can't be dismissed as just a fly in the ointment or just a period of mistaken, political adventurism, or anything like that. Far from it."

Many of the government's initiatives endure to this day, even after a generation or more of other governments committed to dismantling them, Mitchell said. "There's been a staying power for some of the impulses associated with the Barrett administration that has been underestimated." For all its sloppiness and carelessness, the pace of pent-up reform during the Barrett years amounted to a decade in the political life of the province, according to Mitchell. "It was a period of fascinating public policy development and initiatives we had never seen in a concentrated period like that—before or since in British Columbia." A Vancouver-bound air traveller descending over the city can see the Barrett government's impact in the landscape itself, from the sharp, green edge of the Agricultural Land Reserve to the forest above Cypress Bowl and the SeaBuses crossing Burrard Inlet.

"Are we here for a good time or a long time?" Barrett asked his new cabinet at their first meeting. His answer: "a good time," a time when good people did good things. In hindsight, they all wished it could have been longer. Forty years later, Levi would still encounter strangers who would stop him to say, "you were the best government we ever had, a breath of fresh air." He would reply, "Well, you're only a good government if you're in government, and three years, three months and two days is not really much experience as government." But no one regretted what they had done, or the wonderful times. Sitting in his spacious west-side living room, Gary Lauk would light up at the memory of his few years in government. "I look back fondly. They were my comrades," he recalled. "I actually loved them." It was, he said, a revolutionary government—"revolutionary in the sense that you overthrow the old, the conservative, and you bring in a new form of governance. That's revolutionary." Bob Williams would recall Barrett saying, "'Williams, there's never been another government like us in the history of this province.' And he was right. He was absolutely right. There was never, and there hasn't since, been a government like that in the history of this province."

Appendix

Legacy of the Barrett Government (a partial and subjective list)

1. Hansard.
2. Daily question period in the legislature.
3. Increased funding for opposition parties.
4. Chairmanship of the Public Accounts Committee was given to a member of the opposition.
5. Restored and spruced up Parliament Buildings.
6. Minimum wage raised from $1.50 to $2.50 an hour.
7. Mincome for those over sixty.
8. Pharmacare.
9. Provincial sheriffs service.
10. Preservation of BC farmland for agriculture, through the Agricultural Land Reserve.
11. Strap banned from public schools.
12. Arbitrary ceiling on teacher wage increases lifted.
13. Government-owned auto insurance.
14. Neighbourhood pubs.
15. Drinking age lowered to nineteen.
16. Columbia Cellulose, Crown Zellerbach's Ocean Falls pulp mill, Plateau Mills, Kootenay Forest Products and Panco Poultry bought by the government.
17. Full collective bargaining and the right to strike for government employees.
18. Far-reaching Human Rights Code.
19. Landmark Labour Code that virtually ended court's jurisdiction over picketing and greatly facilitated unions' ability to organize.
20. Powerful Labour Relations Board given unprecedented jurisdiction over all elements of collective bargaining in the province.
21. Government-funded art bank to purchase BC art.
22. BC Energy Commission, which regulated private utilities and monitored oil and gas prices.

23. BC Petroleum Corporation, cutting the government in on profits from sale of natural gas.
24. MLA pay doubled to $25,000 a year.
25. Elected community resources boards.
26. Provincial ambulance service with licensed paramedics.
27. Dramatic expansion of community colleges.
28. Pay toilets abolished.
29. Right to sue the Crown restored.
30. Province's first ministry of housing, designed to encourage affordable and co-op housing through the purchase of Dunhill Development.
31. Islands Trust Act to protect the Gulf Islands against uncontrolled development.
32. Rent controls.
33. Rentalsman to oversee tenant rights.
34. Refurbished Royal Hudson steam locomotive for rail trips between West Vancouver and Squamish.
35. Amalgamation for both Kelowna and Kamloops.
36. Purchase of Seattle–Victoria ferry, the *Princess Marguerite,* plus Victoria harbourfront.
37. First Native school board in the province, Nisga'a Tribal Council.
38. Expanded daycare spaces and increased subsidies.
39. Farm Income Assurance Act.
40. Reduced teacher–student ratios.
41. Purchase of 1.1-million shares in BC Tel, later resold for a large profit.
42. Boycott of non-union grapes at all government-owned institutions.
43. Union wages mandated for publicly funded construction projects.
44. Independent boards of review to decide Workers' Compensation Board appeals.
45. Improved WCB pensions.
46. Annual federal grant of $700,000 restored to the school system.
47. Mandatory kindergarten.
48. End of grade 12 province-wide exams.
49. BC Rail boxcar manufacturing plant in Squamish.

50. Using money saved by cancelling Third Crossing between Vancouver and the North Shore for more public transit buses and SeaBus service (finished under Social Credit).
51. Cancellation of downtown Vancouver government office tower planned by W.A.C. Bennett, setting in motion what eventually became Robson Square.
52. Preservation of Cypress Bowl for recreation.
53. Independent board of governors at BC Institute of Technology.
54. Provincial police commission to set policing standards.
55. *Public Officials and Employees Disclosure Act*, requiring elected and appointed officials to disclose their financial holdings.
56. Increased funding for the arts.
57. Expansion of provincial parks from 7.1 to 9.4-million acres.
58. End to logging and mining in provincial parks.
59. BC lottery launched.
60. Financial aid to enable City of Vancouver purchase the historic Orpheum Theatre.
61. Stalling of Skagit Valley flooding.
62. BC Day.
63. Full-time human rights officers.
64. BC Human Rights Commission.
65. Closure of Willingdon School for troubled girls.
66. BC Ferries shipbuilding.
67. Expansion of legal aid.
68. Province's first consumer services ministry, and Canada's best consumer protection legislation.
69. Significant financial aid for Native fisheries co-op in northwest BC.
70. Legislation allowing BC to establish its own bank.
71. Quashing of proposed bulk-loading coal port for Squamish.
72. Removal of succession duties from farms passed from parents to their children.
73. Freeing civil service pensions funds to be invested in stocks.
74. *BC Police Act* to handle public complaints against the police.
75. *Mineral Royalties Act*, boosting royalties on metals, and increasing government take on windfall profits resulting from spike in world metal prices.

76. Burns Lake Development Corporation.
77. Provincial Status of Women Office.
78. Raising corporate taxes from 10 to 12 percent.
79. Increased renter's grants.
80. Increasing coal royalties from 25¢ to $1.50 per ton.
81. Removal of sales tax from books.
82. Amassing of $38.8-million in Crown corporation profits.
83. *Timber Products Stabilization Act*, enabling government to regulate the price of wood chips sold by sawmills to pulp mills.
84. Prohibition of raw log exports.
85. Boosting welfare rates 20 to 40 percent, with total human resources spending going from 8.5 per to 15.1 percent of the budget.
86. BC Development Corporation to assist BC industries with $100-million fund.
87. Community health centres.
88. BC Cancer Control Agency.
89. Air ambulance service.
90. Land freeze, development study and creation of Whistler as a resort municipality, first of its kind in Canada.
91. Investment in Sun Valley Foods.
92. Labour Relations Board given unique power to designate essential services to be provided during strike by fire, police or health care workers, allowing them to strike but with restrictions.
93. Municipal assessment reform.
94. Doctors' extra billing banned.
95. *Sexual Sterilization Act* repealed.
96. Acquisition of Shaughnessy Veterans' Hospital, later to become B.C. Children's Hospital.
97. Funding of women's shelters, rape relief centres and women's health collectives.

Acknowledgements

Although many, many veterans of the Barrett government and the movements that brought it to power remain active in the life of the province, harnessing their recollections is a massive undertaking. Finding agreement among them on key issues of that term in government is even more elusive.

Apart from Barrett's own memoirs, and Kavic and Nixon's *The 1200 Days: A Shattered Dream,* published in 1978, there are almost no overviews of those remarkable years from 1972 to 1975. There are, on the other hand, many accounts of specific controversies during that period and the massive archive of the BC Project, held by the University of Victoria, for those with the time to review its remarkable range of working papers and interviews. Our challenge was not only to review this enormous mass of material, including the thousands of newspaper accounts from the period, but to create a narrative structure that was true to the time.

Two people made extraordinary contributions to make this possible.

Researcher Robin Folvik volunteered many, many hours of her time to assist us in tracking down sources, organizing our materials and charting a way forward. This book simply could not have been completed without her selfless assistance.

Peter McNelly was the second person to make a spontaneous and indispensable contribution by offering unfettered access to his extraordinary personal journal, which he himself had not reread since he made the final entries in early 1975. Few writers have had access to such relevant, beautifully written and insightful material from a privileged witness to truly remarkable events.

Harbour Publishing promised to publish the book on the basis of a letter and a chapter outline. This show of confidence was critical to keeping us on task. Silas White proved a hard-nosed, well-informed and patient editor.

During the research phase, the authors received a research grant from the United Food and Commercial Workers, Local 1518, and a contribution to research expenses from Brooke and Carol Sundin. Again, many thanks.

Dave and Shirley Barrett were the first to hear of the plans for this project and were immediately supportive. Dave Barrett sat down for interviews with both authors on different occasions but never sought to influence the direction of what was bound to be a searching look at this critical part of his career.

The names of many others who gave time for lengthy interviews are included in the bibliography. What was striking to us as we pursued various leads was how ready everyone from that crazy time was to help ... and how much their lives had been changed by the experience.

A Note on Sources

Although no full-length account of the Barrett government has been attempted since 1978, there is a rich collection of personal archives, academic research and media accounts that cover many aspects of those turbulent years. In the course of the research for this book, the authors relied on three main sources of information.

The first was media reports, particularly in the Vancouver and Victoria daily papers that were indexed in the files of the legislature library. This daily coverage of Dave Barrett's government provides a vivid and detailed account of his three years in power from the outside. It reflects the story that most British Columbians heard, whether they were hardcore Socreds or committed New Democrats.

These sources were supplemented by the archives of the BC Project, a multi-year 1980s research project headed by Walter Young of the University of Victoria that produced a series of twenty-two peer-reviewed academic papers on a wide range of the Barrett government's policies and practices. The BC Project collection, now housed at the University of Victoria's Archives, includes transcripts of a remarkable series of interviews with leading elected officials and civil servants about key events of that period.

The third and perhaps most critical source was the journal kept by former *Province* columnist and then-Barrett aide Peter McNelly, who sat down about once every two weeks to record life inside the Barrett leadership team in gripping detail. McNelly's four-hundred-page manuscript, typed on legal sheets and never before reviewed or published, is literally a first draft of history, written with extraordinary passion and insight.

John Saywell's *Canadian Annual Review of Politics and Political Affairs* provided an indispensable summary of events at the provincial and national level. Whenever possible, sources are noted in the text.

Notes

Preface

"... more substantial legislation ... than any other administration before or since." Jean Barman, *The West Beyond the West* (Toronto: University of Toronto Press, 1991), 323. Barman, in her history of BC, estimated that three-quarters of Barrett's legislation was of great significance, and argued that Bennett's defeat "marked a watershed in British Columbia history."

Barrett asks for chance to give BC a 'fair shake.' *Vancouver Sun*, August 29, 1972.

"... a time of positive change." Terence Morley et al., *The Reins of Power: Governing in British Columbia* (Vancouver: Douglas and McIntyre, 1983).

Barrett's government as a "hiccup" is from George Woodcock, *British Columbia: A History of the Province* (Vancouver: Douglas and McIntyre, 1990). Barrett as a "loser" who "poisoned politics in the province" is found in David J. Mitchell's *Succession: The Political Reshaping of British Columbia* (Vancouver: Douglas and McIntyre, 1987), 20, 66. "Tried to do everything at once" and "anomaly" from Barman, *The West Beyond the West*, 323.

"... a double calamity." Martin Robin, *Pillars of Profit: The Company Province, 1934–1972* (Toronto: McClelland and Stewart, 1972), 121.

The Twenty Years' War

Martin Robin, *Pillars of Profit: The Company Province, 1934–1972* (Toronto: McClelland and Stewart, 1972), 171, 180, 209; Ian MacAlpine, "Young Socreds Salute Bennett," *Vancouver Sun*, February 22, 1965; Tom Hazlitt, "Elite bow and Bennett beams," the *Province*, February 17, 1965; David J. Mitchell, *Succession: The Political Reshaping of British Columbia* (Vancouver: Douglas and McIntyre, 1987), 15, 17; Paddy Sherman, *Bennett* (Toronto: McLelland and Stewart, 1966), 300, 303; Walter D. Young, "The Legislature Under W.A.C. Bennett" (BC Project working paper, University of Victoria Archives, 1983), 3,4; David J. Mitchell, *W.A.C. Bennett and the Rise of British Columbia* (Vancouver: Douglas and McIntyre, 1983).

"... will see no real alternative." The New Democrats won two additional seats with a 5.82 percent increase in the popular vote. It was symptomatic of the province's imbalanced vote distribution that W.A.C. Bennett needed only 342,751 votes to win thirty-three seats. The NDP's 252,753 vote generated only sixteen seats and the hapless Liberals, who ran in all but two ridings, racked up 152,155 votes but tallied only six seats, all in the Lower Mainland. For details of the platform see Karen Jackson, "Ideology of the NDP in BC: Manifest Socialism 1966, 1969 and 1972 Election Campaigns" (BC Project working paper, University of Victoria Archives, 1983), 8–21; *Vancouver Sun* editorial cited by Jackson is from August 6, 1966.

"... who once flamed with ambition." "NDP Shoestring Resists Juggernaut," *Vancouver Sun*, September 13, 1966. As Barrett noted in his memoir, this election did accelerate the process of renewal, seeing Tom Berger and Bob Williams elected to the new caucus. Dave Barrett, *Barrett: A Passionate Political Life* (Vancouver: Douglas and McIntyre, 1995), 45; "New Democrats Jubilant–'Wait Until Next Time,'" *Vancouver Sun*, September 13, 1996; "NDP sees victory even in minority," the *Province*, September 13, 1966.

Thomas R. Berger, *One Man's Justice: A Life in the Law* (Vancouver: Douglas and McIntyre, 2002), 69; Carolyn Swayze, *Hard Choices: A Life of Tom Berger* (Vancouver: Douglas and McIntyre, 1987), 103–106; "Strachan keeps grip on NDP leadership," the *Province*, June 5, 1967; Lorne Kavic and Garry Nixon, *The 1200 Days: A Shattered Dream: Dave Barrett and the NDP in BC, 1972–1975* (Coquitlam, BC: Kaen Publishers, 1978), 17; Barrett, *Barrett: A Passionate Political Life*, 10, 15, 26–27, 42–44; "Intrigue Web Surrounds Cypress Bowl Promoters," *Vancouver Sun*, March 16, 1965; "North Shore MLAs Battle Barrett Over Bowl," *Vancouver Sun*, March 28, 1965; "Raw Face of Fascism," *Daily Colonist*, June 12, 1966; "Liberal, NDP clash over W. Vancouver Bowl," the *Province*, July 20, 1965; "City of Madness Plan Criticised by Barrett," *Vancouver Sun*, March 23, 1966.

Doug Collins, "Govt Fires Pro-CCF Jail Worker," *Vancouver Sun*, July 27, 1959; Barrett, *Barrett: A Passionate Political Life*, 32. Barrett was immediately hired by the John Howard Society, where he met Norm Levi, another social worker who would serve in his cabinet in 1972.

Allan Fotheringham, *Vancouver Sun*, April 5, 1969; Barrett, *Barrett: A Passionate Political Life*, 46; "Strachan tells NDP 'Bob Williams is the best man,'" *Vancouver Sun*, April 12, 1969; Allan Fotheringham, *Vancouver Sun*, April 14, 1969; Kavic and Nixon, *The 1200 Days*, 18–19; "Phone Takeover Pledged by Berger," *Vancouver Sun*, April 14, 1969; "Barrett predicts 35 seats for the NDP," *Vancouver Sun*, August 15, 1969; Allan Fotheringham, *Vancouver Sun*, August 15, 1969; Mitchell, *W.A.C. Bennett and the Rise of British Columbia*, 389; "We are not a labour party," *Victoria Daily Times*, May 31, 1969.

Inside the Gates

"Barrett attacks with a smile," *Vancouver Sun*, August 19, 1972.

The account of the 1972 election— buildup, campaign and aftermath— is drawn from extensive newspaper coverage of the events; interviews with Peter McNelly, John Fryer and Shirley Barrett; David J. Mitchell's *Succession: The Political Reshaping of British Columbia* (Vancouver: Douglas and McIntyre, 1987) and *W.A.C. Bennett and the Rise of British Columbia* (Vancouver: Douglas and McIntyre, 1983); and Dave Barrett's own account in *Barrett: A Passionate Political Life* (Vancouver: Douglas and McIntyre, 1995).

The Only episode and Barrett's cabinet considerations are based on interviews with Bob Williams and Shirley Barrett.

John Saywell, ed., *Canadian Annual Review of Politics and Public Affairs, 1972* (Toronto: University of Toronto Press, 1974), 202.

The account of the meeting with the CPR's Ian Sinclair is drawn from Alex Macdonald's *My Dear Legs* (Vancouver: New Star Books, 1985), 29. Macdonald puts this incident in 1973, but the bill was passed in the emergency session of 1972.

Vancouver Sun, the *Province*, the *Victoria Daily Times*, June–December 1972.

Awesome, Sweeping Powers

"Barrett laughs at car insurance ads," *Vancouver Sun*, January 8 1973; "Barrett sets out to be 'people premier,'" *Daily Colonist*, January 14, 1973; Paul St. Pierre, "Barrett's days," *Vancouver Sun*, March 29, 1973; "Mr. Barrett and the promised land," January 23, 1973; "Dave Barrett's pragmatic socialism," Sherman et al., the *Province*, January 20, 1973.

John Saywell, ed., *Canadian Annual Review of Politics and Public Affairs, 1972* (Toronto: University of Toronto Press, 1974), 189, 202–204, 229, 256–258, 293–294, 361; Lorne Kavic and Garry Nixon, *1200 Days* (Coquitlam, BC: Kaen Publishers, 1978), 132–33; Dave Barrett, *Barrett: A Passionate Political Life* (Vancouver: Douglas and McIntyre, 1995), 68–69.

The account of the ALR legislation is drawn from Andrew Petter, Christopher Garrish, news accounts and Hansard, as well as interviews with Harold Steves and Bob Williams.

Bob Hunter, *Vancouver Sun*, October 11, 1972; "Accord reached on pollution curbs," *Vancouver Sun*, November 15, 1972; John Clarke, "Pricing powers for energy board?" *Globe and Mail*, February 3, 1973; Marjorie Nichols, "Expected gas price boost to help BC, says Barrett," *Vancouver Sun*, February 16, 1973; Peter McNelly, "BC will fight Alaska pipeline," the *Province*, February 16, 1973.

The story of the ICBC legislation has been told by G. Lewis Seens, "Automobile Insurance in BC, 1968–1979, or, Almost Everything You Ever Wished to Know About Insuring Your Four-Wheeled Mistress in Beautiful BC" (BC Project working paper, University of Victoria Archives, 1979).

Malcolm Turnbull, "Land controls cover province," the *Province*, February 22, 1973; "Barrett meets farmers' body, hints at land act changes," *Daily Colonist*, March 8, 1973; "Land bill suffered from bad PR: Barrett," the *Province*, March 17, 1973; Ian Street, "Divided house supports land bill principle," *Daily Colonist*, March 29, 1973.

Andrew Petter, "Background Paper on Robert Williams," *BC Project background paper*, unpublished, nd.: 29–30.

The Democrat, March–April 1973; Saywell; Nick Hills, "For whatever a New Democrat may be . . . ," the *Province*, March 13, 1973; Paddy Sherman, "Is governing too big a job for Barrett and Co.?," the *Province*, April 6, 1973; "Left turn for BC–at the gallop," *Vancouver Sun*, April 21, 1973; Jack Wasserman, *Vancouver Sun*, April 14, 1973.

Patrick Scott (*Toronto Star*), cited in Allan Fotheringham, *Vancouver Sun*, April 28, 1973; Allan Fotheringham, *Vancouver Sun*, May 17, 1973.

Jerry Hammond, "How bad is Barrett's bite," *Vancouver Sun*, April 4, 1973; "Barrett cool to the idea it's Chile outside," the *Province*, April 4, 1973.

MiniWAC, Little Chief and the Northern Kingfish

Dave Barrett, *Barrett: A Passionate Political Life* (Vancouver: Douglas and McIntyre, 1995), 68–69; "Barrett's bull-slinging skill astounds," *Vancouver Sun*, July 3, 1973.

Peter McNelly, "An offer most never get ... to refuse," the Province, August

21, 1973; Lorne Kavic and Garry Nixon, *The 1200 Days: A Shattered Dream: Dave Barrett and the NDP in BC, 1972–1975* (Coquitlam, BC: Kaen Publishers, 1978), 53–58; many of these names of public servants mean little to people today, but it was a very talented crew.

Gerry Scott's thesis ("Beyond Equality: British Columbia New Democrats and Native Peoples, 1961–1979," MA thesis, Simon Fraser University, 1991) on the NDP and aboriginal policy provides background on Calder and the Nisga'a case, as does Thomas R. Berger, *One Man's Justice: A Life in the Law* (Vancouver: Douglas and McIntyre, 2002), and Carolyn Swayze, *Hard Choices: A Life of Tom Berger* (Vancouver: Douglas and McIntyre, 1987); Marjorie Nichols, "Calder fired from cabinet: Barrett cites 'lost confidence' as reason for minister's ouster," *Vancouver Sun,* July 31, 1973; Peter McNelly, "Opposition shocked: Barrett fires Calder," the *Province,* August 1, 1973; Michael Finlay, "What the hell are they worrying about? 'This is not Watergate,' says Calder," *Vancouver Sun,* August 1, 1973.

The main accounts of the reorganization on the right are found in David J. Mitchell's *W.A.C. Bennett and the Rise of British Columbia* (Vancouver: Douglas and McIntyre, 1983), 428, 429–430, 432, and Mitchell's *Succession: The Political Reshaping of British Columbia* (Vancouver: Douglas and McIntyre, 1987) and Bob Plecas's *Bill Bennett: A Mandarin's View* (Vancouver: Douglas and McIntyre, 2006), 45–47, as well as in Barrett's own memoirs, *Barrett*; "Tanned Bennett out to tan NDP," the *Province,* March 3, 1973; G.L. Kristianson, "The Non-partisan Approach to BC Politics: the Search for a Unity Party—1972–1975, *BC Studies* 33 (1977): 15.

Andreas Killen's *1973 Nervous Breakdown: Watergate, Warhol and the Birth of Post-Sixties America* (New York: Bloomsbury, 2006), 132–134 provides some context for changes in politics and culture in 1973.

Energy policy is summarized in G. Lewis Seens' BC Project working papers on natural gas and petroleum policy (including pp. 16–18, 20–21); Barrett, *Barrett,* 78–84.

John Saywell, ed., *Canadian Annual Review of Politics and Public Affairs* (Toronto: University of Toronto Press, xxxx); interviews with Harold Steves and Bob Williams.

Barrett, *Barrett*; Kavic and Nixon, *The 1200 Days*; Patrick McGeer, *Politics in Paradise* (Toronto: Peter Martin Associates, 1972); Mitchell, *W.A.C.*; Peter McNelly, personal journal, February 17, 1974; Kristianson, "The

Non-partisan Approach..."

Roy/Saywell 227; "Halt or delay fast time switch," *Vancouver Sun*, January 4, 1974; "Hickory dickory," *Vancouver Sun*, January 4, 1974.

Barbara McLintock, "Robin Hood Budget," the *Province*, February 9, 1974; Bob McMurray, "The Money Rolls in," the *Province*, February 12, 1974.

Eileen Dailly, interview with Walter Young, BC Project archives, 22; Kavic and Nixon, *The 1200 Days*, 165–67; John Bremer secured an apology from Barrett in 1976. Dailly speculated some years later that Barrett had been upset by criticism of Bremer from teachers he had met earlier that day during a visit to a Coquitlam high school. Bremer's work had been unsatisfactory and speculation about his fate had circulated for days, but no one expected the news to be released on live television.

The Chicken and Egg War

Marjorie Nichols, with Jane O'Hara, *Mark My Words: The Memoirs of a Very Political Reporter* (Vancouver: Douglas and McIntyre, 1992); Jack Webster, *Webster!* (Vancouver: Douglas and McIntyre, 1990).

Carol Gamey and Jeremy Wilson produced BC Project papers on media coverage.

Interviews: David Anderson (BC Project interview and personal interview), Barb McLintock, George Oake (BC Project interview), Ron Thomson (BC Project interview), Ernie Hall (BC Project interview) and Malcolm Turnbull. Correspondence exchanges with Michael Finlay, Peter McNelly and Scott Dixon.

Newspaper articles 1973-1975, the *Vancouver Sun* and the *Province*.

Peter McNelly's personal journal, 1974. McLintock

Patrick McGeer, *Politics in Paradise* (Toronto: Peter Martin Associates, 1972), 232; G.L. Kristianson, "The Non-partisan Approach to BC Politics: the Search for a Unity Party—1972–1975, *BC Studies* 33 (1977): 20; David J. Mitchell, *W.A.C. Bennett and the Rise of British Columbia* (Vancouver: Douglas and McIntyre, 1983).

The Engineer Who Made the Grade

Paul Weiler's *Reconcilable Differences* (Toronto: Carswell Legal Publications, 1980) remains the leading source on the Labour Code and its creation.

Alan F.J. Artibise, Michael Moetki and Carol Gamey's BC Project papers are the leading academic analyses of the Barrett government's labour legislation. William Cochrane's BC Project papers offer some media and statistical analysis.

Interviews with Carolyn Askew, Colin Gabelmann, Peter Gall, Ron Johnson, Clive Lytle, Ray Haynes, John Fryer, Bill King, Jim Matkin, Jack Munro and Sharon Yandle, plus correspondence exchange with Bob Plecas.

Dave Barrett, *Barrett*; (Toronto: Peter Martin Associates, 1972).

Lazarus, Morden. *Up From the Ranks: Trade Union VIP's Past and Present.* Toronto, Ontario: Co-operative Press Association, 1977.

The Godfather and the Tank Driver

Andrew Petter's "Working Paper on Bob Williams" provides an overview of Williams' work (including pp. 10, 13, 16–19, 30–34); Alan Fotheringham, "Williams is 67.3 percent of government," *Vancouver Sun*, June 7, 1975; Malcolm Gray, "The driving force behind Barrett and BC socialism," *Globe and Mail*, November 12, 1975; "Northwest plan: 'environmental disaster?'" *The Democrat*, April 1974.

Lorne Kavic and Garry Nixon, *The 1200 Days: A Shattered Dream: Dave Barrett and the NDP in BC, 1972–1975* (Coquitlam, BC: Kaen Publishers, 1978), 73; On forestry: Marchak and Wilson, Forest Conservation in British Columbia…

Peter McNelly, personal journal, May 13, 1974 and June 16, 1974; John Saywell, ed., *Canadian Annual Review of Politics and Public Affairs 1974* (Toronto: University of Toronto Press, 1975), 230.

Interviews with Bob Williams and Norm Levi.

Bridget Moran, *A Little Rebellion* (Vancouver: Arsenal Pulp Press, 1992), 132–33 details the condition of social services before the NDP.

The story of Norm Levi's reforms of social services can be found in Michael Clague, Robert Dill, Roop Seebaran and Brian Wharf's *Reforming Human Services: The Experience of the Community Resources Boards in BC* (Vancouver: UBC Press, 1984).

McNelly, personal journal, September 29, 1974.

Quotes on community resources boards by Elgin Ruddell, cited in Stan Persky, *Son of Socred* (Vancouver: New Star Books, 1979), 168–69.

Health, Housing and Human Rights

A perspective on Dennis Cocke's work can be found in Michael Clague, Robert Dill, Roop Seebaran and Brian Wharf's *Reforming Human Services: The Experience of the Community Resources Boards in BC* (Vancouver: UBC Press, 1984); "in the words of one ministry official": Pallan cited in Clague et al., *Reforming Human Services,* 125; Cocke and Dr. Richard Foulkes from Clague et al., *Reforming Human Services,* 126.

Housing section based on Beverley Jean Grieve, "Continuity and Change: Provincial Housing Policy in BC, 1945–1985" (MA thesis, UBC, 1985); Dallard Runge, *Housing and Rent Control in BC: A Report Prepared by the Interdepartmental Study Team on Housing and Rents* (Victoria: Queens Printer, 1975); interview with Lorne Nicolson; NDP party platform.

Dominique Clement's *Canada's Rights Revolution: Social Movements and Social Change, 1937–82* (Vancouver: UBC Press, 2008) puts the *Human Rights Act* legislation in context.

Interviews with Dennis Cocke (BC Project, January 28, 1981, School of Social Work); Clay Perry, Kathleen Ruff, Lorne Nicolson and William Neilson.

The Life of the Party

Richard Gwyn, "BC and the election," *Regina Leader-Post,* May 30, 1974; Marjorie Nichols, *Vancouver Sun,* June 28, 1974; July 9, 1974; Hans Brown, "Federal election: where the votes went and why," *The Democrat,* July 1974.

Interviews with Mike Lebowitz, Colin Gabelmann, Gary Lauk, Harold Steves, Gene Errington, Cynthia Flood and Sharon Yandle.

Rosemary Brown, *Being Brown: A Very Public Life* (Toronto: Random House, 1985), 88, 99); *Priorities,* issues 1:9; 1:11; 2:6; 2:8; *The Democrat,* October 1974; December 1974.

Peter McNelly, personal journal, September 8, 1974.

How They Forgot the Future

R.H. Payne's "Corporate Power and Economic Policy-making in BC, 1972–1975: The Case of the Mining Industry" (MA thesis, McGill University, 1979), 11, 30–53, 60, 100, 240–245, 249, on the mining industry remains the only comprehensive account; "Pay royalties or leave ore—Barrett," the

Province, April 13, 1974; "1,000 Stewart area residents protest mine royalty," the *Province,* April 4, 1974; "Mining town joins royalty fight," the *Province,* March 28, 1974; "Nimsick says: 'We don't have to have Japs,'" the *Province,* April 26, 1974; Terry Hammond, "Mortal blow aimed at BC mining," *Vancouver Sun,* June 13, 1974.

The story of the start-up of ICBC has been told by G. Lewis Seens, "Automobile Insurance in BC, 1968–1979, or, Almost Everything You Ever Wished to Know About Insuring Your Four-Wheeled Mistress in Beautiful BC" (BC Project working paper, University of Victoria Archives, 1979).

Peter McNelly, personal journal, June 20, 1974, March 2, 1975, March 1975 and February 19, 1975.

Interview with Marc Eliesen; Dave Barrett, *Barrett: A Passionate Political Life* (Vancouver: Douglas and McIntyre, 1995), 95–96.

Christina Newman, "In Wild Kingdom of Bee-Cee, an Unlikely Hero," *Victoria Daily Times,* February 15, 1975; Rick Prashaw, "Not a dime without debate," *Vancouver Sun,* May 15, 1975; Alan Fotheringham, "Nasty byplay in house over procedural wrangling"; Neale Adams, "Convention refuses to buy Barrett's slate," May 20, 1975; "Wallace blasts Bennett," *Vancouver Sun,* February 25, 1975.

David J. Mitchell, *Succession: The Political Reshaping of British Columbia* (Vancouver: Douglas and McIntyre, 1987); G.L. Kristianson, "The Non-partisan Approach to BC Politics: The Search for a Unity Party—1972–1975," *BC Studies* 33 (1977); Paul Tennant, "The NDP Government of British Columbia: Unaided Politicians in an Unaided Cabinet," *Canadian Public Policy* 3, no. 4 (1977).

Back to Work

Kristianson, "The Non-partisan Approach to BC Politics: The Search for a Unity Party—1972–1975," *BC Studies* 33 (1977), 26, 28; Gary Mason and Keith Baldrey, *Fantasyland: Inside the Reign of Bill Vander Zalm* (Toronto: McGraw-Hill Ryerson, 1989); "Wallace blasts Bennett," *Vancouver Sun,* February 25, 1975.

Dave Barrett, *Barrett: A Passionate Political Life* (Vancouver: Douglas and McIntyre, 1995); Stan Persky, *Son of Socred* (Vancouver: New Star Books, 1979); Peter McNelly, personal journal, October, 1975.

Interviews with Bill King, Colin Gabelmann and Jack Munro.

Vancouver Sun and the *Province*, August–September, 1975.

And Good Luck to Us All

The election has been documented in David J. Mitchell's *Succession: The Political Reshaping of British Columbia* (Vancouver: Douglas and McIntyre, 1987); *Dave* Barrett's *Barrett: A Passionate Political Life* (Vancouver: Douglas and McIntyre, 1995); Lorne Kavic and Garry Nixon's *The 1200 Days: A Shattered Dream: Dave Barrett and the NDP in BC, 1972–1975* (Coquitlam, BC: Kaen Publishing, 1978); Stan Persky's *Son of Socred* (Vancouver: New Star Books, 1979).

Peter McNelly, personal journal, October–December, 1975.

Interviews with George Oake, Bob Williams, Bill King, John Fryer, Gary Lauk and Scott Dixon.

Vancouver Sun, the *Province* and *Victoria Daily Times,* September–December, 1975, plus CBC-TV for November 3 election announcement.

Other Sources

Colin Preston of CBC Vancouver kindly provided access to the CBC's television news archives for the Barrett era. Robin Geary shared her complete set of *Priorities.* Mike Lebowitz provided a copy of a BC Waffle position statement.

Bibliography

Books

Anderson, James. *British Columbia's Magnificent Parks: The First 100 Years.* Madeira Park, BC: Harbour Publishing, 2009.

Barman, Jean. *The West Beyond the West: A History of British Columbia.* Toronto: University of Toronto Press, 1991.

Barrett, Dave. *Barrett: A Passionate Political Life.* Vancouver: Douglas and McIntyre, 1995.

Bellamy, D.J., J.H. Pammett and Donald C. Rowat. *The Provincial Political Systems: Comparative Essays.* Toronto: Methuen, 1976.

Berger, Thomas R. *One Man's Justice: A Life in the Law.* Vancouver: Douglas and McIntyre, 2002.

Brown, Rosemary. *Being Brown: A Very Public Life.* Toronto: Random House, 1985.

Clague, Michael, Robert Dill, Roop Seebaran and Brian Wharf. *Reforming Human Services: The Experience of the Community Resources Boards in BC.* Vancouver: UBC Press, 1984.

Clement, Dominique. *Canada's Rights Revolution: Social Movements and Social Change, 1937–82.* Vancouver: UBC Press, 2008.

Clyne, J.V. *Jack of All Trades: Memories of a Busy Life.* Toronto: McClelland and Stewart, 1985.

Dunn, Christopher. *The Institutionalized Cabinet: Governing the Western Provinces.* Montreal–Kingston: McGill-Queen's University Press, 1995.

Dyck, Randall. *Provincial Politics in Canada: Towards the Turn of the Century.* Toronto: Prentice-Hall, 1996.

Foster, Leslie. *People, Politics and Child Welfare in BC.* Vancouver: UBC Press, 2007.

Gutstein, Donald. *Not a Conspiracy Theory: How Business Propaganda Hijacks Democracy.* Toronto: Key Porter, 2009.

Hayter, Roger. *Flexible Crossroads: The Restructuring of BC's Forest Economy.* Vancouver: UBC Press, 2000.

Kavic, Lorne, and Garry Nixon. *The 1200 Days: A Shattered Dream: Dave Barrett and the NDP in BC, 1972–1975*. Coquitlam, BC: Kaen Publishers, 1978.

Killen, Andreas. *1973 Nervous Breakdown: Watergate, Warhol and the Birth of Post-Sixties America*. New York: Bloomsbury, 2006.

Lazarus, Morden. *Up From the Ranks: Trade Union VIP's Past and Present.* Toronto: Co-operative Press Association, 1977.

Legislative Assembly of BC. *Hansard (Debates)*. Victoria: Queen's Printer, 1972–75.

Macdonald, Alex. *My Dear Legs*. Vancouver: New Star Books, 1985.

Marchak, Patricia. *Green Gold: The Forest Industry in British Columbia.* Vancouver: UBC Press, 1983.

Mason, Gary, and Keith Baldrey. *Fantasyland: Inside the Reign of Bill Vander Zalm*. Toronto: McGraw-Hill Ryerson, 1989.

McGeer, Patrick. *Politics in Paradise*. Toronto: Peter Martin Associates, 1972.

McLean, Bruce. *A Union Amongst Government Employees: A History of the BC Government Employees' Union, 1919–1979*. Vancouver: BCGEU, 1979.

Mitchell, David J. *Succession: The Political Reshaping of British Columbia.* Vancouver: Douglas and McIntyre, 1987.

—. *W.A.C. Bennett and the Rise of British Columbia*. Vancouver: Douglas and McIntyre, 1983.

Moran, Bridget. *A Little Rebellion*. Vancouver: Arsenal Pulp Press, 1992.

Morley, Terence, Norman Ruff, Neil Swainson, Jeremy Wilson and Walter Young. *The Reins of Power: Governing in British Columbia*. Vancouver: Douglas and McIntyre, 1983.

Neufeld, Andrew and Andrew Parnaby. *The IWA in Canada*. Vancouver: New Star Books, 2000.

Nichols, Marjorie, with Jane O'Hara. *Mark My Words: The Memoirs of a Very Political Reporter.* Vancouver: Douglas and McIntyre, 1992.

Perksy, Stan. *Son of Socred*. Vancouver: New Star Books, 1979.

Plecas, Bob. *Bill Bennett: A Mandarin's View*. Vancouver: Douglas and McIntyre, 2006.

Robin, Martin. *Pillars of Profit: The Company Province, 1934–1972.* Toronto: McClelland and Stewart, 1972.

Roy, Patricia E. and John Herd Thompson. *British Columbia: Land of Promise.* Don Mills, ON: Oxford University Press, 2005.

Runge, Dallard. *Housing and Rent Control in BC: A Report Prepared by the Interdepartmental Study Team on Housing and Rents.* Victoria: Queen's Printer, 1975.

Saywell, John, ed. *Canadian Annual Review of Politics and Public Affairs, 1972.* Toronto: University of Toronto Press, 1974.

—. *Canadian Annual Review of Politics and Public Affairs, 1973.* Toronto: University of Toronto Press, 1974.

—. *Canadian Annual Review of Politics and Public Affairs, 1974.* Toronto: University of Toronto Press, 1975.

—. *Canadian Annual Review of Politics and Public Affairs, 1975.* Toronto: University of Toronto Press, 1976.

Sherman, Paddy. *Bennett.* Toronto: McLelland and Stewart, 1966.

Swayze, Carolyn. *Hard Choices: A Life of Tom Berger.* Vancouver: Douglas and McIntyre, 1987.

Webster, Jack. *Webster!* Vancouver: Douglas and McIntyre, 1990.

Weiler, Paul. *Reconcilable Differences.* Toronto: Carswell Legal Publications, 1980.

Weyler, Rex. *Greenpeace: How a Group of Ecologists, Journalists and Visionaries Changed the World.* Vancouver: Raincoast Books, 2004.

Woodcock, George. *British Columbia: A History of the Province.* Vancouver: Douglas and McIntyre, 1990.

BC Project materials

The BC Project was a five-year research program funded by the Social Sciences and Research Council from 1978 to 1983 to study the changes in BC's political life and governance from 1972 to 1976. Directed by University of Victoria professors Terry Morley, Neil Swainson, Norman Ruff and Jeremy Wilson, it published more than twenty working papers and conducted dozens of in-depth interviews. The BC Project materials are stored in the Archives of the University of Victoria.

Working papers

Cochrane, William. "Labour Disputes and the Metropolitan Press: A Catalogue of Editorial Reaction." *BC Project Working Paper*, n.d.

—. "The Labour Code of BC and the Labour Relations Board: Review of Amendments to the Labour Code." *BC Project Working Paper*, 1983.

Gamey, Carol. "Collective Bargaining and the Excluded Employee in the BC Public Service." *BC Project Working Paper*, 1981.

—. "Comparative Cabinet Committee Systems: Canadian Developments." *BC Project Working Paper*, 1983.

—. "Government Media Relations: Bennett–Barrett–Bennett." *BC Project Working Paper*, 1980.

—. "The Impact of Collective Bargaining on the BC Government Nurses (The RNABC Record)." *BC Project Working Paper*, 1983.

Jackson, Karen. "Ideology of the NDP in BC: Manifest Socialism 1966, 1969 and 1972 Election Campaigns." *BC Project Working Paper*, 1983.

Lapper, Robert. "The Creation of Administrative Agencies in British Columbia, an Overview: (Independence and Accountability)." *BC Project Working Paper*, 1981.

Petter, Andrew. "Background Paper on Bob Williams." *BC Project background paper*, unpublished, n.d.

Seens, G. Lewis. "1972–1975, Political and Economic Change in the Province of British Columbia: An Overview." *BC Project Working Paper*, 1980.

—. "Automobile Insurance in BC, 1968–1979, or, Almost Everything You Ever Wished to Know About Insuring Your Four-Wheeled Mistress in Beautiful BC." *BC Project Working Paper*, 1979.

—. "'Awesome, Sweeping Powers': *The Land Commission Act*, 1973; the *Mineral Royalties Act*, 1974 and Other 'Blank Cheque' Legislation: The NDP Years 1972–1975." *BC Project Working Paper*, 1983.

—. "Natural Gas—A Finite Resource." *BC Project Working Paper*, 1979.

—. "Petroleum and Politics: NDP and Socred Policies in the Seventies." *BC Project Working Paper*, 1980.

Wilson, Jeremy. "Government and Opposition Use of a Changing Legislature: An Analysis of the Battle for Media Coverage." *BC Project Working Paper*, 1983.

Young, Walter D. "The Legislature Under W.A.C. Bennett." *BC Project Working Paper*, 1983.

Interviews

Transcripts of these interviews are held in the University of Victoria Archives

David Anderson, October 30, 1978

W.R. Bennett, September 23, 1987

Linda Coady, November 6, 1979

Dennis Cocke, January 28, 1981

Eileen Dailly, March 3, 1980

Marc Eliesen, July 8 and 9, 1980

Ernest Hall, January 30, 1979

Ray Haynes, August 5, 1980

Alex Macdonald, July 24, 1979

Angus McPhee, June 17, 1980

Jack Munro, August 6, 1980

Paddy Sherman, March 6, 1980

David Vickers, July 18, 1979

Scott Wallace, October 24, 1979

Theses and academic articles

Artibise, Alan F.J. "'A Worthy, if Unlikely, Enterprise': The Labour Relations Board and the Evolution of Labour Policy and Practice in British Columbia, 1973–1980. *BC Studies* 56 (1982): 3–43.

Erickson, Lynda. "Women's Rights Committee Note." In *Politics, Policy and Government in British Columbia,* edited by R.K. Carty. Vancouver: UBC Press, 1996.

Garrish, Christopher. "Unscrambling the Omelette: Understanding British Columbia's Agricultural Land Reserve." *BC Studies* 136 (2002): 25–55.

—. "Okanagan Fruit Growers and the Abandonment of Orderly Marketing." MA thesis, University of Saskatchewan, 2002.

Grieve, Beverley Jean. "Continuity and Change: Provincial Housing Policy in BC, 1945–1985." MA thesis, UBC, 1985.

Groen, James P. "British Columbia's International Relations: Consolidating a Coalition-Building Strategy." *BC Studies* 102 (1994): 54–81.

—. "Provincial International Relations: Case Studies of the Barrett and Vander Zalm Governments in British Columbia." BA paper, Simon Fraser University, 1988.

Harris, Christopher J. "British Columbia 1972–1975: The Genesis of a Two-Party System." MA thesis, UBC, 1987.

Koenig, Daniel J., Gary R. Martin and H.G. Goudy. "The Year That British Columbia Went NDP: NDP Voters Support Pre- and Post-1972." *BC Studies* 24 (1974): 65–86.

Kristianson, G.L. "The Non-partisan Approach to BC Politics: The Search for a Unity Party—1972–1975." *BC Studies* 33 (1977): 13–29.

Mackenzie, Bruce Allen. "Party and Press Portrayals of the British Columbia CCF–NDP: 1937–1979." MA thesis, University of Victoria, 1977.

Martin, Eryk. "When Red Meets Green: Perceptions of Environmental Change in the BC Communist Left, 1937–1978." MA thesis, University of Victoria, 2006.

Moeti, Michael. "The Structural Role of the Workers' Compensation Board in the Industrial Economy of British Columbia." MA Research Project, UBC, 1988.

Neilson, William A.W. "Consumer Protection and Public Administration: Some BC Notes." *Canadian Business Law Journal* 2, no. 2 (1977): 169–181.

Payne, R.W. "Corporate Power and Economic Policy-making in BC, 1972–1975: The Case of the Mining Industry." MA thesis, McGill University, 1979.

Persky, Stan. *Days of Social Democracy: A Memoir.* Dooneyscafé.com, August 24, 2004.

Petter, Andrew. "Sausage Making in British Columbia's NDP Government: The Creation of the *Land Commission Act*, August 1972–April 1973." *BC Studies* 65 (1985): 3–33.

Resnick, Philllip. "Social Democracy in Power: The case of British Columbia." *BC Studies* 34 (1977): 3–20.

Schwindt, Richard. "The Pearse Commission and the Industrial Organization of the BC Forest Industry." *BC Studies* 41 (1979): 3–35.

Scott, Gerry. "Beyond Equality: British Columbia New Democrats and Native Peoples, 1961–1979." MA thesis, Simon Fraser University, 1991.

Tennant, Paul. "The NDP Government of British Columbia: Unaided Politicians in an Unaided Cabinet." *Canadian Public Policy* 3, no. 4 (1977): 489–503.

Wilson, Jeremy. "Forest Conservation in British Columbia: Reflections on a Barren Debate, 1935–1985." *BC Studies* 76 (1987): 3–32.

Wolfe, L.D.S. "The High Ross Dam/Skagit River Controversy: The Use of Public Hearings in the Management of a Public River." MSc thesis, UBC, 1974.

Articles and papers

Agricultural Land Commission. *10 Years of Agricultural Land Preservation in BC*. Queen's Prints, Victoria, 1983.

Campbell, Charles. *Forever Farmland: Reshaping the Agricultural Land Reserve for the 21st Century*. Vancouver: David Suzuki Foundation, 2006.

David Suzuki Foundation. *Land Reserve for the 21st Century.* Vancouver, 2006.

Manning, Edward, and Sandra S. Eady. "The Land Reserves in BC: An Impact Analysis." Ottawa: Environment Canada, 1978. VPL.

Marchak, M. Patricia, Scott L. Aycock and Deborah M. Herbert. *Falldown: Forest Policy in British Columbia*. Vancouver: David Suzuki Foundation and Ecotrust Canada, 1999.

McNelly, Peter. Personal journal, December 26, 1975–February 24, 1984. Unpublished.

Quayle, Moura. "Stakes in the Ground: Provincial Interest in the Agricultural Land Commission Act." Victoria: Ministry of Agriculture and Lands, September 25, 1998. http://www.agf.gov.bc.ca/polleg/quayle/index.htm.

Smart Growth BC. *State of the Agricultural Land Reserve*, 2004.

Voice of BC (transcript), Dave Barrett and Vaughn Palmer, June 29, 2005.

Yearwood-Lee, Emily. *History of the Agricultural Land Reserve.* Background Paper, Legislative Library of BC, January 2008.

Newspapers

Most of the newspaper articles consulted for this book were indexed by the Legislative Library. A microfilm copy of that card index is available at the Vancouver Public Library Central Branch. All records for Dave Barrett and Bob Williams were reviewed. A number of articles from the *Globe and Mail* were also reviewed.

Vancouver Sun, 1959, 1969–1975

The *Province,* 1972–1975

The Victoria *Times,* 1972–1975

The Democrat, 1972–1975

Priorities, 1974–1975

Interviews

Interviewed by Geoff Meggs and Rod Mickleburgh:

Marc Eliesen, April 23, 2011

Colin Gabelmann, June 2010

Clive Lytle, July 9, 2011

Norm Levi, Victoria, August 2010

Alex Macdonald, September 11, 2010

Harold Steves, June 20, 2010

Gerry Scott, February 9, 2012

Bob Williams, July 2, 2010

Sharon Yandle, September 18, 2010

Interviewed by Geoff Meggs:

Carolyn Askew, August 27, 2010

Dave Barrett, August 26, 2009

Gene Errington, by telephone, April 22, 2011

Cynthia Flood, April 2, 2011

Colin Gabelmann, June 29, 2010

Robin Geary, August 25, 2010

Mike Lebowitz, April 19, 2011

Lorne Nicolson, May 2012

Ken Novakowski, March 29, 2011

Clay Perry, Vancouver, May 10, 2012

Kathleen Ruff, May 6, 2011

Interviewed by Rod Mickleburgh:

David Anderson, May 2012

Dan Barrett, June 2012

Dave Barrett, December 2009

Shirley Barrett, March 2012

Michael Coleman, May 2012

Scott Dixon, March 2011

John Fryer, March 2011

Peter Gall, March 2012

Ron Johnson, March 2012

Ray Haynes, May 2012

Bill King, September 2010

Gary Lauk, September 2010

Jim Matkin, March 2012

Barbara McLintock, April 2012

Peter McNelly, December 2010

Jack Munro, February 2012

Bill Neilson, June 2012

George Oake, June 2012

Malcolm Turnbull, April 2012

Correspondence exchanges with Michael Finlay and Bob Plecas, May and June 2012

Index